Finding Peace

through

Spiritual Practice

The Interfaith Amigos' Guide to Personal, Social and Environmental Healing

Pastor Don Mackenzie, Rabbi Ted Falcon
and Imam Jamal Rahman

Walking Together, Finding the Way®

SKYLIGHT PATHS®
PUBLISHING

Nashville, Tennessee

Finding Peace through Spiritual Practice:
The Interfaith Amigos' Guide to Personal, Social and Environmental Healing
2016 Quality Paperback Edition, First Printing

Library of Congress Cataloging-in-Publication Data
Names: Mackenzie, Don, 1944- author.
Title: Finding peace through spiritual practice : the interfaith amigos' guide to personal,
    social, and environmental healing / Pastor Don Mackenzie, Rabbi Ted Falcon and Imam
    Jamal Rahman.
Description: Quality Paperback Edition. | Woodstock, VT : SkyLight Paths Publishing, 2016.
    | Includes bibliographical references.
Identifiers: LCCN 2016018330 | ISBN 9781594736049 (pbk.) | ISBN 9781594736087 (ebook)
Subjects: LCSH: Peace of mind—Religious aspects. | Religions—Relations. | Religious life.
    | Spiritual life.
Classification: LCC BL627.55.M33 2016 | DDC 204/.4—dc23 LC record available at
    https://lccn.loc.gov/2016018330

10 9 8 7 6 5 4 3 2 1

Manufactured in the United States of America
Cover design: Michael J. Myers
Interior design: Tim Holtz
Cover art: shutterstock/Grisha Bruev

SkyLight Paths Publishing is creating a place where people of different spiritual traditions come together for challenge and inspiration, a place where we can help each other understand the mystery that lies at the heart of our existence.

SkyLight Paths sees both believers and seekers as a community that increasingly transcends traditional boundaries of religion and denomination—people wanting to learn from each other, *walking together, finding the way.*

SkyLight Paths, "Walking Together, Finding the Way" and colophon are trademarks of LongHill Partners, Inc., registered in the U.S. Patent and Trademark Office.

Walking Together, Finding the Way®
Published by SkyLight Paths Publishing
An imprint of Turner Publishing Company
Nashville, Tennessee
Tel: (615) 255-2665   Fax: (615) 255-5081
www.skylightpaths.com
www.turnerpublishing.com

We wish to dedicate this book to all who are willing to open their minds, their hearts, and their hands to the peace that needs to be, and we seek to honor these spiritual activists from our Abrahamic faiths whose courage and compassion have inspired our work:

Abraham Joshua Heschel (1907–1972)
Martin Luther King Jr. (1929–1968)
Abdul Ghaffar Khan (1890–1988)

And in honor of the work of
Malala Yousafzai (1997–)
Who brings great light for the road ahead.

Contents

Introduction

On the Way
to Peace

This book is about helping us all find greater inner and outer peace. But before we can even begin to think about achieving this peace, we need to name the truths of our condition. Naming the truth is the first step toward healing.

We've got problems, and plenty of them. The world is a beautiful but, all too often, increasingly dangerous place. Environmental degradation threatens drought, mass flooding, and challenges to food crop production. Serious air pollution damages the lungs and lives of many across the globe. Racism is once again revealed as a serious issue in the United States and elsewhere. The dwindling middle class and the economic chasm between the rich and the rest of us threatens the foundation of our entire social system. The destabilization of governments in the Middle East has led to an international crisis, as refugees fleeing violence and poverty strain the economic stability of Europe as a whole. And terrorist violence aimed at civilian populations has prompted fear and the radical intensification of Islamophobia. Yes, we've got problems.

Many of us have spent a good portion of our lives trying to make things better yet, clearly, we don't seem to be resolving the basic social justice and environmental issues. We sponsor conference after conference, hold program after program, hear from expert after expert. One political party is in power, and then another. And, sometimes, the very actions meant to heal just make things worse.

As social activists working to change the world for the better, striving to forge a sustainable peace, we need to strengthen our

1

spirits so that our work can be even more effective. We want to fortify our belief that personal, social, and environmental healing is possible to achieve. This book is focused on increasing our sense of purpose and our hope for the future.

Why Has Significant Personal, Social, and Environmental Change Been So Difficult?

Many of our actions that are meant to fix things in the world ultimately fail because, while we have focused on making things better "out there" in the world, we have ignored the nature of the environment "in here" in our hearts. It is becoming increasingly clear that without inner change, alterations in the outer world will not endure.

Social activists often become frustrated when the changes toward which they have devoted time and energy happen slowly, if at all. Often galvanized by anger and self-righteousness, those pushing for social justice frequently wind up fueling anger rather than defusing it. People working for societal and environmental healing are best served with a spiritual foundation and they need spiritual resources to best accomplish the changes they seek.

On the other hand, spiritual seekers who have avoided taking action to mend the world have slowed the pace of positive change. Spiritual practices are useful and important for individuals striving to connect with the Divine, decrease tension in their lives, lower their blood pressure, and strengthen their community. But without action in the world, those seekers do not contribute to the real changes that we need to make. We believe that authentic spiritual practice is always expressed through compassionate action in the larger world.

That's the premise of this book: Spiritual practices can give advocates for social change greater success in their pursuits, and concrete actions in the world can deepen the experience of spiritual seekers. We can maximize positive personal, social, and environmental change by supporting activism with spiritual practices, and we can encourage spiritual seekers to recognize that true spirituality demands action. We all want greater peace, and that requires both inner and outer action.

What Is Peace, Anyway?

Have you ever thought about it? Most of us seem to equate peace with the absence of war and the absence of fear. We might say, "Peace means all children can sleep without fear" and "Peace means we no longer have to go to war." To many, peace means we are safe, living in a place without violence, perhaps even without pain and fear.

But pain is part of human experience. We actually need pain to keep ourselves safe—to teach us to refrain from touching the hot burner. And, to be able to navigate our environment safely, we need some elements of fear as well. Without fear, we would be far less vigilant when driving, and we would not build adequate shelters against the sun, wind, rain, and snow.

Many think that peace is the absence of conflict, yet conflict, managed successfully, is a requirement for positive change. Couples often believe that an ideal relationship is one with little conflict, but those conflicts provide the context in which relationships can grow deeper and mature. We need conflict to grow.

So, if peace is not the absence of conflict, fear, and pain, what is it?

The three of us believe that true peace is a way of living in which our conflicts lead us to more meaningful relationships, fear awakens us to live with greater safety, and pain reminds us of where we need support. Peace is an environment in which we help each other become the very best we can be.

Peace is when conflict no longer leads to violence, disagreement no longer requires us to dehumanize and demonize the other, and we enjoy finding new ways to support others and welcome their support of us.

But peace in the world is not possible until we learn to be peaceful beings ourselves, and spiritual practices can support our awakening to the peace that is already part of our being. Inner peace refers to equanimity and resilience in our responses to conflict. Inner peace flows from our connection to the greater wholeness of our being.

Interfaith Dialogue, Spiritual Practices, and Social Activism

The three of us are an unlikely trio: Don Mackenzie is a pastor; Ted Falcon, a rabbi; and Jamal Rahman, an imam. We have been called the "Interfaith Amigos," but getting to this point—learning from each other, understanding our differences, working through the difficult matters, and forging a genuine friendship—has been an eye-opening journey over the span of many years. Today we use every avenue we can to share the power of interfaith collaboration and understanding. We speak and write about our friendship and lead workshops to help others find the same richness that we have. We believe we offer a living message that it is possible to move beyond the separations and suspicions that could divide us by listening to each other's stories and genuinely getting to know each other. We do not seek to minimize our differences, but to learn from them. Together, we seek to discover and to celebrate the life that we share. We have some appreciation that we are each forging a path toward deepening community. As we do, we are discovering that our roots in our own traditions deepen. We are each more committed than ever to our own path, perhaps because we are able, through the lens of another's tradition, to appreciate hidden depths within our own faith.

Our interfaith work throughout our careers, and as a team since 9/11, has always been aimed at dialogue in the service of more effective social and environmental action. Interfaith dialogue can help us create a common foundation to support such action, as we recognize the significant universal ethical teachings our disparate traditions share. We have also found that it is important to acknowledge and deal with the challenges in each tradition that make such cooperation and collaboration more difficult.

But along the way, we have come to appreciate that interfaith dialogue is only part of the process. We also need to encourage spiritual practices that can nurture the inner environment to support the outer actions we take. Ultimately, spirituality is the ground supporting us all, and spiritual practices help us become more sensitive to that more inclusive reality.

In our first book, *Getting to the Heart of Interfaith*, we identified and explored five stages in a deepening interfaith dialogue process. We summarize them briefly here so readers can best appreciate the addition of spiritual practice as the sixth stage in this pursuit.

The Five Stages of Effective Interfaith Dialogue

1. **Creating a context in which we can meet each other as human beings.** For many of us, our religious identity is an important aspect of our lives. But we are more than that religious identity. We share many of the challenges and opportunities, the wins and the losses, that all human beings encounter in their lives. Listening to another's story can most effectively build bridges of understanding as the focus turns toward religious identity.

2. **Exploring our understanding of a core teaching of our tradition.** Each tradition contains teachings, beliefs, texts, rituals, and practices that define that tradition in its uniqueness as well as its universality. Even those without a formal religious identity can point to a central teaching that guides their lives. Such a teaching applies more broadly than a specific belief system, and we encourage consideration of a central teaching against which we can measure other aspects of our tradition and our lives.

3. **Honoring what supports that core teaching and what does not.** Meeting each other as human beings and sharing a core teaching allow us to openly examine those aspects of our own traditions that are in keeping with that core teaching, and those aspects that seem to conflict with that teaching.

4. **Entering into more difficult conversations.** The history of interfaith relationships has not been without serious conflicts and challenges. Supported by the first three stages of a developing dialogue, it becomes possible to address historical as well as current sources of pain. Without this foundation, for example, many Abrahamic interfaith groups falter when the conversation turns to the conflict between Israelis and Palestinians. Yet such conversation is absolutely necessary if we ever hope to move beyond violence toward healing.

5. **Walking another's path.** We believe that interfaith dialogue is not about conversion but about completion—becoming a more complete human being. We also believe that every authentic spiritual path is an avenue to a shared Universal. If this is so, might it be possible to celebrate that Universal through the rituals of another's tradition? To us, such opportunities radically support a deeper understanding of rituals in our own tradition.

These first five stages of interfaith dialogue expand a conversation of personal experience, sharing traditional wisdom, and increasing understanding and the ability to talk about difficult issues. They encourage us to meet another's path. But what truly unites us is far more than an intellectual or an emotional sharing. So now it is time for us to acknowledge the necessary sixth stage of an evolving interfaith dialogue.

6. **Engaging in and sharing spiritual practices.** In awakening to more spiritual dimensions of consciousness, we can enter an environment of a far more profound sharing. While celebrating the rituals of other faith traditions is a beautiful way to deepen interfaith understanding, there is an even greater depth when we share personal spiritual practices. These are more private, more subject to each person's preferences and unique spiritual history. They are also the avenue through which most of us experience the true transformation that the rituals of our faith express and celebrate.

This sixth step forms the focus of this book. We will be exploring specific practices that relate to obstacles within us that inhibit effective and enduring change in our inner as well as outer world.

Is There Hope?

Who among us has not had moments of pessimism, when we found ourselves believing that humankind is, indeed, on a path of self-destruction? In the face of seemingly random violence, how can we avoid the suspicion that there is no real solution? As spiritual leaders ourselves, we have such thoughts, and we appreciate how those very beliefs carry us toward that conclusion.

Yet we have hope. It's not a hope that some heavenly hand will come down to perform the miracles of peacemaking. It's not even a hope that a particular human being will arise to save us. Our hope rests on the ground of an inner knowing, an inner place of reconciliation of opposites and awakening to the reality of the peace we seek.

This is the inner peace that needs to blossom in the world, and we are all the vehicles through which that peace must flow.

What You Will Find in This Book

Here is a spirituality that inspires action, and a spirituality that supports activists. It's rooted in multiple faiths, and can be integrated into a life of any faith—or no faith. No matter your spiritual history or current practice, we believe you will find these practices to be helpful and nourishing. We hope you will be empowered to continue whatever work it is you do in the world, strengthened by renewed spirituality. We hope you will be inspired to live out your spirituality in new, world-changing ways.

Although we are targeting social justice and caring for the environment, you will not find many statistics of injustice and the depletion of resources here. Nor will you find specific action programs. Many other teachers and groups have presented well-documented statistics spelling out the injustices and environmental blights that exist. And numerous wonderful groups are organizing and working for social and environmental change.

This book focuses on what has made necessary changes so difficult, and what we can do to create the inner environment to work through those obstacles. Each chapter of this book contains specific spiritual practices from our traditions—Jewish, Christian, and Muslim—to help us deal with feelings that inhibit successful action in the world.

Chapter 1 focuses on our own personal awakening to the effectiveness of spiritual practice. We want you to have some sense of who we are as the Interfaith Amigos, and how we ourselves realized the need for such practice.

In chapter 2, we explore the issue of polarization, and how that polarization works against the changes we seek. The practices shared are designed to help us move beyond the consequences of the way our minds almost automatically compel us to take one side or the other and increase such polarization.

Chapter 3 looks at freeing ourselves from the past conditioning that prompts us to fear the other and seek safety among people who share our beliefs or background. You will find spiritual practices to help you escape the traps of old conditioning that can unconsciously work against true social justice.

Consideration of environmental problems that loom so large often leads us to despair. In chapter 4, we examine practices that can move us beyond that hopelessness. Spiritual practices help us deal with feelings that inhibit positive action.

Anger and burnout plague the social and environmental activist, so we dedicate chapter 5 to practices that can help us deal with our anger and avoid the pain of burnout.

In chapter 6, we spotlight the nature of our fears, noticing how those fears can lead to violent thoughts and behaviors. Specific spiritual practices offer relief from the kind of fear that erupts into violence, as well as some of the fears that stop us from living freely and happily.

After considering how we can deal with many of the serious negative states that derail effective action, chapter 7 probes the power of love as a positive force for change. We offer practices to help celebrate the awakening of that love within ourselves and our world.

While we focus on specific issues in our lives, we also know that effective spiritual practice must become part of our daily lives. Chapter 8 looks at daily practices, as well as seasonally oriented and life cycle–specific spiritual practices from our faith traditions.

We conclude with some general comments on the nature of spiritual practice, with reminders about how all of us can benefit from them. We close by inviting you into a fuller awakening of hope and a deeper commitment to compassionate action in the world.

A Note about the Perspectives and Practices

While we draw from our own traditions—Judaism, Christianity, and Islam—each of our perspectives also flows from our personal experience. We do not necessarily intend to provide a comprehensive overview of any one topic as addressed by our faith. We do intend to provide compelling spiritual practices that spring from our understanding of our faith. These practices are rooted in tradition but are also often extensions of traditional rituals of our faiths.

A note on our scriptural sources: Rabbi Ted's biblical quotations are his own translations, unless otherwise indicated. Pastor Don's biblical quotations are taken from the *New Revised Standard Version Bible*.[1] Imam Jamal's Qur'anic translations are primarily from *The Meaning of the Holy Qur'an*. Other translations used are *The Message of the Qur'an* and *The Light of Dawn: Daily Readings from the Holy Qur'an*.[2] Throughout the book, we have used the term "Christian Scriptures" in place of the more usual "New Testament" because of the supersessionist nature of the latter. In this book, we mean this term to point specifically to the Christian literature usually called the New Testament. However, it should be noted that for Pastor Don and many others, "Christian Scriptures" includes not only the specifically Christian material in the Gospels and Epistles, but also the Jewish biblical texts.

How to Use This Book

The three of us once spoke during a Sunday service at the Fauntleroy United Church of Christ in Seattle, and one of the topics we touched on was the value of experiencing spiritual practices of other traditions. In the question-and-answer period, a Jewish visitor shared that he once was surprised to see two Muslim men in a restroom prayerfully focused on a purification ritual with water, preparing themselves for the body prayer. With great care, they washed their hands and elbows, rinsed their nostrils, cleaned their ears, splashed their faces and eyes, ran their damp hands over their hair and neck, and washed their feet. With each cleansing motion, they softly intoned prayers, such as "May these hands always be of service to You, my Cherisher and Sustainer," to accompany the washing of hands; or a more specific prayer to follow the cleansing of the ears: "May I refuse to listen to gossip." As that man witnessed them with fascination, he felt a palpable shift in himself. His understanding and appreciation of Islamic body prayers inspired him to say his own Jewish prayers with a deeper sense of purification and presence.

The idea of exploring practices of other faiths is not to judge or compare them but to experience the beauty of the same Spirit that pervades all spiritual practices. Sometimes a spiritual practice of another tradition can touch us so deeply that we want to weave it in into our own. Treasures from another's faith practice can supplement our own practices and help us grow during our spiritual journey. By entering into this kind of experience of the heart, we can soften our fear of what is unfamiliar and different. This journey has its ups and downs. The path is not easy, but the rewards are beautiful. By exploring each other's spiritual practices, we can begin to cultivate an inner spaciousness that allows us to embrace and celebrate the different forms of religious experience so we can discover the universals we share.

This is not about shedding your faith but adding another dimension to your identity. It's a way of experiencing new spiritual practices that reflect the wisdom, the compassion, and the clarity of the ground of another's faith. For the three of us, deepening our spirituality through experiencing these spiritual practices has profoundly supported our individual journeys. We have learned to trust that the words, the melodies and movements, and the meditations of another's way can help us experience flavors of spirituality that enhance us all.

Each chapter in this book addresses a topic we've found to come up again and again in social justice and spiritual action work. Following a brief introduction, we each share perspectives from our particular faith tradition, along with specific practices we've found to be helpful in relation to the chapter's themes. While you are most welcome to read this book from beginning to end, this is the kind of text that does not require that. You can turn to a chapter that addresses a particular need you have in a certain moment, and then come back to read other sections later. The material in the early chapters will broaden your understanding of what follows, but each chapter stands on its own.

Please take your time with the spiritual practices. Read them slowly and ponder them. Even a few moments with them can help you taste their richness. Of course, truly grasping the essence of a particular practice requires more than reading. When you find a practice that appeals to you, take some time to work with it. When you find one that supports you, repeat it. We know that different spiritual practices resonate for different people at different times in their lives, so we encourage you to trust your experience. We also encourage you to go back and explore practices that at first may have seemed unappealing.

In all spiritual practices, the proof is in the doing. It's not enough just to read about a practice. It's necessary to step into it, and discover the difference it makes in your world. We share ideas on "Walking This Practice into the World" to help you bring each practice from a dedicated "spiritual" time into your everyday tasks and encounters.

We hope you will use the practices in this book not only to deepen your own spirituality, but also to connect with others of different faiths and spiritual perspectives. We encourage you to try practices on your own and then discuss your experience in a trusted group, and even to try practices together as a group.

Whether done individually or as a community, no matter the foundation of our path, the spiritual practices shared here can support all of us in deep ways—whatever our faith of origin. There is but one caveat: we have to practice them. We encourage you to journal your experiences so that you can better witness your process and your progress. Be aware of resistances that may arise. Most important, be aware of changes you perceive within yourself or in the world around you.

Spiritual practices from a wealth of traditions can help awaken you to your deeper spiritual identity, to the fullness of your human potential. Because this is so, the very nature of your experience in the world can shift. Not only will you find a rejuvenation of soul, of mind, and of body, but also this final stage of the interfaith process will allow you to celebrate this healing together with other people on the interfaith journey.

This book has been a special challenge and joy for each of us to write. In many ways, we are sharing a great deal about our own journeys through this text. Many of these practices have been deeply meaningful to us and profoundly express the spirituality in our traditions that we cherish. We are delighted to share them with you.

So take a deep breath, release it slowly and fully, and begin this journey with us.

1

Discovering the Need for Spiritual Practice

Inner Change Leads to Lasting Outer Change

"Be the change you wish to see." These words are usually attributed to Mahatma Gandhi, and frequently appear on bumper stickers. His actual words, however, were "If we could change ourselves, the tendencies in the world would also change."[1] This statement is less suited to bumper stickers but conveys even more deeply the reality that true change starts inside ourselves.

Our external changes may take us outside our usual comfort zones, but unless we internally expand those comfort zones, our behavior will inch right back to where we started. This is one of the main reasons that people who lose weight tend to gain it back: Their inner sense of themselves never made the switch to their new body. In personal development, this is sometimes referred to as the difference between cosmetic change and authentic change—cosmetic change gives way to old patterns unless there is an authentic inner identity change. This is also why, over time, many of the advances in areas of social justice tend to revert to injustices thought long past. The outer changes were not accompanied by the changes in consciousness necessary to sustain them in the world.

Spiritual practices encourage the inner change that reinforces the positive impact we have on our personal and communal lives.

Spiritual practices open us to new levels of self-understanding. They help us find deeper meaning in our lives, because they increase our awareness of how powerful our own thoughts, words, feelings, and actions can be.

These practices enhance our relationships with others, because through them we become more aware of our common humanity, so often hidden behind the prejudices of our conditioned minds. When we are not hindered by preexisting judgments, we are better able to authentically respond to others. Spiritual practices also help us open to and recognize a far larger sense of the Life that holds us all, and that thrives within each and every being. Through spiritual practice, we encounter this greater Life as an active experience, rather than a more limited conceptual and intellectual understanding.

And spiritual practices decrease the stress and anxiety that keep us from enjoying so much of our experience in the world. Through social and environmental action, we can accomplish much more when we release the anger and hate that we use to justify dehumanizing, and even demonizing, the other. Spiritual practices can help us realize that we are all in this Life together, and that each of us is responsible for supporting the healing that everyone needs. Our actions in the world are obviously important, but without an inner recognition of our common humanity, they cannot endure.

How We Ourselves Realized the Importance of Spiritual Practices

Rabbi Ted's Story

I was always fascinated by psychology, philosophy, and the nature of consciousness. From an early age, I remember times when I was aware of my utter aloneness and other times when I was conscious of my connection to everything around me.

In the senior year of my undergraduate studies, I discovered the writings of Martin Buber, one of the most important twentieth-century Jewish philosophers and educators. Buber spoke of authentic relationship as I-Thou: meeting another as subject to subject, in which the full presence of the one is alive for the other. This is in contrast to an I-It relationship, where both meet as subject and object, as separate beings. Buber called the I-Thou meeting transformative. Experiencing the depth of that kind of relationship with another transformed me, prompting me to abandon my previous desire to teach English literature and shift to the study and teaching of Jewish philosophy. This change led me to rabbinical school. Little did I know that Martin Buber was not a favorite among the faculty there; his I-Thou philosophy was out of step with their more academic orientation. My further study of Buber had to wait until I had completed the seminary curriculum.

Like all rabbinic students, I spent several years as a student rabbi at congregations unable to hire a full-time rabbi. During the civil rights movement of the 1960s, as a student rabbi at a synagogue in Hattiesburg, Mississippi, I again encountered the power of the I-Thou and the potential promise of spiritual practice. At the very first Bar Mitzvah ritual I conducted as a student rabbi, I stood with the young man before the open ark to convey the traditional Bar Mitzvah blessing. I placed my hands on him and pronounced the ancient Hebrew words of the priestly benediction (Numbers 6:24–26). A sudden, intense connection illuminated the moment, a connection I had never experienced in such a focused way before. Perhaps it was an I-Thou. Perhaps it was an energy transfer. Whatever it was, it was an opening and it was a surprise. The young man and I shared something that we were not able to put into words. That moment, in which something so powerful came alive between us, inspired me to learn more about such events.

After ordination, I become an assistant rabbi at one of the most socially active congregations in the country. In that Los Angeles community, I became active in social causes, but kept returning to the importance of personal relationships, becoming a leader of sensitivity groups and getting training in counseling. It appeared that social activism meant identifying the enemies and working against them and the manifestations of their belief systems. But I found that much of human meaning came from identifying others as potential neighbors, rather than enemies. It seemed we protestors always found more to protest about. Even when external changes did occur, they did not seem to end the problems because the groundwork for those changes in the inner world had not been established.

In December 1969, I took time for a needed personal retreat at the Esalen Institute in Big Sur, on the California coast. Driving back in a rainstorm, rocks suddenly started raining down on my VW bug from the wall of mountain on my left. On my right was a cliff, a sheer drop down to the ocean.

I still treasure the rock that crashed through the driver's–side window and hit me in the back of the neck. In the middle of the rockslide, as a boulder flattened my door and rocks threatened to block my way, I suddenly found I was looking down at the car from far above. In that moment, out of the body, I experienced a radical sense of peace and safety. I thought my body was dying, and I was at ease with that. Only later did I read reports of such experiences from others, and learned that it had a name: an out-of-body experience.

Another level of expanded awareness had opened and I knew it was one I needed to explore. In those days, spiritual exploration and altered states of consciousness fell into the province of psychology, rather than religion. I entered a graduate program in the professional application of psychotherapy that allowed me to openly pursue studies in how altered states of consciousness promote healing.

It became clear to me that a more inclusive meditative consciousness not only enhanced personal psychotherapeutic healing but was needed to support greater social change as well. Along my journey, I discovered helpful meditative practices in Zen Buddhist and Hindu traditions, and I wondered at the absence of meditative teachings in Judaism. It was not that they didn't exist but, at the time, they had been forgotten and ignored, and were certainly not taught at seminary.

So I developed a personal Jewish practice of contemplative meditation that I later learned had a name, *hitbon'nut*, which refers to inviting deeper wisdom, usually through focusing on a text. I would randomly open a traditional Jewish prayer book and contemplate whatever I found. On one such day, the book fell open to the most well-known passage in Jewish worship, the *Sh'ma*: "Listen, Israel: The Eternal is our God, the Eternal is One" (Deuteronomy 6:4). I came close to shutting the book to find something less familiar, but decided to trust the process—after all, *Sh'ma* means "listen." The text continues:

> And you will love the Eternal your God with all your heart, with all your soul, and with all your might. And these words that I command you today shall be on your heart. Repeat them to your children, and speak them when you sit in your house, when you walk on the way, when you lie down and when you rise up. (Deuteronomy 6:5–6)

In the ancient biblical idiom, the heart was understood as the center of thought. So the injunction encouraged us to repeat the words of the *Sh'ma* in our *mind* while at home or away, when going to sleep and when awakening from sleep. *That's all the time.* In truly listening to what the *Sh'ma* was saying, I found myself encountering this well-read text for the first time. I suddenly understood the words to be instructions for a focus for meditation, and it has been a secure foundation for my spiritual practice ever since. The meditative instructions had always been there, hidden in plain sight.

The *Sh'ma* became my mantra, and I later found many other Jewish texts and practices that support spiritual awakening. As a result, in the late-1970s I became one of the first to teach Jewish meditation in the Los Angeles area. Since then, in part because of the deepening relationships with my fellow Amigos, my mind and heart have opened more fully to the spiritual wisdom of the other Abrahamic traditions as well.

Some imagine that with spiritual practice all of life becomes easier, as if the bumps are smoothed. That has not been my experience. But meditative practice has allowed me to better understand the dramas we all face. I have found depths of healing connections with others that simply were not available to me before. The universality of spiritual awareness continues to lead me to greater appreciation for the treasures of all authentic spiritual traditions. I know that a more inclusive consciousness, awakening through spiritual practice, is required to support the kind of social changes that are needed in our world today.

Pastor Don's Story

My Christian path can be traced back to my Scottish, Irish, and German great-grandparents. My great-grandfather, Roderick Mackenzie, was a pastor in Tarbert in the Outer Hebrides of Scotland. It was from his church that the Harris Tweed industry was organized. I can connect to his social conscience as well as to his ministry.

Both of my grandfathers were clerks of session in their Presbyterian churches in Chicago Heights, Illinois, and Leavenworth, Kansas. My father was also an elder in the Presbyterian church and my mother was a member of the choir and an organist. The congregations where we lived and the life of the Christian faith were a part of my life from my earliest memories. I am grateful to all those who have gone before me for this gift of faith.

At the same time, and within this sense of gratitude, I also have a sense of skepticism concerning the church and its ministry. Part of that goes back to the awareness that my father was a conscientious objector during World War II. He based his position on religious grounds and was supported by his minister at the First Presbyterian Church of Chicago. From an early age I assumed that ministers would, in general, be opposed to war. But growing up, I never heard an antiwar sermon and, in fact, I don't remember ever hearing a sermon that in any way challenged the status quo. It became harder and harder to connect what little I knew of Jesus's message to what seemed to be support for the status quo by churches. Not until I entered seminary did I begin to hear challenging sermons and lectures on the relationship between the message of the gospel and social action.

While "spirituality" was a word that I heard frequently from my parents as I was growing up, it was not a word that I heard in church and not a word that I remember much from seminary. So much less so the phrase "spiritual practice." In fact, in the first church I served, after preaching a sermon on prayer, I was informed that prayer was not an appropriate topic for a sermon!

My first memory of a spiritual experience was in the summer of 1965. I had a job as a lifeguard at the Nile Hilton Hotel in Cairo. It was a Macalester College program. When the job ended, I flew to Beirut, where I had made plans to meet with the headmaster of a private school in Sidon, Lebanon. He was also a Macalester graduate. He picked me up at the airport and drove a friend and me up into the mountains to the house they were renting for the summer. When we arrived, he suggested that we take a walk to see the landscape. We did that and, at one point, we came to a promontory, a place where, suddenly, we could see Beirut down below and the Mediterranean on the horizon. It seemed as if, seeing the strip of coast where Beirut was and then such a vast expanse of sea beyond, we could see the entire world at once. In that moment I felt a sense of oneness, of centeredness, though I would not have used those words then. A door opened for me. It was an intensely spiritual moment and has helped define my faith and my ministry. Since then I have dedicated my life to reexperiencing that sense of oneness and helping others become aware of our interconnectedness through spiritual practices.

Imam Jamal's Story

My parents have been my most precious and treasured teachers. As devout Muslims, they taught their children the basics of Islam and because they were both of a spiritual bent, they shared with us a variety of spiritual practices. Over the years we learned exercises to be grateful, to cultivate compassion, to forgive others, and to be conscious of God. My favorite spiritual practice was to reflect on Qur'anic verses chosen by my parents.

As an adult, in my work with projects for social justice causes, I always remember the wisdom of a verse in the Qur'an that my parents taught us. It helps me understand why humans throughout

history have been so susceptible to senseless polarization and violence. In an environment of chronic prejudice, fear, anger, and
hate, of hopelessness and helplessness, "Truly it is not their eyes
that are blind," says the Qur'an, "but their hearts which are in their
breasts" (22:46). Too often, when our hearts become blind to God's
presence in other people, they are also tightly closed against any
feeling of fellowship with those who don't "belong" to our own
small circle of family and friends. The blind and inhospitable heart
is capable of countless ills, starting with simple unkindness and
escalating along a tragic continuum to discrimination, persecution, and ultimately even genocide. In these violent times it clearly
behooves each one of us to open our hearts and acknowledge the
divine essence of our fellow human beings.

But how do we do this necessary work, which is much easier
said than done? Trying to force the heart to open merely causes
it to close up even more tightly. Trying to convince it with sweet
reason is a good beginning, but the ego intervenes, guards its own
biases, and is loath to let them go. Ultimately, only what comes
from the heart can touch and open another heart.

At a recent conference I was profoundly touched and inspired
by the story of an African-American activist who spoke about how
he continually engages the Qur'anic insight about blindness of
heart in his struggle for racial justice. As a child he experienced
the hurt of being called the "n-word," and he responded by hit-
ting the white boy who had called him the hateful word. At home,
his father congratulated him, but his mother tenderly chided him,
saying, "What good did that do?" She continued, "Son, there has
to be a better way." Her words resonated in his young soul, and
he has dedicated his life to finding that better way. To overcome
racism, he combines political action with the continuous sacred
work of opening his heart by becoming a more mindful, compassionate, patient, and inclusive human being. Refusing to demonize people who exhibit racial bigotry, he consciously distinguishes
between their behavior and their being. Only the behavior needs to
be criticized and confronted. The being or essence of every human

is sacred. To heal his pain and soften his anger, he employs a variety of spiritual practices. With compassion, he examines his own biases against other people. He makes every effort to establish a human and personal connection with those who offend him.

I have learned that this inspiring man is practicing what we might call "sacred activism," the art of restoring love and compassion to relationships that have been damaged by fear and hatred, and his story highlights the critical need for spiritual practices. By doing the abiding inner work, one cultivates what Sufis call an "inner spaciousness." From this wellspring of spaciousness will arise ways of thinking, being, and doing that are integrated, whole, and compassionate. The heart knows that no one is born with a genetic predisposition to hate. Even a slight human connection reduces the tendency to dehumanize the other. The work we do to open our own hearts and the efforts we make to touch the hearts of others are two sides of the same coin, called peacemaking. It is a coin of inestimable worth, for the Arabic word for peace, *salaam*, means not only absence of conflict but also "wholeness" and "well-being," and it stems from the same root as "Islam."

Spiritual Resources and Basic Practices in Our Traditions

Each of us approaches the importance of spiritual practice and spiritual consciousness from our own experience. As we have expanded our own awareness, we find ourselves supported by the depth of spiritual resources and practices within our respective faith traditions. We make no claim to the superiority of any tradition, but seek to appreciate the treasures we have discovered and that we can share with each other. Here is some of what nourishes us on our spiritual journey.

Spiritual Resources in Judaism

People often use the word "spiritual" to signify something beautiful, awe-inspiring, overwhelmingly good, and deeply meaningful. All of these meanings are reinforced by Jewish tradition. More specifically, however, spirituality encompasses a more inclusive reality behind, beneath, or even above our normal everyday experience of self and world.

The Four Levels of Awareness

From the early years of the first century CE, these different levels of reality have been identified in Judaism by the acronym PaRDeS, where the capital letters represent four levels of awareness. The word *pardes* (pronounced PAR-days) means "orchard" in Hebrew.

The Hebrew letter represented by the "P" stands for *p'shat*, indicating the simple, surface level of a text or an event. It's where our experience of self and the world begin.

The Hebrew letter represented by the "R" stands for *remez* (pronounced REH-mehz), which means "hint," and indicates a broader context for a text or an event. Understanding something at this level helps us see its more universal themes.

The "D" of PaRDeS represents the Hebrew word *derash* (pronounced deh-RAHSH), which means "explication," an unfolding of meaning that is behind the words. This is the metaphorical level, in which the drama is no longer external but is taking place within each of us. Characters and events reflect aspects of our inner world and the text becomes far more personal. The text lives in us.

The "S" in PaRDeS stands for *sod* (pronounced SODE), which means "secret." This refers to the more profound spiritual mystery, often referred to as the "pathless path." *Sod* calls to mind the ineffable, a realization that cannot be expressed in words.

This PaRDeS model encourages an appreciation of the more spiritual and universal levels of all sacred texts, particularly the Torah, the first five books of the Hebrew Bible. It also offers a map for looking at dreams and even external events of our lives. PaRDeS provides a model for moving from the literal to the figurative, from the specific to the more inclusive spiritual dimension of our lives.

Three Levels of the Soul

Rabbinic tradition also identifies three levels of soul. The *nefesh* refers to the body-self, the personal identity we call the ego, centered in the solar plexus. Our *nefesh* represents our separate self. Behind that persona is our more expansive Self, the *ruach*, often called the Greater Self, centered in the heart. The *ruach* bridges the gap between our separate ego identity, the *nefesh*, and the far more inclusive identity called the *neshamah*. The *neshamah* cannot fit into the confines of the body, but communicates through the *ruach* in dreams, intuition, and spontaneous awakenings.

Spiritual Practices in Judaism

Spiritual practices in Judaism are called *hanhagot*. They help awaken us from the knowledge of the outwardly revealed Torah to the spiritual depths of the sacred text. They help us find the sacred in the seemingly ordinary. At the same time, we become more available for the universal wisdom of our soul. The spiritual goal is called *d'vekut*, best translated as "God consciousness."

Well-known spiritual practices in Judaism include:

Study: Particularly when focusing on sacred Jewish literature, study can be a spiritual practice. By the fifteenth century, Jewish literacy had expanded beyond the scholars and rabbis to the entire Jewish population. Education is still emphasized within the Jewish community—it's one thing that can never be taken away from us.

Prayer: Prayer is another avenue to Jewish spirituality, supported by the rubric of PaRDeS. Many of the spiritual practices relating to prayer involve utilizing the shapes and energies of individual Hebrew letters, words, and phrases as focuses for meditation.

Spiritual Renewal and Shabbat: Shabbat (Hebrew for "Sabbath") is the most important Jewish holiday, creating a weekly space for many spiritual practices. Shabbat reflects this Torah teaching: "The children of Israel shall observe Shabbat ... because on the seventh day, God observed Shabbat and re-souled" (Exodus 31:16–17). Shabbat is meant to support a spiritual renewal of the *nefesh*, the separate self with which we walk in the world.

Singing: Singing is another commonplace spiritual practice, particularly the melodies without words, sung or chanted repeatedly, that are called *niggunim*. A *niggun*, a form popularized by the eighteenth-century Jewish spiritual renewal called Hasidism, is designed to reach deeper than words to open us to the true prayers and aspirations of the soul. Group practices of such soul-singing encourage the celebration of the profound Presence we share.

Blessing: Blessing means saying "Yes!" to existence, and each "Yes!" helps us reach beyond separateness. It is so important a practice that the ancient rabbis prescribed one hundred blessings daily. Spontaneous blessings throughout the day reflect mindfulness and an attitude of acceptance. And if you hear someone else's blessing—someone else's "Yes!"—and say "Amen!" it counts as one of your own hundred blessings.

Meditation: Meditation, of course, is central to Jewish spiritual practice. Study, ritual, prayer, song, and blessing may each have meditative aspects. *Hitbod'dut* is the Hebrew word for meditation, a word that literally means "to be alone with oneself." Most Jewish meditative practices encourage the withdrawal from external focus to the breath, to a Hebrew word or phrase, or to the visualization of Hebrew letters or words. Where once meditation was a hidden treasure within modern Jewish tradition, there are now several schools that offer training for those who wish to teach Jewish meditation.

***Tzedakah*:** *Tzedakah* is the Hebrew word that comes closest to the English word "charity," but *tzedakah* literally means "righteousness." Jewish spiritual practices support compassionate action in the world, and compassionate actions in the world themselves can open us spiritually.

A Basic Jewish Spiritual Practice

A Breath Meditation with the *Sh'ma*

The Torah instructs us to have the six words of the *Sh'ma* "in our hearts" always—when we sit in our homes, when we walk on the way, when we lie down, and when we rise up (Deuteronomy 6:6–7). Using the words of the *Sh'ma* in meditation is a time-tested technique for helping us transcend our attachment to separateness. The words can be paired with the breath.

I began my practice of Jewish meditation by silently repeating the six words of the *Sh'ma* in a period of meditation, and then continuing to silently repeat those words as I went about my daily activities. I still find this practice extremely helpful, particularly in times of stress.

Beginning and ending the day with even a brief time for meditating on the *Sh'ma* reinforces the practice. Living with this proclamation affirms that there is only One. The *Sh'ma* continually reminds us that the two aspects of oneness we perceive—the transcendent One that includes all that exists, and the immanent One awakening within each being—are One. There is only One Life, One Presence, One Being, and we are each a precious and unique expression of that One in our world.

The six words that comprise the *Sh'ma* (Deuteronomy 6:4) are:

Sh'ma: Listen.

> It all begins with learning to listen. We are asked to be still, to release whatever current thoughts and stories, feelings and judgments, sensations and perceptions are now filling our awareness. This first word invites our silence.

Yisrael (pronounced YISS-ra-el): Israel.

> At the time this line was shared and finally written down, there was not yet a country named Israel. There was a people called the children of Israel, descended from Jacob, whose spiritual name came to be "Israel." The name translates either as "one who wrestles with God," "one who persists for God," or simply, "God persists."

Adonai (pronounced ah-doh-NYE): The Eternal; Lord.

> *Adonai* is the word we substitute for the four-letter name of God, the letters transliterated as YHVH, that stopped being pronounced during the days of the Second Temple. YHVH is a form of the Hebrew verb that means "to be," and signifies being without limitation of time or space. When Jews encounter this

four-letter name in scripture or in prayer, we read the replacement word *Adonai*, which means "Lord."

Eloheinu (pronounced el-oh-HEY-new): [is] our God.

This is a possessive form of *Elohim*, translated as "God," which is a unique plural form in Hebrew that is always treated as singular. The word affirms the oneness of God while at the same time recognizing the multiple forms through which that One manifests.

Adonai: The Eternal.

The Name Beyond Speech appears for a second time in this biblical verse. It looks the same, but perhaps this second appearance carries a deeper meaning. We might imagine the progression as an evolving process. First, there is *Adonai*, the One in Whom All Else Is. Then comes the indwelling aspect of that One—the Eternal awakening within each of us as "our God"—*Eloheinu*. What might be perceived or understood or imagined as two are always One, so the progression needs to complete itself with *Adonai*. Outside and Inside are both embraced by *Adonai*. The progression allows us to understand That Which Is Never Separate from Itself. (If you're wondering why I use so many capital letters as I stretch words to contain the uncontainable, capital letters serve as reminders that these words are meant to transcend themselves.)

Echad (pronounced eh-KHAD): [is] One.

As the awareness of this Oneness has awakened over time, many of us understand that everything that exists is a part of this One, and that nothing exists outside of this One. There is One Life, One Consciousness, One Love, One Energy that we all share. All that is, is God, but God is not limited by all that is. We are to strive for that level of awareness in which Oneness is no longer a concept but a lived Reality.

Take a few moments to get comfortable, sitting in a position that frees you to breathe easily. You might take a gentle inventory of the places in your body that are particularly relaxed, and notice any areas of tension. Simply becoming aware, without trying to change anything, has interesting consequences.

Silently and gently imagine saying *Sh'ma* as you inhale. Listening is a taking-in. Then silently say *Yisrael* as you exhale. Inhale with the next word, *Adonai*, and then hear yourself say *Eloheinu* as you exhale. Then inhale with *Adonai* and exhale with *Echad*.

With each breath cycle there are two words; with three breaths, the entire *Sh'ma*. And the process simply repeats. You can set a timer if you like, perhaps starting with even five or ten minutes and working your way up to fifteen or twenty minutes.

When your mind strays, gently return to the cycle by silently repeating *Sh'ma* as you inhale. Using a meditation journal to record your experience will help you appreciate deepening aspects of this practice.

Walking This Practice into the World

Take just the first word, *Sh'ma*, or the English word, "Listen," and silently repeat it to yourself as you go about your daily life. Let this be an inner reminder that brings you into a greater appreciation of the uniqueness of each moment. In conversation, let this inner reminder encourage fuller attention as you become more present and available.

Spiritual Resources in Christianity

In Christianity, spiritual resources are found most visibly in scripture, in the writings of the leaders of the early church, in the writings of the desert fathers and mothers, and in the great medieval, renaissance and modern mystics. These resources are rooted in the Jewish concept of Oneness, are made functional through unconditional love, and point toward compassion.

Spiritual Practices in Christianity

The history of Christian spiritual practices begins with the Gospels' accounts of Jesus's time in the wilderness in prayer, meditation, and fasting (Matthew 4:1–11; Mark 1:12–13; Luke 4:1–11). The story says he spent forty days in the wilderness. The number forty points to the Hebrew concept of forty as a length of time necessary to complete the task at hand. The story goes on to describe three temptations from the devil. The image of the "devil" functions as a metaphor for the needs of the ego. But Jesus's preparation has enabled him to rise above those kinds of things. The failure to tempt him provides evidence that he is ready for his ministry.

Jesus did not invent the idea of spiritual practices. He was drawing on traditions within Judaism—Jesus was a Jew—as well as possibly from Buddhist or Hindu sources. While there is no hard evidence for that speculation, I like to think he was open to the wisdom of other traditions. My evidence for this lies in the Parable of the Empty Jar in the Gospel of Thomas.[2] A woman is on her way home, carrying a jar filled with grain. There is a crack in the jar and the grain is slowly leaking out. She does not realize this until she gets home and sets down the jar, only to discover that it is empty. The parable has a Zen-like quality. Jesus is constantly seeking wisdom to enhance his life, to strengthen his beliefs.

Spiritual practices were also developed by Jesus's followers—both those seeking to make sense of and draw strength from his death and resurrection as well as those seeking understanding from his teachings. These kinds of spiritual exercises were practiced by adherents of the early Christian monastic movements and continued through Christian history, including well-known Christian medieval and later mystics such as Hildegard of Bingen, Julian of Norwich, Teresa of Avila, and Meister Eckhart.

The Protestant Reformation did not place as much emphasis on spiritual practices, apart from prayer, but spiritual practices were kept alive by the Roman Catholic church and the Greek, Russian, and other Orthodox denominations. It is only recently that Protestants have rediscovered these ancient practices of the church. Contemporary theologian Brian McLaren suggests three classifications of practices: personal or devotional, communal or corporate, and missional. There is, he suggests, a linear progression from the personal through the communal to the missional, each needing the previous for wisdom and guidance.[3]

In Christian scripture, spiritual practices are frequently encouraged. For example, in the Sermon on the Mount (Matthew

6:5–15) Jesus teaches the importance of prayer. There are many verses that suggest the idea of living life as much as possible with a spiritual sensibility, as evidenced by such phrases as "pray without ceasing" (1 Thessalonians 5:17). In Romans 12:12 we read, "Rejoice in hope, be patient in suffering, persevere in prayer." In Ephesians 6:18 we find, "Pray always with all prayer and supplication in the spirit, and watch thereunto with all perseverance and supplication for all saints." Understood literally, praying without ceasing is an impossibility. But what is suggested and encouraged is to develop a way of living that carries spiritual practices done privately or in corporate worship into our everyday activities by using key words or phrases or brief moments of meditation to maintain, as much as is humanly possible, a spiritual way of being. This work of spiritual practices—personal, corporate, and missional—is what we three call the inconvenient work, because it demands discipline. But practices are habits and, if they are integrated over time into our other daily habits, they can actually become convenient and wonderful.

A Basic Christian Spiritual Practice

Lectio Divina

Lectio divina is a spiritual practice that derives from the Christian tradition. The dynamics of this practice date back to the early years of Christianity. It was encouraged for monastic use in the sixth century CE by St. Benedict. The four steps were formalized in the twelfth century and are promoted today for general use by all Christians and, I would say, anyone wishing to adapt this practice to another tradition.

Lectio divina means "divine reading," words that point to a greater feeling for and closeness to God. For Christians, this comes because of the ministry of Jesus, which revealed God's purposes with particular clarity. *Lectio divina* helps us return to that clarity.

The four steps of *lectio divina* are: (1) reading a passage of scripture, (2) meditating on that scripture, (3) praying in the context of that scripture, and (4) contemplating the broader message of the scripture, particularly how it increases our awareness of God's presence. *Lectio divina* is not a process of analyzing scripture. It points us toward an understanding of the purposes of God.

Consider the story of the Prodigal Son (Luke 15:11–32). A man has two sons. The younger son asks for his inheritance, travels to a distant country, wastes the money, and, after a period of starvation and menial labor, decides to go back home, hoping for a job on his father's farm. While he is gone, the older son, obeying his father's rule, is left to shoulder the burden of the farm's and family's responsibilities.

When the younger son returns, the father welcomes him with open arms and throws a party in his honor. The older son, because he has yet to come to an understanding of forgiveness, resents the party because, as he says, he has always obeyed the father.

When reflecting on this story through *lectio divina*, the purpose is not to try to understand forgiveness in an intellectual sense. Rather, the process is useful in helping us feel the meaning of forgiveness and better absorb the meaning of God's purposes.

So, to practice *lectio divina*, I invite you to read the story of the Prodigal Son.

Find a quiet place to read and meditate, the first two steps. After you have read the passage slowly once or twice, noticing words or phrases that stand out to you, sit up straight with both feet on the floor and slowly and gently close your eyes and become aware of your breath moving in and out of your nose. This part of the practice does not always come easily, so be patient. One of the purposes of meditation is to empty the mind of superfluous thoughts. But, almost always, those thoughts drift back in. Use a word or phrase from the passage of scripture that you have just read to help you return to the center of your meditation. You might try using "and they began to celebrate," a phrase that describes what happens when the younger son returns to his family. I like this phrase because it suggests an awareness of and a marking of an event of very high importance. You will need to decide just how long to meditate, perhaps aiming for ten to twenty minutes, and set a timer for yourself.

The third step is prayer. When we pray, we use words to communicate with God. But we are not educating God about our needs. That is not necessary. The use of words is an act that helps open our hearts, to manage the activities of our egos so that we can find that balance between our individual needs and the needs of the world. So as you move into prayer, become aware of some words that are suggested by the reading of the story of the Prodigal Son. Use those words in a conscious attempt to be emptied of your narrower concerns and filled with the concerns and purposes of God. This requires practice as well. Do not be discouraged if you feel you have not accomplished this right away.

As you move to the fourth and final step, you can simply listen to your thoughts as you reflect on what has happened in the first three steps. You will experience a similarity between meditation and contemplation because the openness of the mind and the heart is essential to each step. But with the final step, you may experience a feeling of peace, increased spiritual awareness and closeness to God and God's purposes.

Walking This Practice into the World

After you've experienced the full *lectio divina* practice, take the meditation into your daily activities by occasionally repeating the word "celebrate" from the Parable of the Prodigal Son to remind yourself of the miracle that happens with the experience of forgiveness.

Spiritual Resources in Islam

The primary source of spiritual guidance for Muslims is the Qur'an, a collection of divine revelations conceived in silence and mystery. Deep in meditation one night in 610 CE, an illiterate caravan trader named Muhammad was startled by a blinding light that announced itself as the angel Gabriel and commanded him to "Recite." The terrified Muhammad bolted from the Meccan cave but later returned. Again the light appeared and Muhammad, suffering the painful pressure of being squeezed from within, began to utter words of startling beauty. This mysterious transmission of verses in Arabic from Spirit to angel Gabriel to Muhammad, now revered by Muslims as the Prophet Muhammad, continued intermittently for twenty-three years. The collection of these verses constitutes the Qur'an, which informs the daily lives of Muslims on both practical and spiritual levels.

A secondary source of guidance for Muslims is hadith, the collection of the Prophet's sayings and stories about his life and conduct. Since these are based on hearsay, sages caution Muslims to accept only those hadith that conform to the core teachings of the Qur'an.

Yet another source of guidance is the priceless treasury of spiritual wisdom offered by the sages and mystics who abound in Islam. Many of these treasured teachers come from a tradition known as Sufism, which is not a denomination of Islam but rather a spiritual aspiration that focuses on essence rather than form; that is, the spirit of Islam rather than the letter of Islamic law. Sufism emerged very early in the history of Islam, when the nascent religion was experiencing exponential growth and becoming a global empire with all the secular faults and abuses that accompany temporal power. Concerned that the spirituality of Islam was being sullied by the needs of empire building, the early Sufis did their best to focus on purification of the inner self and to be of service to God's creation. No one knows for certain the origin of the word "Sufi," but the root word seems to indicate a combination of material simplicity and spiritual purity. There are both Sunni and Shia Sufis, and even non-Muslim Sufis who draw on Sufi wisdom and practices as they pursue other paths to the Divine. Because they are not wedded to every small dictate of Islamic law, Sufis are accused by conservative Muslims of being overly flexible, but Sufis smilingly reply, "Blessed are the flexible for they will never be bent out of shape!"

At an early age I developed unbounded admiration for the wisdom of the thirteenth-century Sufi sage Jalaluddin Rumi. Because of my father's diplomatic postings, I spent some of my formative years in Iran and Turkey, where Rumi is studied with awe and devotion. My teachers taught me verses of the Qur'an and then invited me to chant and meditate on selected poetry by Rumi. The great sage's utterances are essentially commentaries on the inner meanings of the Qur'an. He often said, "I am a slave of the Qur'an; I am dust on the path of Muhammad."

Spiritual Practices in Islam

In Islam, spiritual practices are usually based on spiritual insights gleaned from the Qur'an, which are then supplemented and complemented by hadith and deepened over time by the writings and meditations of spiritual teachers. For example, one of my favorite spiritual practices is silence, which the Qur'an extols for its majesty and beauty. Speaking of the meditative silence during which the Prophet received the first revelations, the Qur'an says, "Therein come down the angels and the Spirit" (97:4). The Qur'an's praise of silence is validated by stories of the Prophet, who regularly spent time in silence and sometimes even spent forty days and nights in retreat. This combination of Qur'anic verse and hadith leads to the insight that the Qur'an was conceived in the womb of silence, and teachers have expanded that insight by concluding that silence is the language of God. What they mean when they speak of this kind of silence is not the absence of sound but the silencing of the little self. In that pure state, when the ego is surrendered and not nattering endlessly about its own concerns, the heart can hear the whispers of God directly. All the world's self-help books, teachings, and sermons offer but a poor translation of this inner communication with God.

Another practice that follows the pattern of Qur'anic verse augmented by hadith and expanded by spiritual teachers is the core Islamic virtue of compassion. Virtually every one of the 114 chapters of the Holy Book opens with the words, "In the Name of God Boundlessly Compassionate and Infinitely Merciful." The Prophet taught that this oft-repeated invocation, called the *Basmala*, means that we must learn to be compassionate with ourselves and show mercy to others. Expanding on the theme, Sufi teachers use the metaphor of water to illustrate the power and majesty of compassion. Water is life-giving: "Wherever water falls, life flourishes," says

Rumi; "wherever tears fall, Divine mercy is shown." At the same time, water is powerful enough to wash away continents. Thus the compassionate person may seem "soft," but in fact is showing the most authentic kind of strength.

For one last example of the Qur'an-hadith-sages' paradigm of spiritual guidance, let us consider Islam's unique form of prayer. "Bow in adoration and draw closer to God," says the Qur'an (96:19), and so Muslims prostrate themselves in praise and thanksgiving to complete five obligatory prayers a day. The Prophet instructed his followers to perform the prayers "as if you are seeing God and if you cannot see God, know that God sees you." Sufi teachers expound on that insight by pointing out that when we praise God, God does not become holy; we humans do. When we thank our Creator, we tune in to a cosmic chorus of everything on heaven and earth that extols the limitless glory of God. We experience peace and grace because, in the words of a traditional saying, "One prostration of prayer to God frees you from a thousand prostrations to your ego."

A Basic Islamic Spiritual Practice

Islamic spirituality is often centered on the heart, which is mentioned 132 times in the Qur'an and innumerable times in the hadith. We are asked repeatedly to open our hearts. In a beautiful revelation that came to the Prophet in a dream, God says:

> I cannot be contained in the space of the earth
> I cannot be contained in the space of the heavens
> But I can be contained in the space of the pure loving heart
>   of my devotee.[4]

I love the imagery and mystery of Divine Heart being inside human heart! Between the two lie levels upon levels of consciousness, and it is our life work to remove the veils by doing spiritual practices. The goal is to surrender human heart to Divine Heart. By this spiritual process, we create an inner spaciousness that enables us to encompass the bewildering opposites of life, embrace both our joys and sorrows, expand our ability to love, increase our awareness, and practice the golden rule. In so doing, we evolve more and more into the fullness of our being so that we can be of authentic service to God.

Heart Meditation Practice

Reflect on the verse about Divine Heart being inside human heart.

Close your eyes, become silent, and focus on your heart. Touch your heart with one or both hands. Connect for a while with your heartbeat. Remind yourself that the Beloved resides in the chamber of your human heart. God is not only outside of you but also within you. Be present with this astonishing mystery. When you are ready, tell your heart, "I love You" or "Please help me to love You." Say the words with humility and feeling. You might want to say, "Thank You. I am so grateful." Or, "I surrender to You. Please help me." Choose words that resonate for you. No matter how awkward it feels initially, persist and stay with this for a while. Over time, you will find a mysterious divine vibration going from the tongue into the mouth, into the throat, into the chest, deep into the heart, deeper still into the hidden, and then into the "hidden of the hidden," healing and empowering your sacred essence. Faithful practitioners have reported that in difficult times, they have been stunned to hear a reassuring voice mysteriously arising from within and telling them, "I love you," filling their being with calm, joy, healing, and grace.

Walking This Practice into the World

In your waking hours, as you are engaged in speech and action, especially in stressful situations, make it a habit to keep part of your attention focused on your heart space. This will keep you present and centered. Whenever possible, in the course of the day, silently plant words of endearment into your heart. You will feel a deeper connection to your divine identity or authentic Self.

2

Polarization: Our Basic Challenge

What Is It and Why Is It a Problem?

Perhaps you remember the famous cartoon character Pogo Possum's pronouncement in the poster designed by cartoonist Walt Kelly for the first Earth Day in 1970: "We have met the enemy and he is us."

We human beings are the one constant in the unending eruptions of violence that have plagued individuals, groups, and even the planet itself. There seems to be something within the makeup of human beings that permits, promotes, and even perpetuates the pain we bring on ourselves and each other. What makes this even more confusing is that this part of our makeup is also responsible for the compassion, love, and peace in our lives. We are creatures of contrasts. In fact, we know things only *because* of those contrasts. We know hot because there is cold. We know something is soft only because we experience something else as hard.

Knowing through contrasts flows from the very nature of our personalities; it's the basic way our separate self—our ego—operates in the world. Our brain requires comparison to perceive, to understand, and to navigate. We are constructed for a world of separation and distinctiveness.

Problems arise when our awareness of contrast turns into polarization, when one side is valued and the other is not. Or worse, the unvalued side is perceived as wrong, then bad, and, finally, evil.

When we choose sides, like liberal versus conservative, the relationship between the polarities becomes charged. Behind the violence in our world is this basic identification with our side against their side. All of us do it.

Our Personal Self Is a Polarizing Ego

One of the yearnings of the ego, our personal self charged with the survival of our physical being, is to be happy. We long to be healthy, secure, and financially stable. We want to live in a world where everyone gets along. The problem is that such desires lead us to ignore the way our minds operate.

We keep yearning for one side without the other. We want health without sickness and security without endangerment. In some ways, our minds condemn us to this condition. Our minds are judging mechanisms. Charged with protecting us from danger, the mind has to identify where danger lies. In the ancient world, that danger was pretty clear: wild animals and inclement weather. And there were also those other people across the way, the ones who wanted what we had.

Even though we have some understanding of the consequences of polarization, that does not mean we are able to avoid it. As evidence of this, our world today appears more polarized than perhaps ever before. The rejection of the "other side" seems far more severe. We each fervently believe we are identifying with the "right side."

The polarizing nature of our experience of the world has long been seen as a problem to be fixed. Whether by positive thinking, positive imagining, or positive praying, we seek to live in the light and avoid the shadow side of ourselves. But rather than thinking we can destroy one side or the other, we need a more productive way of dealing with the nature of contrasts.

A World beyond Polarization

We know we are polarizing when we see evil on the opposite side of what we believe is right. Much of the time, the evil we find reflects aspects of our own personal self that we want to deny. We might see another's selfishness without fully acknowledging our own, or we might notice dishonesty in another that we do not recognize in ourselves. In psychological terms, this negative and denied aspect of self is called our shadow, and it is a crucial part of our makeup. We may try to deny or destroy our shadow side, but we will always fail because that shadow is part of ourselves. Consider this from the Russian dissident Aleksandr Solzhenitsyn:

> If only it were all so simple! If only there were evil people somewhere insidiously committing evil deeds, and it were necessary only to separate them from the rest of us and destroy them. But the line dividing good and evil cuts through the heart of every human being. And who is willing to destroy a piece of his own heart?[1]

When we deny our shadow, it is virtually impossible to explore the two sides of a polarity without dehumanizing or demonizing. This makes it impossible to bridge the divide. We need to own our shadow. Doing so helps us avoid the natural tendency to identify exclusively with just one side of a polarity. By engaging our whole self, we can listen compassionately to an opposing side and begin to build bridges of understanding that lead to healing.

Beyond polarization lies a world of compromise based on compassionate caring. But our minds alone will not take us to such a place. We need spiritual practices, which have the ability to transform us, opening us to a more inclusive way of relating and a greater capacity for compassion.

Jewish Views of Our Separate Self

The Creation myth in the book of Genesis begins with the contrasts of light and dark, of day and night, and of man and woman. There are regular days of creation and there is the Sabbath. Creation is made up of opposites interacting.

The Midrash—expositions and stories built from biblical events and characters—imagines the first man, alone, as the sun sets on his first day. With the growing darkness, he grows afraid. But God teaches him to light fire, to bring light into the darkness, which eases his fear. In many ways, this story reflects Judaism's approach to dealing with the contrasts that lead to polarization: As the contrasts appear, notice the feelings that accompany them. When one side of the contrast sparks fear, infuse it with aspects of the more comfortable side. Judaism does not deny either one, but rather recognizes that both can live together. Neither, in fact, can exist without the other.

The same is true of good and evil—both are found throughout the world and within ourselves, and both have a purpose. Rabbinic psychology explains this coexistence by saying that our separate self contains two specific urges. There is the *yetzer tov*, the inclination toward good, and the *yetzer ha-ra*, the inclination toward evil. The *yetzer tov* urges us toward paths of Oneness; the *yetzer ha-ra* urges us toward paths of self-satisfaction.

We need both to fulfill our role as part of creation. Martin Buber, one of the greatest Jewish philosophers of the twentieth century, translates from eighteenth-century Hasidic thought:

> But if there were no evil, there would be no good, for good is the counterpart of evil. Everlasting delight is no delight.... For there is no good unless its counterpart exists.... The fact that evil confronts good gives a person the possibility ... of rejecting evil and choosing good. Only then does the good exist truly and perfectly.[2]

Without the evil inclination, rabbinic wisdom says, there would be no progress. There would be no cities and no development. We would not be inclined to reach beyond ourselves.

> And the Eternal One saw all that the Eternal had made, and found it very good—"good" refers to the Good Inclination, the *Yetzer Tov*, but "very good" refers to the Evil Inclination, the *Yetzer Ha-Ra*. Why? Because were it not for the *Yetzer Ha-Ra* no one would build a house, take a wife, give birth, or engage in commerce. (Genesis Rabbah 9:7)

We need the passions contained in that self-serving inclination to support ourselves. Our challenge is to acknowledge and channel the passions of the *yetzer ha-ra* into constructive creations in the world.

From a Catholic priest, Father Robert Spitzer, a former president of Gonzaga University, I learned that the *yetzer ha-ra* can be referred to as the "comparative ego," always functioning in comparison to others, seeking power and position as some form of security in the world. The *yetzer tov* is the "contributive ego," the part of ourselves that can use the energies of the comparative ego to make things better in our lives and in our world. Essentially, the *yetzer ha-ra* asks, "How can I get something for myself?" and the *yetzer tov* asks, "How can I make things better for us all?"

Our greater self, identified with our heart, can bridge the divide between the *yetzer tov* and the *yetzer ha-ra* and hold both as one. On this greater-self level of consciousness, we know that the contrasts are simply needed for the mind to function. Contrasts are the basis of language, since words divide our reality into separate parts, and language is the province of the separate self.

Some years ago I was privileged to teach at a conference on Jewish meditation in San Francisco. One of my contemporaries and fellow teachers, the late Rabbi David Zeller, a traditionally observant Jew, referenced a well-known Jewish teaching that the Messiah will come when all Jews observe Shabbat in the traditional manner. Rabbi David suggested instead that the Messiah will come when those Jews who observe Shabbat traditionally love those Jews who do not, and when those Jews who do not observe Shabbat traditionally love those who do. This is a teaching of the greater self that can hold contrasts, even polarities, as necessary aspects of one reality.

The key to moving beyond identifying with our separate self to identifying with the greater self is acceptance, and true acceptance opens us to the path of love. Ultimately, we must accept the inclinations of both good and evil within ourselves, and appreciate how each is a facet of one reality. In that way we can channel the passions of our self-serving ego into compassionate action in the world.

⟋ℐℐℐ— Jewish Spiritual Practices for Reconciling Good and Evil

Spiritual practices support awakening our greater self and a more inclusive identity by helping us accept the inclinations of good and evil within each of us. And they can help us use these seemingly intransigent polarities to steer us to the inclusive path of love.

The Havdalah Candle

One of my favorite rituals is part of Havdalah, the brief ceremony concluding Shabbat on Saturday evening. As part of the practice, we light a special braided candle. Before or during the blessing for this light of Havdalah, we curl our fingers and let the radiance from the candle reflect off our fingernails.

When our fingernails are illuminated in this way, a shadow is cast on the palm beneath. The visual image is clear—both the light and the shadow are evidence of the Havdalah candle's flame.

The image reminds us that both the light and the shadow, the positives and the negatives, of our earthly experience are consequences of a single greater light of consciousness. When we turn contrast into polarization, this visual symbol encourages us to accept the reality of contrasting beliefs and conflicting energies. Conflict situations, though often uncomfortable, remind us that each side creates the other. Neither the light nor the shadow can exist on its own. They need each other. When we are able to see that, we are able to work more effectively to heal rifts caused by feelings generated by polarization. We do not seek to do away with either side, but to work toward the kind of understanding that can bring cooperative and meaningful action.

Whenever you light a candle, you can experiment with this practice. As you stand before the candle's flame, curl your fingers toward your palm, letting the light reflect off your fingernails, noticing the shadow on your palm. It's a visual representation designed to help us accept both the light and the darkness, both sides of the coin of life. Take a moment to simply focus on what you see.

Walking This Practice into the World

At any time, you can notice the interplay of light and shadow in your world. When an artist wishes to portray greater light, she will contrast it with greater darkness. Take moments during your day to simply become more aware of your environment. Notice that contrast is a constant. Perhaps you will observe that you prefer one side of a contrast to the other. You might even consider what it would be like if you were to decide that one side is "good," and the other "evil." Such a practice as you go about your daily life can support a more inclusive consciousness, responding to the contrasts you experience in your life. That greater consciousness can minimize the negative impacts of polarization.

The *Shiviti*

One of the biblical verses Jewish spiritual teachers often give students is Psalm 16:8, "I set the Eternal before me always." The Hebrew verse reads, "*Shiviti Adonai l'negdi tamid.*"

Hasidic teachers of the eighteenth century encouraged students to repeat this verse in meditation and to contemplate it. When the student felt ready, he would share what meaning he had found through this practice. In a way similar to certain Zen Buddhist practices, the teacher would either send the student back to the same verse or move on to the next level of teaching.

Rabbi Israel ben Eleazar, also known as the Baal Shem Tov (the Master of the Good Name [of God]), taught students to take this verse quite literally. He instructed students to write the word "Eternal" on a card and place it in front of them when they were at work or at study. The students were then setting the name of the Eternal before them always.

But the Baal Shem Tov shared a deeper teaching. Although the Hebrew word *shiviti* is usually translated as "I set," the Baal Shem Tov taught that it could also be a form of a word that signifies "equanimity." He suggested a deeper meaning of the verse: that when we have equanimity the Eternal is present in our consciousness. He explained that equanimity is achieved when we receive criticism with the same energy with which we receive applause.

When we seek applause, we wind up being controlled by those from whom that applause is sought. When we seek to avoid criticism, we adjust our message so as not to displease. In either case, we are caught in the needs of the separate self. We are far from equanimity and we are not open to the wholeness and inclusivity of God.

As a spiritual practice, take the entire phrase in English, "I set the Eternal before me always," as a focus for meditation. Repeat it and contemplate it, and let it unfold in its own way within you. Let the words unfold in their own time and in their own way. If you are comfortable with the Hebrew, focus on "*Shiviti Adonai l'negdi tamid* (shee-VEE-tee Ah-doh-NYE l'neg-DEE ta-MEED).

Walking This Practice into the World

It is interesting to repeat this *shiviti* phrase while talking to another person—particularly when it is a person with whom you disagree. The psalm verse can help remind you not to cast another out of your heart because of differences between you, but to remember that you are probably acting out the contrasts of light and shadow. Each of you may see the other as the shadow and yourself as the light—that's natural. But the *shiviti* practice also helps us learn more about those who oppose us, honoring them more fully and creating an atmosphere for more productive and more healing outcomes.

Christian Views of Our Separate Self

One of the most dramatic examples of the need to move beyond the separate self comes in the Sermon on the Mount (Matthew 5:43–44):

> You have heard that it was said, "You shall love your neighbor and hate your enemy. But I say to you, love your enemies and pray for those who persecute you."

Jesus's teaching here has been dismissed as idealistic, not possible or practical. Yet the verse encourages us to ask, "What is real?" If we are truly independent beings and not really connected to each other, then we can remain inside the protection of our personal selves. But if we are connected, all part of one creation, then we must understand reality in a different way.

What is illusion? What is reality? What is the difference? These questions first came to me as a college student reading *Don Quixote*. In this introduction to the Viking Portable edition, Samuel Putnam quotes the great American critic Lionel Trilling:

> Lionel Trilling ... notes that this problem, that of illusion and reality, is the novelist's chief concern. "I will act," says Don Quixote, "as if the world were what I would have it be, as if the ideal were the real." He is under no delusion regarding his lady Dulcinea: "God knows whether there is a Dulcinea in this world. I contemplate her as she needs must be."[3]

The woman is a barmaid named Aldonza Lorenzo. But Don Quixote sees her with eyes of love. And for him she *is* his lovely lady Dulcinea. Which is real and which is illusion? Is Don Quixote a madman? No, says Putnam. He is a poet and a defender of the imagination. And it is from the imagination that things can become real. It is from the imagination that we construct our affirmations and intentions. To me, this suggests that we can choose to see our separateness as the illusion and, having made that choice, we can choose to see and act in accord with the spiritual and physical needs of the world. We can love our enemies.

But most of us love others with conditions, do we not? Often those conditions do not appear on the surface of our consciousness, but they are there. Consider how difficult it is to love without conditions. There would be nothing the other could do to make you stop loving him or her. Nothing. This is at the heart of Jesus's teachings and we refer to it as the core teaching of Christianity. As God tells us in Leviticus, you shall love your neighbor as you love yourself. Jesus clarifies this by telling us that all people, regardless of who they are, are our neighbors. By seeing others in this inclusive way, we make real the interconnectedness of all being.

To illustrate this teaching, Jesus tells the story of the Good Samaritan (Luke 10:25–37). A man is walking from Jerusalem to Jericho, a distance of about twenty miles through a barren wilderness. He is set upon by robbers, beaten, and left for dead. Two people—a priest and a Levite, two members of the Temple establishment—walk by and do not stop to help the man. But a Samaritan, considered at the time to be of a lowly class, is the one who stops. The Samaritan goes to the man who has been beaten, gives him aid, takes him to an inn, gives the innkeeper money, and tells the innkeeper that he will come back. He also notes that if more money is needed to cover the man's care, the Samaritan will provide it. Jesus asks, "Which of these three was neighbor to the man who was robbed and beaten?" The answer comes back, "The one who showed mercy." Jesus responds, "Go and do likewise."

We are all neighbors to each other. No one is excluded.

⌒*ᔕᔕ*⌒ Christian Spiritual Practices for Reconciling Good and Evil

Knowing Your Neighbor

You probably have neighbors. You may know some of them, but maybe not all. You may like some of them and you may not like some of them. Take a few moments to sit quietly, breathe in and out, and focus on your center. Now think about the neighbors you like. Why do you think you like them? How are they good? What have you learned about them that you like? In other words, what are the qualities in a neighbor that make them "good neighbors"?

Similarly, think about the neighbors you do not like. Why don't you like them? How are they not good neighbors? What, if anything, have you learned about them?

Which type of person would you like to be? The bigger question is why?

Finally, is there any way to relate to a bad neighbor that can enable her to become a good neighbor? You have no control over her behavior, over her sense of self, over her desires, hopes, and fears. But you can give her an opportunity to refrain from unpleasant or difficult behavior. The story of the Good Samaritan says it best: Show mercy. In other words, put that person's concerns ahead of your own. Show respect for the essential dignity of her being. Listen to her story and find ways to connect with it. In showing mercy, say "yes" to her. Not "Yes, I agree with you." Rather, "Yes, I honor your life as a person and the integrity of your story, even though I might disagree with some of it." In listening, it is rare that we cannot find some way to connect, some way to say in so many words, "I hear you, I see you, and I respect your being." It is difficult to sustain polarities under such conditions.

Walking This Practice into the World

Keeping in mind the story of the Good Samaritan, meditate on the phrase "Go and do likewise" as a reminder of our essential interconnectedness. "Do likewise" is a good trigger for your memory to reconnect you to this practice.

Connecting through Music

Singing together is a form of spiritual practice that has great potential for helping us access that place in us where we "know" we are a part of the same Being, where we feel our connectedness and understand that the space between us is an illusion. Singing together helps us realize our interconnectedness because the nature of music is to lift us to a place where words only complement rather than dominate. I imagine that the first music was made by some primitive person standing out on a lonely hillside, arms outstretched, crying out. That essential act of externalizing what exists within was and is the very heart of music. In its more popular forms it can express the primary experience of the ordinary (tonic, in music theory terms) moving to the extraordinary (subdominant—either joy or sorrow) and resolving that extraordinary back into the ordinary, making it useful. This parallels the arc of the folktale. As "Once upon a time" moves through the extraordinary, it helps us grow into a resolution described as "happily ever after." But as everyone knows, "happily ever after" does not mean a life of endless bliss.

It means a life where the resources to cope with the experiences ahead are learned and received in ways similar to the dynamics of the story. This is the satisfaction we feel at the end.

In Christian worship there is a similar pattern, reflecting a passage in the book of Isaiah (6:1–13):

> In the year that King Uzziah died, I saw the Lord sitting on a throne, high and lofty; and the hem of his robe filled the temple. Seraphs were in attendance above him; each had six wings: with two they covered their faces, and with two they covered their feet, and with two they flew. And one called to another and said: "Holy, holy, holy is the Lord of hosts; the whole earth is full of his glory." The pivots on the thresholds shook at the voices of those who called, and the house filled with smoke.
>
> And I said: "Woe is me! I am lost, for I am a man of unclean lips, and I live among a people of unclean lips; yet my eyes have seen the King, the Lord of hosts!" Then one of the seraphs flew to me, holding a live coal that had been taken from the altar with a pair of tongs. The seraph touched my mouth with it and said: "Now that this has touched your lips, your guilt has departed and your sin is blotted out." Then I heard the voice of the Lord saying, "Whom shall I send, and who will go for us?" And I said, "Here am I; send me!"
>
> And he said, "Go and say to this people: 'Keep listening, but do not comprehend; keep looking, but do not understand.' Make the mind of this people dull, and stop their ears, and shut their eyes, so that they may not look with their eyes, and listen with their ears, and comprehend with their minds, and turn and be healed." Then I said, "How long, O Lord?" And he said: "Until cities lie waste without inhabitants, and houses without people, and the land is utterly desolate; until the Lord sends everyone far away, and vast is the emptiness in the midst of the land. Even if a tenth part remain in it, it will be burned again, like a terebinth or an oak whose stump remains standing when it is felled." The holy seed is its stump.

When we come into the presence of the Holy, we are emptied of our ego consciousness. We are free then to hear a presentation of God's purposes and we respond with thoughts and actions that, ideally, reflect what we have been emptied to hear. In other words, we are filled and we do something good with that filling.

Music can also give us a sense of movement. We all get stuck. At one time or another, we are all held captive by money, sex, art, politics, religion, and so many other things. Rock, country, R&B, gospel, and the blues can all give us the feeling of getting unstuck. That is why I call that "Getting Out of Egypt" music. The Hebrews were enslaved in Egypt. We like that feeling of getting unstuck. It moves us!

Music in its more complex forms can help us feel the complexity of what it means to be alive on this planet. It can show that to us in ways that make us feel good and make us feel sad; in ways that take us deeper into life's meanings and ways that help shape the way we see life. Music helps us feel. Singing together is one of the best ways to feel our Oneness, our condition of being part of the One. Singing together is the sound of Oneness, a sustainer of Oneness, and a source of strength in the midst of the constant changing of life itself.

As a spiritual practice, listen to music. Almost any kind of music can serve as a spiritual exercise. Even the most inane rock 'n' roll song can help us feel something important. So as you listen to music, ask yourself what you are feeling. Ask yourself how that feeling might be translated into thoughts and actions that could contribute to the world's need for healing. Meditate on a phrase from a song that means something to you.

Walking This Practice into the World

Sing! Sing in the shower, sing while you are working around your home or in your yard. Sing! And, if you can, find people to sing with. There have been times in our history when singing together was more important than it is now. In the 1960s, for example, singing together—what the folksinger Pete Seeger called hootenannies—was popular because it was needed. It brought us together and gave us that healing sense of oneness. And that is why when we sing those songs today we can feel once again the sense of coming unstuck, the sense that a community can support our being, and that we are all part of the same thing, of the One.

Islamic Views of Our Separate Self

In a world currently inhabited by more than seven billion people, the possibilities for different and opposing beliefs and opinions about everything from private life to international relations are endless. The problem lies not in our differences, which could actually be educational and productive, but in our human tendency to insist that our opinions and judgments prevail, even to the point of unreason. We can be adamantly attached to our entrenched positions for the sake of individual or tribal interests and unwilling to make compromises for the common good. When challenged, we sometimes react with meanness, anger, and violence in words and actions in defense of our positions. Thus the root of many of the world's ills is the untamed human ego and its attachment to its position as the center of its own universe.

What is the ego? The word comes from the Latin word for "I," which psychoanalyst Sigmund Freud used to describe the part of the psyche that experiences and reacts to the outside world. Muslims know it by the Arabic word *nafs* and Jews know it by the related Hebrew word *nefesh*, as Rabbi Ted discussed earlier in this chapter. Both *nafs* and *nefesh* imply a spiritual element of animating spirit or soul, as well as the more secular "self" suggested by the word "ego."

The ego is morally neutral, neither good nor bad, but simply a necessary part of our psychological makeup that enables us to interact with the world. Sufi teachers say that the ego is an instrument of the soul. According to the Qur'an, each human being is intrinsically noble. Molded from water and clay, we are also infused with the spirit of God, which inclines us to evolve into higher states of consciousness (Qur'an 32:7–9 and 95:4). Such is the exalted and precious potential of the human being that, in an astonishing revelation, God asks the angels to bow to the human (Qur'an 2:34).

But out of a mysterious and divine design, Divinity has placed into every human what the Holy Book calls a "slinking whisperer," a voice of our lower self that tries to lead us astray (Qur'an 114:4). Our troubles begin when we allow the slinking whisperer to seduce our ego into riding roughshod over our more noble instincts. Much of the polarization and conflict that we experience in the world is a reflection of that inner conflict. If we could heal and reconcile the wars that rage inside of us, there would be no seeds for war in the world around us. But this is easier said than done. The work to tame the ego and align it with our higher self is a lifelong endeavor, requiring constant spiritual work to recognize and transform our inner chaos and dysfunction. According to Sufi teachers, this work to transform the ego is a primary reason for our existence on earth.

By whatever name we call the ego—the "I," the *nafs*, the personality—most religious traditions teach that it is not the essence of who we are and we are not here on earth merely to satisfy its vain desires. Rather than being controlled by the ego, we need to transform it into a helpful assistant for our spiritual journey. In Islamic spirituality, this means that we need to align elements of our ego with the pure essence of our soul. The light of constant self-witnessing slowly diminishes our shadows, opens our hearts, and eventually connects us to Divinity within. In the words of the Prophet Muhammad, "Know thyself and thou shalt know thy Sustainer." Our lifelong work is to make every effort to align our personality with our higher self. "Marry your soul," counsels Rumi. "That wedding is the way."

The Qur'an identifies three stages in taming the ego. In the early stage the ego has an exaggerated opinion of itself. We need to be vigilant about the foolish pride of the ego. In a teaching story, the mulla, on one of his evening strolls on a moonlit night, was alarmed as he peered into a well. The moon had fallen into the well! Worried about the disastrous consequences for Islamic observances, which are based on cycles of the moon, the mulla rushed home to get a rope, tied it to a hook, and returned to rescue the moon. After dropping the hook into the well, he heaved and pulled until something came loose and the momentum threw him on his back. Lying there, he was delighted to see the moon restored to its proper domain in the sky. "Thank God I came along!" he crowed in self-satisfaction.

In the middle stage of taming the ego, the ego realizes that it has the ability to make choices. Ours is a world of opposites. The Qur'an says, "And in everything have We created opposites so that you might bear in mind that God alone is One" (51:49). We are often called to choose between two options. Sugar is sweet, in contrast to vinegar. High is defined by low. Life's events turn us from one feeling to another so that we might learn from opposites and fly with both wings, not just one. Through positive experiences and from our mistakes, we learn about discernment and the power and beauty of making righteous choices. In the process, we connect to an inner voice of conscience and guidance.

In the final stage, through continuous self-witnessing and abiding spiritual effort, the ego is surrendered little by little to divine will. This is not about resignation or giving up; rather, it's about opening up to a Higher Power. The work of transforming the ego opens up the innermost heart and renders it "free of all dross" (Qur'an 3:154). At this stage we begin to experience within a profound calmness and joy. By cultivating an inner spaciousness, we are able to embrace much more love and compassion, which enables us to enfold our pains and sorrows and integrate them into our being so that we become more fully developed human beings.

Coming to Know Each Other

From this place of inner spaciousness we begin to understand the wisdom of the much-quoted Qur'anic revelations that God created us in all our diversity of languages, color, gender, and religions so that we might come to know each other (Qur'an 5:48; 49:13). We are all part of the Oneness of God, but each person is a distinct individual, and connecting with each other is a sacred injunction. It is not always easy, especially when the "other" we are trying to relate to is not a member of our family, tribe, or religion. In a witty revelation, God says, "We have created some of you to be a trial for others" (Qur'an 25:20). However, once we make a personal connection with the other, we are less inclined to demonize or dehumanize. Even if our differences in politics or ideology remain unaltered, we no longer perceive the other as a threat. The importance of personal relationship with an "other" was borne out in a poll about a proposal to build a mosque and interfaith center at Ground Zero. Of the 60 percent who were opposed to the project, not a single person knew even one Muslim personally, whereas of the 26 percent who were in favor, all said they knew at least one Muslim.

Clearly, it is critical to get to know one another in a sincere and abiding way. Our challenge is to find creative ways to connect with the other. One remarkable model is Job Cohen, a Jew and the former mayor of Amsterdam, who regularly made time to drink tea and have honest conversations with Muslims and imams who were considered "radical." His tea drinking was derided, satirized, and criticized by his political opponents, but eventually effusive praise was heaped on the mayor because his outreach had such positive results. At a time of racial and religious violence all over the Netherlands, following the brutal 2004 murder of filmmaker Theo van Gogh by a Muslim, Amsterdam itself remained quiet. Cohen's tea-drinking connection with Muslim radicals was given the credit, and *Time* magazine called the mayor a "European hero" and a "hate buster."

Behavior and Being

What are we to do if someone is adamantly adversarial, even violent, despite our sincerest efforts? The sixteenth-century teacher Kabir offers sage advice: "Do what is right. Protect yourself. Don't allow yourself to be abused. But please, do not leave the other person's being out of your heart." This insight is paramount. Every tradition urges us to differentiate between behavior and being. We all may err and even commit terrible deeds from time to time, but the essence of every human being is divinely sacred. Even when we are locked in mortal combat with each other, we must remember that we are fighting the antagonism, not the antagonist. Just this awareness, as we speak and act, has the power to shift heaven and earth. When we are dealing with someone whose heart is clenched because of fear, anger, or hopelessness, we know that only what comes from the heart can open another heart. When the people who affect our lives—whether at home, at work, or on the political front—cause anger, fear, or hopelessness, we need to remember that "Truly it is not their eyes that are blind, but their hearts" (Qur'an 22:46). We know, from our own reactions, that the human heart responds to force by clenching itself shut. We also know that our closed hearts can't always hear the sweet voice of reason. Only what comes from the heart can open another heart. When we, coming from a place of spiritual awareness, make a distinction between another's behavior and being, we are exercising the power of our heart, and this can open doors. By the grace of God, even an enemy might become a friend (Qur'an 60:7).

Using Compassion to Transform the Ego

To transmute the ego from commanding master to personal assistant, we need to exercise constant self-vigilance. The power of self-vigilance is magnified immeasurably when it is accompanied by compassion. Sufi teachers are tireless in their explanation of the power and majesty of this divine attribute. Invariably, they use the metaphor of water in nature. Nothing is as soft and yielding as water, but for cutting through the hardest stone, nothing is as powerful as water. Thus, compassion reflects genuine strength. Then, observe that every living thing of this created world depends on water for life. Water is life-giving. Thus, compassion is also life-bestowing.

When we attempt to transform the ego through willpower or logic, it responds with imaginative excuses and beguiling reasons of its own. But when we shine the light of awareness on the ego with compassion and mercy, amazingly, the armor and defenses of the ego begin to crumble, allowing the higher self to expand and express its true nature.

Islamic Spiritual Practices for Cultivating Compassion

Of all our relationships, the most fundamental one and yet the most neglected one is the relationship with our own dear selves. Without our even realizing it, we talk to ourselves often and, sadly, much of this self-talk is quite negative. We criticize ourselves for not being smart enough, quick enough, beautiful enough—the list is long and hurtful. If we are serious about pursuing a relationship with our sacred essence, it is helpful to become more aware of our own internal dialogue and practice "spiritual intervention" to transform our negative self-talk by addressing ourselves with affection and compassion.

Sacred Naming

One of the most effective ways of doing this is a simple practice called sacred naming. Choose your own term of endearment, something like "Sweetheart," "Dear One," "Brother [plus your name]"— for example, I say, "Brother Jamal"—or whatever feels genuine and evokes compassion for yourself. It may be a loving nickname used by a treasured grandparent or a favorite aunt. The key is to find a sacred name that brings up feelings of mercy and gentleness. Know that there is sacred beauty and power in being named with affection. If the naming is said in a tone of voice that emanates from the heart, it creates a sacred vibration that leaves an indelible imprint on your soul.

Family members, friends, and congregants who perform this practice report several major shifts. The sharpness of the ego palpably begins to soften and the ego actually enjoys the moments of collaboration with the soul. Also, there is the added benefit that, with continuous practice, you will find yourself naturally naming others with kindness, and this often results in outer harmony and cooperation.

Walking This Practice into the World

At every opportunity, practice sacred naming with yourself, no matter how awkward it might feel initially. You will rejoice in the truth that every relationship outside of yourself is a reflection of the relationship you have with yourself.

Self-Witnessing

"Die before you die," said the Prophet Muhammad, meaning that we should die to all that is false and illusory in us before we come to the end of our lives. This is achieved by making a sacred commitment, here and now, to witness oneself with compassion, awareness, and persistence continuously over a lifetime. The Qur'an says, "There is a watcher within, ever present" (50:18). This holy intention to self-witness switches on a mysterious inner light that, over time, has the power to shine through the many personality masks we wear and to illuminate for us our real face—the divine spark within. Sufi teachers wax eloquent over the breathtaking beauty of our authentic self.

At regular intervals, make an honest evaluation of how well you are tending to your commitment and create a ritual to renew your sacred pledge to continually witness yourself. If you find yourself succumbing to a negative ego quality, use sacred naming to address yourself with compassion and remind yourself that you are more than your personality and that the breath of God resides within you.

Walking This Practice into the World

In the course of your daily life, continue to witness yourself. The moment you become aware that your internal dialogue is beating up on you, immediately intervene by addressing yourself with your sacred name and continue the conversation with the gentler energy that it evokes. Invariably, the direction and content of the negative inner conversations will change for the better.

3

Moving beyond
Past Conditioning
Awakening to Authentic
Social Justice

As all of us look at our role in both social justice and injustice in the world, we begin to appreciate more fully the consequences of the polarization discussed in the last chapter. We become polarized into us/them, making value judgments based on contrasting beliefs and backgrounds. This creates greater struggles that may inhibit the positive changes we seek in our lives and in our world.

But polarization is often grounded in and supported by our past conditioning. This is how, mostly unconsciously, we come to form our value judgments in the first place. We all grow up with attitudes toward ourselves and others that are the product of our environment. We are usually unaware of the pervasiveness of that conditioning, but merely take for granted our ideas about our world and ourselves.

What Is the Problem with Past Conditioning?

It is often difficult to appreciate the degree to which our personal conditioning is reflected in our world. We usually tend to think that our feelings and thoughts are responses to events in the outer world. Someone cuts us off on the freeway, and we get upset; another person allows us to switch lanes in front of him, and we are happy. When things go as we think they should, we feel good. When things do not, to some degree or another, we suffer.

At a certain point, many of us begin to realize that we are not merely victims of the external world. Sometimes, the external world is a victim of our own judgments. That is the case when shared feelings bring people together to oppose others whose actions are viewed as wrong. Nothing brings people together like a common enemy. In such cases, our preconceived ideas and judgments further reinforce our thoughts, our words, and our actions. Our beliefs, many of which are held without our conscious awareness, always impact us. Our experience is limited by preexisting beliefs that can create blind spots. People often say, "Seeing is believing." But it is also true that "Believing is seeing." We tend to see things that substantiate the beliefs we already hold.

We need to become aware of our often hidden past conditioning, so that we can choose another way—our own way—in each moment. That greater awareness can alert us to discover what we had not been able to perceive before.

Social Injustice Often Reflects the Consequences of Past Conditioning

It is not our task in this book to catalog the problems that we confront as humans. Nevertheless, we all need to be reminded of just how pervasive those problems are.

Social injustice is endemic to society, and we function within it according to what we believe to be true. If we have privilege, we usually believe we deserve it. If we do not have privilege, we are likely to be angry and depressed, a condition that is often viewed as laziness. And, underneath it all, are serious questions concerning our own self-worth. We compare ourselves to others and much of the time we believe our worth is lacking. We do things to try to boost our sense of worth and that contributes to our conditioning and to overall injustice. Here are some facts to consider.

Economic Injustice

1. In 2016 the top 1 percent of the world's wealthiest people own half the world's wealth.[1]

2. Just 62 people have as much wealth as the 3.5 billion people in the bottom half of the world's income scale.[2]
3. In the United States, the wealthiest twenty people have more wealth than half the American population.[3]

Racial Injustice

1. Chronic poverty in the United States: Between 2004 and 2006, the chronic poverty rate was 1.4 percent for non-Hispanic whites, 4.5 percent for Hispanics, and 8.4 percent for blacks.[4]
2. Combined statistics for episodic poverty in the United States (living in poverty for fewer than thirty-six consecutive months) and chronic poverty in 2014: 10 percent white, 24 percent Hispanic, 27 percent black.[5]
3. Criminal incarceration in the United States: In 2008, 20 percent of prisoners were Hispanic, 34 percent were white, and 38 percent were black, when African Americans make up less than 13 percent of the population. Black males are imprisoned at a rate that is 6.5 times higher than the imprisonment rate for white males.[6]

Gender Injustice

Throughout much of the twentieth century, the average woman earned about 60 percent of what men earned. In the 1970s that rose to about 80 percent and has remained unchanged since 2005.[7]

LBGT Inequality

Same-sex marriage became legal nationwide in 2015. Military service is possible for gay, lesbian, and bisexual people, but not for transgender people. Discrimination protections still vary by jurisdiction.[8]

Discrimination against and Persecution of Religious Minorities

Although the First and Fourteenth Amendments to the Constitution of the United States guarantee religious rights, historically there has always been negative discrimination against non-Christians. This has occurred even against Roman Catholics by Protestants. The terrorist attacks in Beirut, Paris, and San Bernardino, California, in November and December of 2015 increased hatred and distrust of Muslims. For example, following the massacre in San Bernardino on December 2, 2015, the top Google search in California with the word "Muslims" in it was "kill Muslims."[9] Even so, according to a 2013 report from the FBI, hate crimes against Jews continue to be substantially higher than against any other religious group.[10]

How Do We Discover Our Own Conditioning?

We cannot know the exact degree to which the discrimination, poverty, and powerlessness we experience in our world are supported by our past conditioning. But because we know that our own beliefs and attitudes accustom us to situations that are often grossly unfair, and can blind us to the suffering of others, we need to grapple with our conditioning in order to free ourselves to respond more effectively as we work toward constructive change.

This is not simply a matter of pointing our accusing finger back toward ourselves. It's not a call to encourage guilt, since that is never an effective motivator toward significant change. This is an opportunity to understand ourselves more fully and to free ourselves from the tyranny of our past.

We Keep Ourselves Comfortable

Perhaps you've noticed that we all tend to find evidence to prove what we already believe to be so. Once we have an idea of how things are—and many of those ideas are the result of prior conditioning—what we see will almost automatically support our convictions.

There is a kind of comfort that comes with certainty. Outsiders—which usually means people who look different than we do or see things differently—may have trouble appreciating our point of view. It is far easier for us to notice the closed-mindedness of another than it is to become aware of our own.

Take, for instance, the nature of what you fear or, at least, what you are less comfortable with. Think about the people and situations that are most comfortable for you, and those that are least. Perhaps you are most comfortable with those who are like yourself, and least comfortable with those who are different. You might notice that some situations and some people attract you and others do not, and that you tend to surround yourself with those who basically agree with how you see the world. We all do.

The Reality of the Other

Our past conditioning is largely responsible for our identification of the "other" or the "stranger." For example, if we are among the poor and are food insecure, the "other" includes those who have greater resources. If we are among those who have greater financial resources, the "other" includes those we see in food lines and those who are seeking charity on the streets. If we are among the Christian majority in our culture, the "other" might be the Muslim whom we fear might somehow be aligned with those who seek our destruction. If we are Jewish, the "other" might be the Christian majority whose religious observances are celebrated as national holidays, from which we feel excluded.

No matter who we are, no matter where we are, there are "others" with whom we are less comfortable. Our inability to transcend such divisions forms the foundation for the social inequalities and injustices with which we are living. Until we move beyond fearing or fighting with the "other," there can be no true justice and no true peace in our lives.

Judaism and the Stranger

In some ways, Jews fit a universal archetype of the "other." We have been strangers in strange lands for most of our history. People are often surprised to learn that the first country that gave Jews full citizenship, including the right to vote, was the United States. While there were times we lived relatively comfortably as a minority culture in other countries, we were never afforded equal rights.

Our history helps us understand what it means to be a stranger, what it means to be the other, so that we are often sensitive to the needs of those cast in that position in any society: "Do not oppress a stranger, for you know what it feels like to be a stranger, for you yourselves were strangers in the land of Egypt" (Exodus 23:9). Our identification as the stranger began even earlier, when Abraham had to negotiate with the Hittites to obtain a burial cave for his wife, Sarah. He identified himself as "a stranger and a resident alien among you" (Genesis 23:4). It is no surprise, then, that in the United States Jews have historically been visibly active in social justice causes.

Jewish Exclusivity

It is also no surprise that the conditioning of Jewish consciousness usually includes not only a concern for others, but also a degree of paranoia stemming from a concern for itself. Due to the high rate of hate crimes against Jews and Jewish institutions, there is a reverse tendency, in which the Jewish community withdraws into itself in an attempt at self-protection and thus winds up accentuating its otherness.

The tragedy of persecution is, of course, the wounds inflicted on those persecuted, and the Jewish community bears scars from those wounds. The Holocaust proved that the impossible was possible: A single people, the Jews, were blamed for all the ills of the world and their extermination by the Nazis was intended to cure the world of the disease they represented. While this may strike most of us as bizarre, the manipulation of public opinion in times of stress and turmoil suggests that it could happen again. If not to the Jews, then to others.

But the deeper tragedy of persecution is that those who are persecuted learn behaviors that they themselves might unconsciously inflict on others. While the unequal treatment of Palestinians does not mirror the demonization of Jews in Nazi Germany, it is clear that we Jews have forgotten how blatant unequal treatment felt to us. In Israel, there have been conflicts between ultra-Orthodox communities and less observant Jewish communities in which the traditionalists have thrown stones at those defiling what they consider to be absolute laws of Sabbath observance. Schoolgirls have been spit upon because they wore more modern clothes, deemed inappropriate by some traditionalists.

Similar struggles within the Jewish community occur here in the United States, as Samuel Freedman recounted in his book *Jew vs. Jew: The Struggle for the Soul of American Jewry*. When my family moved to the suburb of Beachwood Village on the outskirts of Cleveland, Ohio, in the 1950s, we were among the very few Jews living there. Fifty-some years later, an enclave of ultra-Orthodox Jews, occupying much of Beachwood, made life for less observant Jewish families challenging by condemning their failure to observe the strict traditions of the Sabbath.

In some ways, Jewish responses to racism and to economic injustice have demonstrated what we have learned as strangers in strange lands. In other ways, we ourselves have become part of the problem of inequality in our actions against Palestinians and people observing differently within our own community. We have much to share with the larger world concerning caring for those needing help, and we have much that we ourselves need to remember about caring for ourselves and each other.

A Jewish Spiritual Practice for Welcoming the Stranger

Honoring Your Holiness

The Torah, the most sacred of Jewish texts, comprises the first five books of the Hebrew Bible. Its emphasis on treating the stranger with justice is clear. "There shall be one law for the native born and for the stranger who sojourns among you" (Exodus 12:49). "You shall have one law for the stranger and for the one of your own country, for I am the Eternal One your God" (Leviticus 24:22).

But justice alone, while critical, is not enough. Love is required as well. "And if a stranger is a resident alien in your land, you shall not wrong him. But the stranger who dwells with you shall be to you as one born among you, and you shall love him as yourself, for you were strangers in the land of Egypt; I am the Eternal One your God" (Leviticus 19:34). And a verse that sums it up, "You shall love the stranger, for you were strangers in the land of Egypt" (Deuteronomy 10:19). We must open our hearts to those considered to be the strangers among us.

It's not simply a matter of ethical imperative, although that imperative is certainly present. It's a matter of identification. We are to be concerned about the stranger because we know what it's like to be a stranger. It is crucial that we remember. The stranger is not "other" to us: The stranger reminds us of our own experience and of our own identity.

Before equality can be fully achieved in any culture, we must learn what it is like to be the other. This is often the missing element in social action projects. We identify those in need and work against those we see creating and perpetuating that need. It is so easy to find an enemy, and to work against that enemy. But even if we "win," our winning is temporary because we have not changed the fundamental way we view the other.

We can easily pinpoint forces in society that contribute to inequality and suffering. It is also easy to identify those who are themselves suffering. In both cases, if we wish to implement true change, we must explore what it is like to be that other. We need to find ways to honor the essential humanity of all those we identify as the stranger and as the other in our world.

But first we need to honor the sacred Presence within ourselves. In some ways, each and every one of us *is* the other, each and every one of us is the stranger. At the same time, each and every one of us is holy. The Torah tells us, "You are holy, for I, the Eternal One your God, am holy" (Leviticus 19:2). This reminder of holiness was to be inscribed on a golden disk hanging from the high priest Aaron's headdress. The disk was to be engraved with the Hebrew words *Kodesh L'Adonai*, "Holy to the Eternal One." It is time for the high priest to awaken within each of us.

In your own meditative space, welcome the priestly archetype. This is the part of you that carries the awareness of the Sacred, the part that is awake to the holiness of your being.

Imagine that there is a golden disk between and just a little above your eyes. The disk reads, "Holy to the Eternal One."

But the writing on this disk is not turned outward toward those looking at you. Rather, the words are turned inward toward yourself. The words gently penetrate your consciousness to reach the place where they always reside. At the heart of your being, you know that the Life awakening through you is holy. Release yourself to the gentle embrace of this Presence. Allow yourself to be nurtured, nourished, rejuvenated, and renewed. Breathe that Presence into every cell and every level of your being.

Remain in this sacred knowing as long as you wish, and then gently, with intention and with love, walk that holiness into your world.

Walking This Practice into the World

Imagine that there is a golden disk on the forehead of each person you meet. Imagine that inscribed on each disk are the words "Holy to the Eternal One." Each and every person is holy. Holiness is our nature. Behind the mask of individuality, behind our particular history, behind all our past conditioning, we are holy.

As you confront another, notice that there is often a slight brightness between and just a little above his eyes. This is the place of that disk. In the presence of a stranger, an outsider, even an enemy, focus on that area between the eyes. When you focus your attention there, you tend to avoid the call of the separate self. The other person will not be able to tell that you are not looking him in the eye, but you may find it more conducive to meeting him as your neighbor.

Christianity and the Stranger

The Christian attitude toward the stranger flows directly from the aspects of Jewish tradition that Rabbi Ted has described. In Matthew 25:34–40 we read:

> Then the king will say to those at his right hand, "Come you that are blessed by my Father. Inherit the kingdom

prepared for you from the foundation of the world, for I was hungry and you gave me food, I was thirsty and you gave me something to drink, I was a stranger and you welcomed me, I was naked and you gave me clothing, I was sick and you took care of me, I was in prison and you visited me." Then the righteous will answer him, "Lord when was it that we saw you hungry and gave you food, or thirsty and gave you something to drink? And when was it that we saw you as a stranger and welcomed you, or naked and gave you clothing? And when was it that we saw you sick or in prison and visited you?" And the king will answer them, "Truly I tell you, just as you did it to one of the least of these who are members of my family, you did it to me."

Christian Exclusivity

Christian exclusivity has its roots in three places: (1) tribalism, (2) a more rigid understanding of how choices are made, as either one way or the other, eclipsing subtlety and nuance, and (3) the deep need to affirm self-worth. Christian exclusivity grew out of a culture that took for granted the concept of "us against them," a concept that supports the illusion that "we" are better than "they."

In Christian scripture there are conflicting verses concerning exclusivity. How do we decide what to believe? From the work Ted, Jamal, and I have done together in identifying unconditional love as the core teaching of Christianity, I take unconditional love to be the standard against which to measure the relative value of verses and practices in my tradition. For me, verses that illustrate a consistency with unconditional love include "In everything do to others as you would have them do to you; for this is the Torah and the prophets" (Matthew 7:12); "Love your enemies and pray for those who persecute you" (Matthew 5:44); and "Love one another as I have loved you" (John 15:12).

These verses emphasize a sacred inclusivity. In Matthew 7:12, which is easily recognized as the Christian articulation of the golden rule, we see the need for civility as a necessary component for creating and sustaining a sense of oneness that enables us to help each other and not hurt each other. Within such a sensibility there is no room for thinking of ourselves as better or worse than others. We all have the same value, even though we do and think different things. The golden rule creates a framework for understanding why exclusivity is not consistent with unconditional love, loving without conditions, or grace.

Matthew 5:44 states what most people regard to be an impossibility: Love your enemies. Without unconditional love, loving your enemies is impossible. If we are to love our enemies, we can only do it by loving them without conditions. This is very difficult and requires a great deal of practice and discipline. Think of how difficult it would be for peoples marginalized by negative discrimination or persecution to love their enemies. Yet Jesus tells us that it is possible.

In John 15:12, Jesus encourages his disciples to "love one another as I have loved you." On first reading, this seems like a reasonable request. That is, of course, what Jesus would say. But stop to think about the behavior of the disciples. They knew that Jesus was saying important things and the sense of Jesus as a healer must have been extremely compelling. They thought the healing was a mark of power and that made them certain that Jesus would lead a revolt against the Roman occupation. That shows just how little of Jesus's wisdom got through to the disciples. (Scripture suggests, however, that the women, not counted in the original twelve, understood Jesus's wisdom.) Jesus had to have loved the disciples unconditionally, that is, without conditions. The text takes on a much deeper meaning now. Jesus is asking the disciples to love each other unconditionally.

While these verses illustrate a call for inclusivity in the scriptures, other verses seem to advocate a position of exclusivity. There is a subtle (and sometimes not so subtle) stance of, "We are correct and they are wrong. It is us against them."

For example, "I am the way, the truth, and the life. No one comes to God except by me" (John 14:6). This is one of the most powerful examples of the basis for Christian exclusivity. It seems to be saying that following Jesus and his ministry is the only way to salvation, to healing. In historical context, this was likely a defense against other competing religious movements following Jesus's death. It articulates the need to be correct and it seeks self-affirmation at the expense of others who choose other spiritual paths.

Much of what we see as the inability of people to embrace the lives of those who are in any way different comes from the framework above. This line of thinking has conditioned us to fall back on the us/them dichotomy. Among the effects of this kind of thinking is negative discrimination against racial and ethnic minorities, against people in the LBGT community, against religious minorities, and against women. It prompts negative discrimination against poor people and against poorly educated people. Among Christians, we see negative discrimination against fundamentalists by progressives and vice versa as a result of this kind of worldview. Each of us desperately needs to find ways to be reassured of our worth, our value, our essential dignity in order to take a position of "My way is the only right way." We often use violence and oppression as tools to reinforce our positions, and we choose to be blind to the tragedy, the danger, and the inconsistencies with our deeper values when we do so.

Our past conditioning—"I am right and they are wrong"—leads us to see stereotypes based in words such as *white* or *black*, *liberal* or *conservative*, *Christian* or *non-Christian*. Yet underneath these identities are deeper features that, if made known, would help us forge a strong bond with other people.

It takes imagination, empathy, and compassion to break out of Christian exclusivity and the suffering it causes. Let's look again at John 14:6: "I am the way, the truth, and the life. No one comes to God except by me." How else might we understand this? An important part of our Interfaith Amigos presentations is to remind people that "I am" is the name of God revealed to Moses at the burning bush:

God said to Moses, "I am as I am." He said further, "Thus you shall say to the Israelites, 'I am has sent me to you.'" (Exodus 3:14)

God is Being. In both Hebrew and Aramaic the verb "to be" in the present tense is understood but not spoken or written. So the verse in John 14:6 could be understood as I am *is* the way, the truth, and the life. Or, God (not Jesus) is the way, the truth, and the life. In other words, spiritual wisdom is rooted in a sense of the interconnectedness of all being.

We need spiritual practices to cultivate imagination, empathy, and compassion in our lives, to help us break free from our past conditioning, and to strengthen our spiritual identities and our spiritual awareness that we are One. Spiritual practices also help us fortify our spiritual communities, which prompt us to act and help sustain us in our actions.

A Christian Spiritual Practice for Welcoming the Stranger

Opening Your Eyes to Social Injustice

It is deeply important to develop an awareness of social injustice. So many of the words and images we hear and see—along with our past conditioning—obscure this reality. It is not just hearing and seeing the reality of social injustice but also learning to penetrate the curtain of advertising and extreme self-interest that so often eclipses a general awareness that not everyone is being given the same opportunities. All is not well for many, many people. While we all bring different gifts to life here on earth, we all deserve the encouragement to grow and to develop our gifts, not just for ourselves but also to contribute in large and small ways to the common good.

1. Following a period of meditation, read a newspaper and ask yourself if you are seeing evidence of injustice. Much of the media focuses on stories of violence and conflict. In those

stories are suggestions that some people are evil, and, by extension, others are good. That is contrary to the teachings of the Christian church, which suggests that all people have the same value but do and think things that are sometimes good and sometimes evil. In a journal, make a list of injustices you read about. Reflect on how your awareness of social injustice is being strengthened.

2. Following a period of meditation, think about your life and the patterns you find to be distracting. Some distractions are good and even inspiring, but others are numbing. Life can be intense and difficult, and we need brief vacations from it. But numbing can eventually decrease our awareness to the point of having no sense of social injustice at all. Make a list of your good distractions. Make a list of your numbing distractions. Reflect on how that balance might be shifted in favor of a stronger awareness of social injustice.

3. Develop a plan to read the four Gospels—the books of Matthew, Mark, Luke, and John—and in your journal note passages that pertain to the need to address social injustices. We can be strengthened by an awareness of Jesus's concerns both for the less fortunate and for the systems that oppress. Reflect on the impact Jesus's ministry might have on your life.

Walking This Practice into the World

As you go about your daily activities and see the faces of other people, practice saying to yourself, "I am seeing the face of the Holy One of Being." As this becomes a habit you will be making use of your spiritual practices and preparing yourself for social activism with a spiritual foundation.

Islam and the Stranger

In this section I talk about religious exclusivity in the Islamic faith, patriarchal bias in the treatment of women, homophobia on the subject of same-sex relationships, and intrafaith conflict among

Sunni and Shia. In the Qur'an, the second most used word after "Allah" is *ilm*, which means "knowledge." According to the Prophet, the highest form of knowledge is self-awareness. It is absolutely essential to become aware of our conditioned prejudices. How else can we honor God's revelation in the Qur'an: "Everywhere you turn is the Face of Allah" (2:115)?

Islamic Exclusivity

One day, according to a well-known interfaith fable, a holy prophet received sublime revelations from the Divine. The prophet shared those revelations with a few followers and soon a faith community began to form. And then the devil came along and said, "Here, let me organize that for you." Thus was born the first institutional religion, and over the millennia many more have sprung up all over the globe. Sadly, wherever humans organize themselves into groups, whether secular or religious, the human drive to be superior to others and to dominate often asserts itself. The culprit is pride, one of the deadliest sins of the untamed ego. "Beware of pride," warned the Prophet Muhammad. "It is the major cause of wrongdoing."

To the proud egos in my religious tradition, Islam is a superior religion because it is based on the Qur'an, which is the only true and unadulterated version of divine revelation. Other revelations had been sent earlier, but were corrupted by the Jews and Christians who received them. It cannot be denied, however, that Qur'anic revelations, too, have been corrupted by self-serving clerics and scholars who have misinterpreted verses and fabricated sayings of the Prophet to serve the interests of empire building or to protect the privileged status of men in Muslim society.

Misplaced pride in one's religious beliefs can cause unnecessary distress and violence. For example, Muslims believe that the Prophet Muhammad is the "Seal of the Prophets" (Qur'an 33:40), which is traditionally taken to mean that he is the last prophet of revelation until the Day of Judgment. When, from time to time, other religious leaders claim to have received divine revelation, they are met with condemnation and cruelty. But why do some of us get so agitated? If these claimants are committing a grave error, it only goes into their ledger of accounts, not into ours. The Qur'an says, "Indeed, God will judge between you on the Day of Resurrection concerning everything about which you would differ" (Qur'an 22:69). It behooves Muslims to remember that when the Prophet was asked to curse nonbelievers, he replied, "I have not been sent to curse people, but as a mercy to all humankind."

When we proclaim that our religion is superior to any other, this is not religion speaking but our prideful ego, refusing to respect the divine plan for the human race. The Qur'an says that God could easily have made us one single community but chose to create diversity so that we might come to know one another (5:48; 49:13). Thus, honoring diversity is a sacred obligation and we are virtually required to gain an appreciative understanding of other people's pathways to the same spiritual goal.

Many American Muslims lament that their non-Muslim counterparts view Islam as a violent religion. They wish that fellow Americans would learn that true Islam is a religion of peace and social responsibility. But have we Muslims made the same efforts in our mosques and homes to cultivate an appreciative understanding of Christianity, Judaism, or other religions? We could take a lesson from Mariyam Siddiqui, a twelve-year-old Muslim schoolgirl from India who made international news when she won a national competition on the subject of Hindu scriptures. Her parents, who are practicing Muslims, encouraged her to study Hinduism "so she can think for herself and no one can ever mislead her." Referring to religious riots in India, they regretted that they could not control what was happening in parts of India. But they could make a difference in the one place where seeds of intolerance are first sown: the home. "If everyone does the same," they said, "then there is a real chance for peace."[11]

Our essential work, mandated in the Qur'an, is not to dispute with others about true religion or religious beliefs. We humans debate and fight over religion, even kill for it; we do everything but live its precepts. This inner work is sacred and essential, says the

Qur'an: "God will not change the condition of a people unless they change what is in their hearts" (Qur'an 13:11).

Our little self tells us that we gain merit in heaven for converting others to our tradition. Enlightened teachers ask us to pause and reflect on how we choose to spend our precious time on earth. I once had an unforgettable conversation with an elderly Christian missionary who had spent forty years in Africa trying to counter the efforts of Muslim preachers who were converting locals to Islam. Now, in retirement, he mourned the years he had wasted in scheming to undermine one religion for the sake of another. It was like serving the kingdom of Caesar, he said, and he wished he had spent more time serving the kingdom of God, becoming more like Jesus and less like Caesar. The missionary confided that now, in his later and wiser years, he relishes the Sufi story of the zealous monkey who made it his mission to go to neighborhood ponds and pluck fish out of water to save them from a watery grave.

 We are all deeply conditioned beings by virtue of what we hear and learn from our family, culture, community, and religion. We inherit and often pass on our biases and preconceptions. A large part of our work on earth is to break this cycle by deconstructing our negative conditioning and expanding our awareness.

We can take comfort in the fact that even prophets have to do the work of expanding their consciousness to evolve into the fullness of their beings. What endears Muhammad to Muslims is his humility and his insistence that he was human. When some followers called the Prophet "Master," he would reply, "God is your Master."[12] When overly praised, he would say, "Do not exceed reasonable bounds in praise."

In the early days of Qur'anic revelations, Salman Farsi, a companion of the Prophet Muhammad, inquired of him about the afterlife status of non-Muslims. His closest friends, whom he loved and admired, were non-Muslims. According to one tradition, the Prophet replied, "They are in hell." The Prophet's understanding of the Qur'an at that time was limited to revelations he had received thus far. But immediately after that response, the Prophet received a new Qur'anic revelation that expanded his understanding: "Those who follow the Jewish faith, and the Christians, and the Sabians— all who believe in God and the Last Day and do righteous deeds— shall have their reward with their Sustainer; and no fear need they have, and neither shall they grieve" (2:62).

Based on the universal teachings of the Qur'an and the conduct of the Prophet, Sufi teachers ask us to ponder the insight that if the relationship between me and my religion gets in the way of my relationship with you, it will surely get in the way of my relationship with God.

Muslim Women

We are blessed to have a number of devout and knowledgeable Muslim women in our congregation who have pointed out the primary cause of injustice imposed on women in many Islamic societies: bewildering patriarchal bias in direct contradiction to revelations in the Qur'an.

In the Arabian Peninsula, where women were considered mere property in the seventh century, Qur'anic revelations granted women revolutionary property, divorce, and inheritance rights. The Prophet declared, "The rights of women are sacred. See that women are maintained in the rights granted to them."[13] But following the death of the Prophet, as Islam spread to feudal societies, male jurists reclaimed their dominance over women and this tribal bias continues today. Over the centuries, a number of Muslim legal scholars have blatantly misinterpreted Qur'anic verses so that they oppress the very women the verses were meant to protect. An extraordinary number of false and biased hadith on women have cropped up in the Islamic tradition. For example, in the story of the primeval humans' fall from grace, the Qur'an places equal blame on both Adam and his wife for succumbing to Satan and disobeying God; subsequently, both husband and wife are graciously forgiven by God. However, in the exegesis by traditional scholars, including the well-respected Sahih Al-Bukhari and Sahih Muslim, Adam's wife is portrayed as the guilty party responsible for the downfall, again in direct contradiction of the Qur'an's account.

The Muslim women in our Interfaith Community Sanctuary have taught us that patriarchal bias starts at home and is reinforced by elders and authorities in the community and in mosques. It is critical, they insist, that we open a sacred dialogue in which men and women listen to one another's pain and suffering and become aware of our conditioned responses, passed down through the generations. We Muslim men must strive to create an environment at home and in the community where the women in our lives feel safe to express their feelings on the issue of inequality without fear of judgment and retribution. The women have also made us aware that interpretations of the Qur'an have traditionally been published exclusively by male scholars and it behooves us to listen carefully to the growing number of female scholars who are challenging traditional patriarchal interpretations that have become institutionalized. Lastly, in our community, when talking about God, we make conscious efforts to refer to Divinity in the feminine gender as often as in the masculine gender.

Homophobia

The topic of homosexuality is controversial and difficult for Muslims because of conditioned views, inculcated by social and religious institutions, that same-gender sexual relations are perverse and wrong.

As a young Muslim, I was taught to be compassionate toward homosexuals. I believed that, through persistent inner work and by God's grace, they could overcome their "addiction." Some years ago, a Muslim family brought me their gay son to help heal him through Sufi practices. God was giving me an opportunity to set this young man on the right path! With great fervor I worked with him for weeks on end but to no avail. He felt closer to God but he still felt the same-sex attraction. At a certain point, sensing his pain, I let go of my agenda and was finally able to listen to him. I was amazed. For the first time I heard the depth of his anguish: His mother wanted to commit suicide; his father was ready to move the family to another state; he agonized over the pain he was causing his loved ones; he did not want to be gay but could not help himself in spite of heroic efforts. Something opened in me: I moved, as Sufis say, from knowledge of tongue to knowledge of heart. I became convinced that his sexual orientation was not by choice but by natural disposition.

In the process of initially advising my gay Muslim client to apply himself diligently to seek help from God and do the inner spiritual work to overcome his dysfunction, it struck me that maybe it was I who was in desperate need of heeding my own advice. I need to make continuous exertions to follow the Qur'anic injunctions of "Open for me my heart" (20:25) and "O God, advance me in knowledge" (20:114). Expansion of consciousness is a sacred duty and there can be no limit to our capacity for compassion. How do we accomplish this?

The first step, I realize, is to put aside the old stereotyping of homosexuals as people who are damaged and perverted. We need to connect with them on a human level and make space in our hearts to acknowledge that all humans long for love and relationship in different ways.

It is also important to let go of exclusive interpretations of our sacred texts and ask how gay Muslims interpret verses of the Qur'an about homosexuality. Like their Jewish and Christian counterparts, they point out that the story of Sodom and Gomorrah in the Qur'an is not about homosexuality but about male assault and rape. And, like all decent people, they condemn these acts of violence. Like most heterosexuals, they also believe in the sacredness of union based on love, respect, and tenderness with their same-sex partners. They believe that out of a need for diversity, God created them as they are. They did not choose their orientation; God chose it for them.

Healing the Sunni-Shia Split

The religious conflict between Sunni and Shia Muslims is based on a historical conflict about choice of successor or caliph after the Prophet's death in 632 CE. One group chose Abu Bakr, a close companion of the Prophet; another group chose Hazrat Ali, the cousin and son-in-law of the Prophet. The former prevailed and called themselves Sunnis. The latter are called Shias. Today, 85 percent of Muslims in the world are Sunni and 15 percent are Shia.

This seventh-century historical dispute caused conflict in the community, culminating in the Battle of Karbala in which the Prophet's grandson was savagely killed by an opposing Sunni army. The date of that battle in 680 CE is a day of immense lamentation in the Shia world.

A group of committed Sunnis and Shias in Seattle have been meeting regularly at Interfaith Community Sanctuary to heal this intrafaith divide. We initially gathered to participate in what we call three cups of tea: Listen, respect, and connect. Through friendship and the willingness to be vulnerable we moved to the next step: Listen to the anguish of the other and engage in more difficult conversations. Some of the Sunnis were surprised and profoundly touched to hear of the deep wounds caused by the Karbala event; some Shias expressed surprise that there were Sunnis who shared the pain of the Shia community. There have been tears, hugs, and honest admissions of ignorance and arrogance.

The conversations have distilled into one major question: What can I do to heal the hurt my community and I have caused you? At the time of this writing we are in the process of creating rituals of forgiveness, especially by Sunnis asking forgiveness from Shias. Simultaneously, the depth of friendships built over time has enabled us to pray together, led by rotating Sunni and Shia prayer leaders, and we have begun collaborating on social projects.

Islamic Spiritual Practices for Welcoming the Stranger

Self-Awareness

A time-honored way to overcome our prejudices and tame our ego is to become aware of both our ego traits and our divine qualities, and strive to diminish the former while expanding the latter. Keep a small notebook in your pocket and record the ego qualities that you see yourself manifesting in the course of the day, especially your biases, prejudices, and stereotyping. Review them each evening and express gratitude to God for your growing awareness of these traits that need to be diminished. The practice of regular awareness is like a sacred sun that gradually diminishes our shadows.

Create a ritual of purification and release of your ego traits. For example, at the end of the week you could write down the traits you have observed, put the list in a fireproof bowl, and burn it with a prayer for divine assistance in the coming week.

In the same notebook, also record the divine qualities that you have observed each day. Perhaps you chose to speak the truth, even though it was inconvenient. Express gratitude to the Source for the specific divine qualities flowing through you, and pray for them to grow and flourish in your heart.

Walking This Practice into the World

By becoming aware of your ego traits and divine qualities, you will be able to make choices that enable you to grow spiritually. You will, by grace of Spirit, experience authentic power and joy.

Connecting with the Other

Make it a spiritual practice to consciously connect with someone who is the "other." Start with someone in your extended family or circle of acquaintances. Maybe it's someone whose political or religious views differ from yours. If there is antagonism, remember that you resent the antagonism, not the antagonist. The individual's behavior or opinions might seem unacceptable, but the person's being is sacred and divine. Remind yourself that just keeping this discernment in your heart, between behavior and being, has the power to shift heaven and earth.

Start by meditating in silence about that person and sending light flowing from your heart to her heart. Tell yourself that you are transmitting light to that person's soul, not to her personality. Speak to her in your meditation. Express your intention to connect on a human level. Pray for guidance.

When you feel ready, take the initiative in your wakeful state, little by little, to connect with the other, maybe by opening a conversation with her. Be sincere and humble. Your essential goal is simply to connect on a human level. Send light from your soul to her soul in the conscious state. If you feel awkward initially, please persist. Sufi teachers say that with this tried-and-true technique, there is the promise of doors opening up, literally and metaphorically.

Walking This Practice into the World

Daily, witness yourself in your dealings with others. Allow your awareness to be like a compassionate sun gently shining on your awkwardness and preconceptions. Allow yourself, as the Sufis say, to be like melting snow. Wash yourself of yourself.

4
Overcoming Despair

Carrying on in the Face of Overwhelming Environmental Problems

There are times when issues we face seem insurmountable and we feel powerless to deal with them in any meaningful way. Working for peace in the world may leave us feeling powerless, and this feeling of powerlessness often leads to hopelessness. But even though we feel overwhelmed, the work we do to address issues such as discrimination, disenfranchisement, and persecution is important. Spiritual practices can help support and restore us as we work to bring about peace.

The increasing danger to the environment of our planet is one area in which the problems seem far greater than possible solutions. Glaciers are melting and the sea levels are rising; 2015 was the hottest year ever recorded. Weather patterns are changing and adversely affecting agriculture and populations in low-lying areas of the world. Environmental air pollution has reached record levels, threatening health in many regions of the earth. Overpopulation strains resources, and we are already consuming more natural resources than are available on our besieged planet. Waste disposal has contaminated our oceans as well as many less developed countries to which our waste is sent. Biodiversity is decreasing as species are becoming extinct, and deforestation is further threatening environmental decay.

Elevated ocean acidification and ozone depletion increase the threat to our planet and our own lives.

While the 2015 global environmental conference in Paris brought greater cooperation from more countries than ever, major groups, particularly within the United States, are dedicated on ideological grounds to fighting any environmental standards meant to decrease pollution. In various ways, many people are refusing to acknowledge the seriousness of the threats we are facing.

When we feel trapped, we respond emotionally and physically. Sometimes we figure out ways to fight our way out. But when we find ourselves in a seemingly no-win situation, confronting powers far greater than ourselves, one of our responses is despair. Because of the nature of our environmental crisis, this condition is not uncommon in environmental advocacy. Hopelessness is a doorway to despair, and despair is the path of inaction. When we decide that there is simply nothing we can do that will make a significant difference, we tend to turn inward in denial. In some ways, it seems like the degradation of our planet has gone too far to be healed, and we find good reason to despair.

What do our faith traditions tell us about despair, and about the environment? Is despair a condition simply to be denied? If not, how are we to deal with it? Can despair itself be a path to healing? How can spiritual practices of our faith traditions fortify us against despair as we work to save the planet?

How Judaism Views Despair

Jews have known despair. How many other peoples, through the centuries, have had their powerlessness demonstrated in such painful ways? Jews have been evicted from their homes, their property confiscated by the dominant powers. In 1182, Jews were expelled from France; from England between 1262 and 1290; from Spain in 1492; and from Portugal in 1496. In fact, since 250 CE, Jews have been kicked out 109 times from nearly every country in Europe and many others. Jewish communities flourished in Iraq since the fourth century CE, and they are no more. History reflects brutal massacres, often motivated by those offended by the unwillingness of Jews to convert to another faith.

And then the twentieth-century Holocaust taught millions of Jews that they were not safe. They were victims not only of Nazi persecution but also of the inaction of those who watched and did nothing. According to journalist Jeffrey Goldberg:

> France's 475,000 Jews represent less than 1 percent of the country's population. Yet last year, according to the French Interior Ministry, 51 percent of all racist attacks targeted Jews. The statistics in other countries, including Great Britain, are similarly dismal. In 2014, Jews in Europe were murdered, raped, beaten, stalked, chased, harassed, spat on, and insulted for being Jewish.[1]

At the same time, Jewish tradition challenges us to resist the temptation to despair. Even in the severest circumstances, in a concentration camp during the Holocaust, Austrian neurologist and psychiatrist Viktor Frankl (1905–1997) taught, "Everything can be taken from a man but one thing: the last of the human freedoms—to choose one's attitude in any given set of circumstances, to choose one's own way."[2]

For the Baal Shem Tov, living at a time of severe pogroms, joy was the key to fending off despair.

> The Baal Shem Tov didn't limit joy to prayer, study, and performance of mitzvahs. Consistent with his guiding principle that God is everywhere and can be found in all things, he taught that every event that befalls a person, everything a person sees or hears, all present an opportunity to know the Creator and to serve Him. There can be no time, no circumstance and no place in which you cannot connect with the Infinite. And if so, there is no excuse at any time not to be happy—since joy is the key to all divine service. And perhaps most fascinating: the Baal Shem Tov understood joy as a device to repair the world, as a key to redemption.[3]

For Rabbi Nachman of Breslov (1772–1810), a great-grandson of the Baal Shem Tov, despair was the greatest of sins. His famous teaching has been made into a song: "All the world is just a narrow bridge, and the main principle is not to be afraid of it all" (Likutey Moharan II:48).

Jewish Spiritual Practices for Overcoming Despair

A Psalm for Greater Vision

Despair, hopelessness, and depression are universal human feelings. Biblical texts show us those who have encountered difficult experiences and found ways to move beyond them. One of my favorites is Psalm 121:

> *Esa aynai el he-harim*
> *May-ayin yavo ezri?*
> *Ezri mayim Adonai,*
> *Oseh shamayim va-aretz.*
>
> I lift up my eyes to the mountains,
> From where shall my help come?
> My help comes from the Eternal One,
> Maker of heaven and the earth.
> (Psalm 121:1–2)

The psalmist speaks from a place of despair, but then lifts his eyes upward, beyond the particular circumstances of his life. He affirms that he is connected to something greater, an Eternal Presence whose power dwarfs earthly conflicts. The Creator of all that exists embraces us, especially in the midst of our difficulties.

We can do the same, using these words. Such lines function best when committed to memory, either in English or in Hebrew, so their energy can lift us beyond the despair of the moment to an expanded awareness of the potential for true healing. Repeat these words gently in your mind, and allow them to carry your vision beyond the specifics of a difficult situation to the images of healing and wholeness that you seek. Allow a Universal Presence to awaken through you with a profound sense of peace and hope.

Walking This Practice into the World

Gently repeat the words of these verses from Psalm 121 in your mind as you walk your way into the world. Remember that there is a greater reality that includes and harmonizes all that you see and all that you experience. Notice what happens when you repeat these phrases during difficult and stressful times.

Moving into Conscious Action

Despair gets in the way of constructive action in both the inner and the outer world. Action is the antidote to that kind of despair: action of the body through energetic movement, action of the mind through constructive visioning, and action of the spirit through the opening of the heart.

The heart is seen as the physical correlate of *ruach*, the more inclusive soul that can know unconditional acceptance and love. The heart is also the place of *tiferet*, the "beauty" that forms the center of the mystical Tree of Life. Walking healing into the world energizes the heart-centered greater self through physical, mental, and spiritual dimensions.

When encountering seemingly intractable problems, get moving. Get your body out of the chair and move, or, if you're unable to stand, simply move your arms, head, and torso. Create your own dance with or without music. Get your physical heart beating and energize your breath. If you are in a setting where spontaneous dancing isn't appropriate, take a quick walk, go up and down a stairway, or engage in some kind of activity to get your blood flowing and your breath moving.

Then stop, and feel the energy flowing through your body. Feel the life and the vitality flowing through you. As you stand still or sit, imagine the problem areas clearing. Perhaps the fog of pollution dissolves and the air clears. Perhaps the forests grow more full, rebalancing the oxygen in the air. The waters are purified, and animal life begins to thrive once again. In the silence, imagine what the mind may have decided was impossible. Let healing begin.

As the greater Presence awakens within you, the body comes to new life, the mind conjures up images of healing, and the Presence flows through you to embrace it all. Realize that you are a vehicle through which the Universal Presence seeks impact in the world. Let that Presence imbue the images of healing you provide, so that you might use your energies in the service of that healing. Conclude by focusing on the area of your heart, where compassion and love arise, to nurture the purification and the renewal of your world.

Walking This Practice into the World

When you find yourself overwhelmed, perhaps stuck, take a moment to stop and breathe. Feel the aliveness of your breath. Feel the breath bringing energy to every cell of your body. Know that visions of healing and wholeness can awaken in the present moment. Affirm that the Greater Presence naturally flows through your breath to bring about the greatest good. Place a hand over your heart, confirming the opening to new possibilities.

How Judaism Views the Environment

The recognition that the domain of the environment is so much greater than the realm of human beings is illustrated by an ancient midrashic tale. When God created the first human beings, God led them around the Garden of Eden and said: "Look at my works! See how beautiful they are—how excellent! For your sake I created them all. See to it that you do not spoil and destroy My world; for if you do, there will be no one else to repair it" (Midrash Kohelet Rabbah 1 on Ecclesiastes 7:13). From our vantage point, it appears that we have hardly heeded that ancient warning. We have participated in the destruction of the precious resources of our planet.

Jewish tradition continually affirms, "The earth is the Eternal's, and all that fills it; the world, and those who dwell in it" (Psalm

24:1). We are part of a single ecosystem, interconnected and inter-dependent. We human beings are here to serve, to care for, and to nurture creation. But when we surrender to our evil inclination (*yetzer ha-ra*), when we seek our own individual satisfaction only, we use resources solely for our own benefit, without consideration of the greater consequences.

The words of the prophet Jeremiah, speaking in the sixth century BCE, are sadly pertinent today: "And I brought you into a land of fruitful fields to eat the fruit thereof; but when you entered, you defiled My land and made My heritage an abomination" (Jeremiah 2:7).

Again and again, Jewish tradition, like other authentic spiritual paths, notes that we human beings are not acting with consciousness in our care of the earth. We need reminders. Shabbat, that most important observance of Jewish tradition, is given to all creation as a weekly reminder of the One Being and the One Life we share; it is the link between care of human beings and care of the environment.

> Speak to the people of Israel, and say to them, When you come into the land which I give you, then shall the land keep a sabbath to the Eternal. Six years you shall sow your field, and six years you shall prune your vineyard, and gather in its fruit. But in the seventh year shall be a sabbath of rest to the land, a sabbath for the Eternal; you shall not sow your field, nor prune your vineyard. (Leviticus 25:2–4)

We need to appreciate that we are not separate from our environment. We are dependent on it for our very lives, and it depends on us to be proper caretakers, to protect it from constant strain and overuse. We will not be able to support the healing of our environment until we realize that we are all interconnected. This is the ultimate meaning of the Oneness we celebrate as the core teaching of Jewish tradition.

How can we awaken from our slumbers, from our unconsciousness, so that we might act with greater care in our world? Perhaps by expanding our self-definition to include not only human beings but our struggling planet as well. We can also energize our efforts through compassionate action, which promises far better results than attacking those we think are wrong.

𝒪𝑓𝑓 Jewish Spiritual Practices for Environmental Healing

Rabbi Nachman's Walking Meditation

When we visited Poland several years ago, I anticipated a land devoid of beauty. The Jewish community there had suffered horrible destruction at the hands of the Nazis and their Polish collaborators, and the awareness of this history had colored my images of the country in shades of gray and brown. Instead, I found beautiful countryside, and realized another dimension of what the Polish Jewish community had lost. The verdant fields and forests reminded me of one of the great spiritual practices of the late-eighteenth-century Hasidic teacher, Rabbi Nachman of Breslov.

He called it *hitbod'dut*. The word itself means "being alone with oneself," and has become the Hebrew word for all meditative practices. The specific practice Rabbi Nachman taught encouraged students to walk in the natural world—in a forest, if possible—by themselves. As they walked, they were to talk to God aloud, freely communicating their feelings, their problems, and their desires. They were to empty themselves as if they were sharing their concerns with their closest friends. Nothing, Rebbe Nachman taught, was too insignificant to share.

Surely, the practice of walking alone in the beauty of the natural world refreshes our spirit and rejuvenates us. But adding to this the actual verbalization of our deepest—and even our most trivial—concerns deepens this experience. We are reminded that we are always in the presence of the One Life we share. We are part of that Life. We communicate not only with the Universal but also with the trees and the grasses. They are part of us and we are part of them. As we allow them to feel some of our own anguish, as well as our own joys, we might become more conscious of their anguish, caused by our unconscious destruction, and of their joys as they grow and flower freely.

Walking This Practice into the World

When walking in your world, consider your neighborhood to be your forest. Think of the people you meet on the street as the trees in that forest. Each is a precious expression of a shared Life, whether they are aware of it or not.

As you move through your day, imagine praying for the very best for each and every person. Look into the sky and affirm greater purification. While not spoken aloud, your prayers for healing and wholeness can make a difference. See how they impact your own experience.

Connecting Heaven and Earth

Find a comfortable place to sit where your feet rest on the floor. Allow yourself to settle in, then begin a body scan: Imagine traveling through your body and noticing how each part feels. You might begin with your feet and stay with them until you feel them soften and relax. Then slowly scan up your legs to your knees. Allow your awareness to focus on each of your knees and, once again, feel them soften and relax. Continue up your thighs and through your hips. Notice how you are held by your chair, and allow yourself to melt into its supportive surface.

Move up through your belly and your lower back until you reach the area of your heart. That is the center; remain there for a moment, noticing your breathing. Then focus on your fingers and hands, allowing them to gradually soften and release. Move up your arms and into your shoulders, and then center once again in the space of your heart.

Finally, begin at the very top of your head, becoming aware of your scalp. Let your scalp soften, and move down to your forehead and the back of your head. Focus on your eyes and then your cheeks. Notice your jaw, your tongue, and your lips. Then move gently down your neck, centering once again in the space of your heart.

Once you feel calm, imagine that a deep earth energy reaches upward into the bottom of your feet. The energy rises up like roots, connecting you to the earth. Allow the sense of that earth energy to ascend through your body until it reaches the area of your heart. Breathe it in quietly, affirming the connection and the grounding to the earth beneath you.

Then imagine a flow of energy from above that enters you at the very crown of your head. That cosmic energy connects you to the universe, and moves gently down through your head and neck to meet in the area of your heart. Breathe the energies of the heavens and the energies of the earth into their meeting place in your heart.

Realize that you are a being who connects heaven and earth. You are like a human tree, with roots deep in the earth and branches reaching into the sky. And your heart is the place of connection.

Breathe into this connection for as long as you like. When you are ready, take several deep breaths and allow your eyes to open. Move your body gently, and take a moment before arising.

Walking This Practice into the World

When you are out and about, pay attention to the trees that you see. Their roots reach down into the earth for the nourishment to be found there, and their branches and leaves reach upward to nourish the air we breathe. Appreciate that, like you, the trees are living beings deserving of love and compassion. Even a blade of grass reflects this same connection. All of life takes nourishment from the earth and brings forth fruits to be shared physically, emotionally, mentally, and spiritually. As we become more conscious of how we treat each part of ourselves, we recognize that we are part of one living Being.

How Christianity Views Despair

There is a suggestion within Jesus's teachings that despair is commonplace. But in Matthew 11:28 Jesus says, "Come to me, all you who are weary and are carrying heavy burdens, and I will give you rest. Take my yoke upon you, and learn from me; for I am gentle and humble in heart, and you will find rest for your souls. For my yoke is easy, and my burden is light."

Despair is natural, but its effects can be devastating. Yet it is part of being human. Even Jesus experienced despair, showing just how human he was. When he was dying on the cross, he cried out, "My God, my God, why have you forsaken me?" (Matthew 27:46). He was quoting the first line of Psalm 22. Nonetheless, relief can be found in the spiritual wisdom of Jesus.

In 2 Corinthians 4:8–9, Paul writes, "We are afflicted in every way, but not crushed; perplexed but not driven to despair; persecuted, but not forsaken; struck down but not destroyed." He is suggesting that the substance of Jesus's ministry can help us in our most desperate moments, because we are never alone in our despair. God is always with us.

In Romans 5:1–5, Paul also writes,

> Therefore, since we are justified by faith, we have peace with God through our Lord Jesus Christ, through whom we have access to this grace in which we stand; and we boast in our hope of sharing the glory of God. And not only that, but we also boast in our sufferings, knowing that suffering produces endurance, and endurance produces character, and character produces hope, and hope does not disappoint us, because God's love has been poured into our hearts through the Holy Spirit that has been given to us.

Jesus's ministry has the power to lead us through despair to a place of hope because, once again, God is always with us.

A Christian Spiritual Practice for Overcoming Despair

I Am Not Alone

During meditation, use two focus phrases to call yourself back to your center. Remembering Jesus's message to the disciples at the end of

Matthew (28:20) "I am with you always, to the end of the age," say, "I am not alone. I have the power to move from despair to hope."

Walking This Practice into the World

Practice using the phrase "I am not alone" as you move through your day. It is a habit that can provide strength and courage. Remember your relationship not just to God through this teaching of Jesus, but also to other people through the preciousness of relationships and to all of creation. We are all part of the One.

How Christianity Views the Environment

Are there Christian teachings concerning the stewardship of the environment? Yes. Are there teachings of Jesus concerning the stewardship of the environment? Yes and no. Let's start there.

Two thousand years ago, the earth had not sustained the damage from human hands that it has sustained today. Historically, there had been environmental damage—from the impact of meteorites, for example, and other "natural occurrences." So Jesus's teachings were focused on a broad way of understanding the relationship between human experience and the natural world (*kosmos*). When we read "world," we might also read "universe" or "creation." The theme of the sacredness of creation is at the center of Jesus's understanding of the environment and is rooted in Genesis 1:26, where we read that people are to be good stewards of creation, to have "dominion." As it is read in English, it can easily slip in our awareness from *dominion* to *domination*, which is quite a different matter. In fact, domination accounts for much of our current predicament.

But where does domination come from? It comes from our egocentric sense of entitlement to the resources of our natural world. We arrived at this difficult moment because of the sense that we have the right to dominate and that we can do as we wish with creation. The evidence is clear that we are capable of destroying life on the planet if we do not make some changes.

What evidence do we find in scripture for Jesus's understanding of the sacredness of creation? Consider this verse from the Sermon on the Mount, a collection of the teachings of Jesus: "Do not think that I have come to abolish the law and the prophets; I have come not to abolish but to fulfill" (Matthew 5:17). What is Jesus saying?

When we read the word "law" in English, we should not think "legality." Much too much has been made of the mistaken idea that Judaism is about law (in the sense of legalism) and Christianity is about love. This is not true, and has caused untold suffering. The word "law" is a translation of the Greek *nomos*, which can have three meanings. It can mean legality, but Jesus would not put that together with "the prophets." It can mean *Torah*, or "the teachings," a reference to the first five books of Hebrew scripture. It can also mean Jewish religion in general. I think the word "law" is an unfortunate and damaging reference to the latter two because it fuels an anti-Semitic sense that Christianity is better than Judaism because it is about love and not about law. In other words, Jesus is saying (or people are saying about Jesus) that we are being called back to the substance of Jewish religion, made known especially in Torah, the teachings, which encompass an awareness of the oneness of all of creation and the interconnectedness of all being. I think this is the context of other teachings of Jesus that can be related to the environment and to the physical universe. It would include an awareness of the teaching in Genesis that humankind is to be given dominion over all of creation. We are to be good stewards of the environment.

Here are four scriptural references that help make up my sense of how Jesus felt about the sacredness of creation:

"God so loved the world that he gave his only son" (John 3:16). This is so important that I am prepared to set aside a masculine and otherwise narrow view of this verse. The Greek word that is translated as "so" means "in this manner." In other words, this verse does not express quantity as much as quality. And though quantity may be important and relevant, it is good to remember how God chose to make known God's love. I would translate the verse this way: "This is the way God loved the world. A person was chosen to make known God's purposes for all of creation."

Jesus's role was both prophetic and healing. And because he was, at one level, just a person, God's purposes became more accessible to people. God loved the world. Once again, the Greek *kosmos* can be translated as "world," "universe," or "all of creation." John 3:16 reveals Jesus's awareness of the depth of God's concern for all of creation. This awareness would have been rooted in Torah. It would have framed the substance of Jesus's entire ministry. And I think it would have been possible for Jesus to see the need for forgiveness among people mirroring the need for healing in anything that exists. This describes a way of understanding experience, a sensibility that was the basis for Jesus's ministry.

"And who is my neighbor?" (Luke 10:29). In the same way, the need for compassion suggested by the parable of the Good Samaritan reflects Jesus's understanding that we are all to be neighbors to each other in terms of both humanity and all of creation. It suggests a need to take care, to stop and notice, to give thanks, and to help, whenever possible, with the care of the planet. We are called to be neighbors, not just to each other but to all of creation.

"This son of mine was dead and is alive again; he was lost and is found" (Luke 15:24). The need for forgiveness expressed in the parable of the Prodigal Son, when the father welcomes home and forgives the wayward son—an action rooted in unconditional love—reflects an additional and deeply important aspect of the way God needs us to see the world. Healing depends on forgiveness, and forgiveness of people can also mirror how we need to take care of the earth. We will always make mistakes. We will harm the earth (as we are doing right now) and we will need to feel forgiveness to summon the energy and the strength to move forward. Forgiveness is necessary for healing and healing is what we need: personal, social, and environmental.

"Mary took a pound of costly perfume, made of pure nard, anointed Jesus's feet, and wiped them with her hair" (John 12:3). In this story Judas criticizes Mary for using expensive perfume instead of selling it and giving the money to the poor. Jesus suggests that while the poor need direct service, we must also be concerned about the need to be good stewards—stewards of property, stewards of money, stewards of compassion. To Jesus, the concept of good stewardship is central to the way we live our lives as people of faith. Good steward-ship is a way of recovering our centers and using that to contribute to the common good.

Being a good steward is not easy. Many people have forgotten or refuse to acknowledge Jesus's teachings on the sacredness of the natural world and our roles in protecting it. Yet, Jesus says, "But strive first for the realm of God and God's justice and all these things will be given you as well" (Matthew 6:33).

Christian Spiritual Practices for Environmental Healing

The goal of these spiritual practices is to gain a deeper sense of our relationship to the environment, to its sacredness and its connected-ness to All Being. So often we are either not aware of the environment or we see it as separate from ourselves. That is the sensibility that con-tributes to the destruction of the environment. It is important to over-come that sensibility and, through repetition, develop a deeper and stronger sense of our relationship to all of creation.

To do that we must become mindful of creation and of our place in it. With a deep breath and an awareness of breathing in and out, focus on the relationship between your being and your natural surroundings. This can be done outside but also inside in a place where the outside is visible. A verse from scripture can help bring us back to our centers. I like the second part of Luke 21:30: "Know that summer is already near." This is important because in summer we find a presence that is different from other seasons. In the fall we are anticipating winter. In winter we are hoping for spring. And in spring we are looking for-ward to summer. But in summer we are here and, ideally, more present with fewer obsessions about the past and less anxiety about the future. "Know that summer is already near."

Each of the following practices is designed to provide an opportunity to be centered in your spiritual being and, within that sense of centeredness, to forge a complete and sacred relationship to the natural world. While nature by itself cannot create, sustain, or redeem us, it is an intimate and completely interrelated facet of Being.

What follows is a list of practices to use as a focus for that deeply needed appreciation and thanksgiving for our natural world.

Greeting the Light with Thanksgiving

Upon arising and experiencing the light of day, repeat this ancient Jewish prayer of thanksgiving: "I thank you, Living and Eternal Being, for you have mercifully restored my soul within me. Your faithfulness is great." (Rabbi Ted's translation)

Remembering That Water Is and Supplies Vitality

As you turn on the water, remember that it comes not just from plumbing but from the rain that showers the earth. Imagine it coming down from the sky, filling the lakes and streams, flowing into the infrastructure that transports it to your home. Imagine it soaking into the dry places in you and bringing you new life.

Recognizing the Meditation That Is Constant for Trees and Other Plants

The photosynthesis of sunlight and the manufacture of oxygen combine in a miraculous "breathing" to replicate our best attempts at meditation. In the context of the sacredness of all of creation, the centeredness of trees and plants can be an inspiration for us. As you breathe, imagine a symbiotic relationship between your breathing and the breathing of trees and plants.

Appreciating the Life That Is in Animals

What does it mean to say that humanity is the highest form of life? We cannot know the highest but we can accept our responsibility to be good stewards of creation and to see the animals as our kin. Of course, some animals are dangerous and there will be particular situations where that sensibility will be difficult. But the universal is key. We are all related. Focus on the memory or the reality of a pet and acknowledge its life. Give thanks for it.

Locating Ourselves among the Stars

If you gaze at the night sky and see the infinite clusters of matter that shine on us, you will also see yourself in a relationship with the physical universe. While we know more and more, we discover at the same time that we grasp very little of what might actually be known. The night sky becomes an invitation to humility—not to diminish ourselves but to see ourselves in relation to an unimaginably larger whole.

Walking These Practices into the World

Remembering Jesus's commitment to the stewardship of creation, make a schedule so you carry out each one of these actions on a revolving schedule. Use the phrase "I have been given dominion over creation" as you move through your days. Look for opportunities to observe others engaged in these same kinds of activities. As we practice, we need the reassurance that others are practicing in similar ways.

How Islam Views Despair

All of us, at some point in our lives, will experience some degree of depression and despair. Whether it be the death of a loved one, the loss of a relationship, or a radical shift in life circumstances, the difficulty can be overwhelming. What Muslims will do, in their pain, is turn to their Holy Book, just as Jews and Christians turn to the Holy Bible for comfort or guidance. And on the topic of despair, the Qur'an offers a powerful example of both comfort and guidance in a single revelation: "Truly by token of time, human beings are in loss, except those who have faith and do righteous deeds, and encourage each other in the teaching of truth and in patient perseverance" (103:1–3). Elsewhere the Qur'an reminds us, "Don't you see that God has made in service to you all that is in the heavens and on earth and has made His/Her bounties flow to you in abundant measure, seen and unseen?" (31:20).

Sometimes it is hard to see the abundant goodness of God when we are faced with relentless and extensive suffering caused by natural disasters or by unspeakable human cruelty, greed, and indifference. How can we believe in a God who is supposed to be all aware, infinitely powerful, and boundlessly compassionate, yet allows pain and distress to occur indiscriminately? Why do bad things happen to innocent people? There is no human logic that will satisfy the mind in response to this conundrum.

An even greater mystery, however, is the inclination of the human heart to grow faith and gratitude in the midst of pain and suffering. As a spiritual counselor, I often sit with people who feel so brutalized by life and betrayed by God that they ask me not to mention God in the healing sessions. I meticulously honor their request, but, amazingly, as they begin to heal, they themselves bring God into their lives and develop an unshakable relationship with the Divine. Some become so passionate about their love of God that they remind me of a tongue-in-cheek Sufi song from South Asia: "O God save me from all these God lovers!"

The "time" verse cited above (103:1–3), with its combination of comfort and advice, could help explain the mystery of how my clients have drawn closer to God even in the midst of their despair. In moments of deep anguish, when he felt abandoned by God, the Prophet Muhammad received a revelation with a similar combination of verses. First came the comfort, tenderly reminding him, "Your Sustainer has not forgotten you ... and, truly, that which comes after will be better for you than the present" (93:1–4). And then came the guidance: "So do not be harsh with orphans, and nor turn away one who asks something of you" (93:9–10). In other words, ongoing acts of righteousness and service even while struggling with personal difficulties can protect us from sinking into a self-focused quagmire of hopelessness and depression. The revelation concludes with a glorious line—"The Bounty of thy Lord rehearse and proclaim!" (93:11)—and this is exactly what I have seen my clients do in the course of their healing work!

To counter despondency, we are also advised to gather in communities that honor truth and teach us to be patient. By hearing the stories of people we trust, we realize that we are not privy to the larger story when distressing circumstances occur in our lives. "Of knowledge it is only a little that is communicated to you," says the Qur'an (17:85). In times of difficulties, the Prophet prayed, "O God, save me from its harm but do not deprive me of its good." Wise friends counsel us to be patient. Sufi well-wishers remind one another that it takes time for the crescent moon to become full. We are encouraged "to hold fast to the rope of God" (Qur'an 3:103) and take refuge in the repeated promise of God that "verily with every hardship comes the easing" (Qur'an 94:5).

An Islamic Spiritual Practice for Overcoming Despair

To God We Belong

To become conscious of God in times of uncertainty and despair, the Qur'an asks us to recite the words, "To God we belong and to God we shall return" (2:156). We can repeat the verse like a mantra while focusing on the heart. Or, alternatively, we can focus on our breath, saying with every inhalation, "To God we belong," and upon exhalation, "to God we shall return."

Walking This Practice into the World

In the course of your day, strive to remain conscious of Divinity as often as possible. In times of difficulty, the Qur'an promises that God "prepares a way of emergence and provides in ways" that cannot be imagined (65:3). Rumi says that in times of affliction, God sends a "stretcher from Grace."

How Islam Views the Environment

"Honor and protect the earth," said the Prophet Muhammad; "the earth is like your mother." This attitude of reverence for nature is highlighted in more than seven hundred verses in the Qur'an. Many chapters are named after natural phenomena and some chapters start with mysterious invocations whereby God takes an oath invoking nature: "By the fig and the olive" or "By the dawn."

Considering the reverence shown by the Qur'an to Mother Earth, it behooves us to pay attention to Qur'anic teachings about stewardship of the planet earth.

Vice-Regency and *Amanah*

The Qur'an teaches that every human being is a representative or "vice-regent" of the Divine, and our assignment is to protect and preserve the sanctity of our environment and the earth community. To that end, each of us in primordial time signed on to an *amanah*, a covenant of trust, in which we promised to exercise awareness and free will to "enjoin good and forbid evil" and "not to sow corruption on earth." "True servants of the All Merciful are those who walk softly on the earth," says the Qur'an (25:63), and "do not walk upon the earth with proud self-conceit; for, truly, you can never rend the earth asunder, nor can you grow as tall as the mountains" (Qur'an 17:37). Too often in our pursuit of pleasure and wealth we assume that we are masters of all we survey and the earth is ours to plunder, but the Qur'an begs to differ. In an astonishing verse, the Holy Book reveals: "Assuredly, the creation of the heavens and the earth is a greater [matter] than the creation of men, yet most people understand not" (Qur'an 40:57).

The concepts of vice-regency and *amanah* were taken seriously by the early Muslims, who developed the environmental ideas of *haram* and *hima*, which later were incorporated into Islamic law. These are two types of inviolate zones on the perimeter of watercourses and towns. In the *haram* zones, space was provided around watercourses, to safeguard water from pollution, create resting areas for livestock, and make room for irrigation facilities. Around towns and cities, in the inviolate zone, people could neither cut nor burn trees. *Hima* zones were specifically placed around cities for conservation of forests and wildlife. Traditional Muslim cities, such as Fez, were exemplary in their delineation of inviolate zones and utilization of water within and around the city. Classical Sufi literature such as *Gulistan (Rose Garden)* and *Bustan (The Fruit Garden)* by thirteenth-century poet Saadi Shirazi extolled nature and conservation. Such was the reverence for nature as teacher and healer that the first hospitals in the world, located in Iran and Iraq in the Middle Ages, were built around water fountains, trees, foliage, and flowers. The sights, sounds, fragrances, and energies of nature were considered an integral part of healing modalities for patients.

Such heightened consciousness about nature no longer exists in contemporary Muslim societies for a variety of reasons, including the decline of Islamic civilization, the effects of colonialism, and the race for modernization at any cost.

What Can We Do?

To some it seems that we have reached a hopeless stage of no return regarding the health of the environment—the damage is close to impossible to reverse. But, as spiritual people, we must nurture hope, lest we sink into futile despair. In this time of overwhelming environmental distress, Sufi teachers ask Muslims to study seriously and urgently the ecological insights of the Qur'an and implement them in our individual and collective lives. We are caretakers of God's creation. Nature is sacred and infused with consciousness; we are all interconnected. We cannot be authentic vice-regents until we feel in our hearts love and reverence for creation. Remember, we humans were created with such potential for goodness that the angels were asked to bow before our primordial selves. We may indeed sink to the depths of selfishness and irresponsibility, but the Qur'an reminds us that we also have the potential to rise to the heights of virtue and selflessness.

Reframing

We might start by reframing some of our current difficulties. Pollution, droughts, and famines are not harbingers of doomsday but are, as the Buddhist teacher Thich Nhat Hanh suggests, "bells of mindfulness," serving to wake us up. We need to awaken to the truth that the materialistic dream of every individual in the world possessing a car, a house, a computer, and other worldly acquisitions is unsustainable. Experts tell us that humanity would require five more planets in addition to planet earth to make this dream possible for every person on earth.

Even if this dream were sustainable, all religions agree that the source of happiness does not lie in possessing more material goods. Our ego needs are insatiable. If we were presented with two valleys of gold, we would yearn for a third. The Qur'an criticizes "those who amass wealth and hoard it, thinking that wealth could make them immortal" (104:1). We need to reframe our aspirations so that the focus is on simple living, love, compassion, awareness, the joy of sharing, collaborations, friendships, and loving relationships. These are the elements that define true success and happiness.

So what will heal the environmental crisis? We must implement righteous actions but, most of all, we need to stop taking Mother Nature for granted and instead experience in our beings the astonishing love, selflessness, nurturance, and wisdom that she provides. Once we restore our connection with and reverence for Mother Earth, we will of our own accord want to protect and honor our planet by changing our lifestyle, modifying our methods of production, and curbing our relentless consumption of resources.

⟡ Islamic Spiritual Practices for Environmental Healing

Prayers and Projects

One immediate way to repair and honor this tender connection, say the Sufis, is to hold our planet earth in our prayers, just as we would our mother or other loved ones. In your supplications, place the planet in your heart, enfold it with love and compassion, ask for forgiveness for our neglect and desecration, and pray for the earth's healing. Do this with sincerity, humility, and fervency. You may choose to focus on your heart and send light and love to trees, rivers, oceans, mountains, and animals, both in meditative prayers and in the course of your everyday wakeful life. These prayer practices are no small matter. Imagine how a person who has been abused for decades might feel and respond even if one person acknowledged that survivor's pain, offered that person love and compassion, and prayed for healing and empowerment. Practitioners of this daily exercise report that within a short time, their beings feel palpably graced and caressed with mysterious blessings and sweet affection.

Another way to connect with Mother Earth is to initiate or support creative projects and programs that restore harmony, balance, and love in nature. For instance, follow the example of the Prophet, who encouraged people to plant trees whenever possible. "Even if you fear that the Last Day has arrived," he said, "plant the sapling you hold in your hand." Islam considers the planting of a tree an act of worship to be accompanied by a special prayer.

The transformative power of planting a tree is illustrated by the story of an amazing village called Piplantri in Rajastan, India, where villagers band together to plant 111 trees every time a baby girl is born. Not only does this beautiful tradition foster a deep appreciation for females in the village, but it also instills a remarkable sense of environmental stewardship. The practice of planting trees every time a girl is born also ensures that the local environment will be able to support a growing population. The trees become a symbol for the baby girl, and the villagers work just as hard to take care of the trees as they do to protect the girls from all the hardships of life. Over the course of six years, a quarter of a million trees have been planted in Piplantri. Villagers credit the harmony that this tradition has brought to their community with the dramatic drop in crime, along with their renewed adoration of little girls. The writer, Kate Wood, who reported this story on March 26, 2015, in the newsletter of onegreenplanet.org, concluded by saying that you might not think something as insignificant as a sapling could change the world, but remember, that sapling will one day grow into an enormous tree.

Reflections on Divine Signs in Nature

Another way to connect to the sacredness of nature is to reflect on divine signs in nature. Not only does nature graciously and generously provide for our critical needs, but she also provides constant examples of divine wisdom, order, and compassion. To underscore this point, the Qur'an repeatedly tells us that there are "signs of God in nature," and persons of understanding will learn from the insights, guidance, and inspiration humbly provided by nature.

In a rhapsodic verse about the beauty and divine wisdom of creation, the Qur'an reveals, "And the earth We have spread out (like a carpet); set thereon mountains firm and immovable; and produced therein all kinds of things in due balance" (Qur'an 15:19). "Due balance" refers to the way in which the mineral kingdom supports the vegetable kingdom, which in turn supports the animal kingdom, all in mutual dependence and economy of purpose. Indeed, all of nature is so intricately intertwined that every injury we inflict on the environment is an injury that we are inflicting on our selves. We take earth's awesome gifts for granted, little realizing that something so seemingly simple and ubiquitous as water is absolutely essential for life itself. Everything that lives is made of water, says the Qur'an (21:30), yet how profligate and heedless we are in the way we waste this precious resource! In a beautiful metaphor of divine providence, the Qur'an describes the winds as tidings heralding the grace of God, carrying the heavy-laden clouds to a "dead land" and causing rain to descend upon it so that it will "bring forth fruits of every kind" (7:57).

Trees are mentioned at least twenty-six times in the Qur'an. Describing the value of truth, the Holy Book says, "A true word is like a good tree, firmly rooted, reaching its branches toward the sky, always yielding fruit, by consent of its Sustainer" (14:24–25). To fully appreciate the nobility of generosity, notice how the tree does not consume its own fruit; it yields to our needs again and again, to rich or poor. To understand humility, see that it is the tree laden with fruit that bows down. To awaken us to our incredible potential, observe the tiny acorn growing into a mighty oak tree. To comprehend unity in diversity, notice that the branches of a tree sway differently in the wind, but they are all connected at the roots.

For those with eyes to see (to use the language of the Qur'an), the endless variety of nature in all its forms is proof enough that our Creator delights in variety. If this is true of the natural world, how can we not honor the splendid mix of religions, cultures, races, and opinions of our fellow vice-regents? "God has created in the earth varied hues; most surely there is a sign in this for a people who are mindful" (16:13).

Nature can help us understand and overcome the religious exclusivity that causes unnecessary suffering and violence. Sufi teachers ask us to meditate on the following metaphor and insight: All rivers flow into the ocean. You may follow one river. But please, do not mistake the river for the ocean.

Tree Meditation

One of my favorite exercises is the tree meditation. Sit comfortably under a tree with your back resting against the trunk of the tree. (Alternatively, if you are unable to sit under an actual tree, create one in your imagination and "feel" yourself sitting at its base.) Close your eyes and settle into silence. You might want to focus on your nostrils and be mindful of in-breath and out-breath. Stay with this for a few minutes. Feel the support of the tree trunk and thank the tree for its sacred presence. Bring your attention to rest on the roots of the tree. The life force energy of the roots slowly and lovingly begins to flow upward and enters you. Be open to receiving it. Feel the sap of vitality flow joyously through you. Stay with this for a while. Then, become aware that a supreme consciousness is perched in the topmost branches of the tree. Mindful of your precious presence at the base of the tree, the consciousness swoops down and envelops you with unimaginably beautiful love, tenderness, and affection. Be willing to receive it. In your heart express gratitude for the gift of the tree.

This meditation will reward you with a surprising sense of rejuvenation and joy.

Walking These Practices into the World

Encompass planet earth in your daily prayers and reflect on the insight and wisdom offered by nature. Support and participate in programs to heal the earth. Most of all, remind yourself repeatedly of the Prophet's saying that the earth is like your mother. Make a personal commitment to respect and care for the earth.

5

In the Face
of Failure

Dealing with Anger and Burnout

Anger is a primary and natural emotion that we all experience to varying degrees throughout our lives. Objectively, it is neither good nor bad, mature nor immature. It is simply a response to danger, attack, injustice, or some other sense of something gone wrong in our world. What we do with that anger is where maturity and morality enter the picture.

From a spiritual perspective, there are two kinds of anger. Anger of the higher self arises from the perception of major problems in the world around us, such as social injustice and environmental degradation. When we see abject poverty, income inequality, child labor, domestic abuse, human trafficking, gun violence, denial of climate change, and sheer meanness in the world of politics, righteous anger of the higher self can energize us with a sense of urgency that compels us to take action to help combat the evil that we perceive.

Anger of the lower self is rooted in fear, emotional wounds, and frustrations suffered in a very personal way by our own egos. For instance, some strongly resent the presence of immigrants and refugees in their neighborhood because of the perceived threat to the prevailing culture and way of life; many of us dwell on ways of retaliation against those we feel have wronged us; others harbor feelings of pain, neglect, and hopelessness in a society rife with chronic discrimination, lack of economic opportunities, and indifference by those in power. Teachers from virtually all spiritual

How do you respond to anger

traditions warn us to be mindful and vigilant about this kind of anger, for it produces both moral and physical imbalance, deadens our emotions, and eclipses rational thinking. Under the influence of this kind of anger, we forget about compassion and oneness with our fellow beings and, instead, become vengeful and unreasonable in both word and deed. The wounds underlying such anger cannot simply be wished away. We need to employ spiritual practices that will help us acknowledge these feelings so that we can soften, heal, and integrate them—not only for our own good but also to empower us to take righteous action to serve the common good.

A prime example of the power of transformed anger is the story of Mahatma Gandhi. In May 1893 in South Africa, he was physically ejected from a train because he had dared to sit with the white passengers. As he shivered with cold and rage on the railway platform, his lower self dreamed of revenge for the injustice and humiliation he had suffered. His higher nature, however, convinced him to use spiritual practices to heal and transform his anger, and this he did to such an extent that he claimed he no longer felt rage against his oppressors no matter how they treated him. The result of Gandhi's intense spiritual work was the practice of *satyagraha*, or nonviolent resistance, which proved enormously beneficial to his people in their struggle for Indian independence from their colonial overlords.

In this chapter we will explore how our traditions can help us deal with anger and rage, whether it is our personal reaction to prejudice, racism, homophobia, anti-Semitism, Islamophobia, and countless other forms of bigotry directed our way, or the moral outrage we feel when we see others being subjected to that kind of abuse. Of course, we need to protect ourselves and our loved ones from such abuse, but beyond that we need to acknowledge and heal our own feelings of fear, anger, and the desire for revenge. By doing the spiritual work of transmuting those feelings, we will be able to make righteous choices that serve both ourselves and the common good.

As if the negative effects of anger alone were not destructive enough, untreated anger can derail our peace-seeking efforts altogether in the form of burnout. Later in the chapter we will address feelings of being overwhelmed—whether by workload, the enormity of our responsibilities, or feelings such as anger and rage—and offer spiritual practices that help us cope before burnout sets in.

How Judaism Views Anger

The path to successful collaboration and action toward social justice and environmental care is often blocked by the consequences of anger. Anger can turn friends into enemies and further distance those who already disagree with one another. It can turn constructive dialogue into destructive name-calling, and bring possible action to a standstill. Unbridled, anger can cause great destruction and chaos in your personal life and to those around you. It has always been so.

Not many of us enjoy people being angry at us, yet all of us have felt the rush of righteous indignation when we catch others in their misdeeds. Anger is simply a basic human feeling that we all experience and that we all need to deal with. In Jewish tradition, even God is perceived as expressing anger. As the children of Israel watch from across the sea, Pharaoh's chariots follow after them, but God destroys them: "You sent out Your anger, and it consumed them like stubble" (Exodus 15:7).

Moses, too, expresses anger on many occasions. When he descends the mountain with the first set of tablets and finds the people dancing around the golden calf, he is furious and shatters the tablets in his rage (Exodus 32:19). Later, despite God's instructions, Moses angrily strikes the rock to bring forth water. For this, he is punished by God, and denied entry into the Promised Land (Numbers 20:12).

People become angry, prophets become angry, even God becomes angry. Sometimes that anger arises to call people back from paths of wrongdoing. But most of the time, our anger is far more personal—and far more problematic.

Anger can destroy relationships, upset family life, and lead to violent behavior. Anger-induced mental, emotional, and physical violence tears at the very heart of our society. Because of this, anger is seen not only as antithetical to peace but also as idolatry, the greatest of sins in the Jewish tradition.

Anger as Idolatry

According to the Talmud, the great fifth-century compendium of rabbinic discussion, anger has the power to make a person an idolater: "Consider one who tears his clothing or breaks his vessels or scatters his money in his anger as an idolator" (Shabbat 105b).

The teaching in the Talmud continues, outlining the consequences: "When a person gives in to anger, if he is wise, his wisdom leaves him. If he is a prophet, his power of prophecy leaves him; if greatness was decreed for him from heaven, anger will cause him to be degraded." And more to the point of idolatry, "When any man gives way to rage, even the Divine Presence abandons him" (Nedarim 22b).

Our anger serves the god of our personal self, the god of our own ego. It is a god of separation, a god of hate and violence. Our anger distances us from the awareness of connection to those at whom we are angry. It allows us to polarize, demonize, and dehumanize the other. In other words, our anger blinds us to the sacred in all of us. We become blind to the Presence within the other when we are angry. Anger is idolatrous because it represents worship of our personal self and its self-righteousness. In a very real sense, our anger holds us hostage to separateness, which is the core of idolatry.

We Are to Avoid Anger

Nowhere in Torah are we commanded not to get angry. Rather, we are encouraged to become aware of our anger and learn to control it. If we feel anger and simply allow the feeling, it can be honored like any other feeling. For example, the Talmud tells us not to discipline our children when we are angry, since at such a moment we are serving our anger, rather than the needs of the child (Moed Katan 17a).

We are reminded that not only will the object of our anger suffer but we who bear the anger will suffer as well. While suppressing our anger and pretending it does not exist is neither emotionally nor physically healthy, the constant expression of anger harms us all. So we are asked to be "slow to anger and easy to pacify" (Ethics of the Fathers 5:14).

Restraining our anger is seen as noble and desirable, as the second-century sage Ben Zoma states in Ethics of the Fathers (4:1): "Who is strong? He who subdues his evil inclination, as it is stated, 'He who is slow to anger is better than a strong man, and he who masters his passions is better than one who conquers a city' (Proverbs 16:32)."

But angry outbursts and angry actions seem to defy rational decisions to avoid them. Our anger rises faster than the speed of thought, and sets us one against the other. Spiritual practices can help us move beyond our anger when it occurs, and help us keep that anger from ruling us.

Jewish Spiritual Practices for Moving beyond Anger

Immersion in a Pool of Peace

Stepping into a ritual bath, called a *mikveh* in Hebrew, is seen to provide a spiritual cleansing. It is the ritual from which baptism emerged in the Christian tradition. In traditional Judaism, visiting a *mikveh* is required by Jewish law for brides prior to their wedding, for women following menstruation, and when converting to Judaism. Today, people are welcome to visit a *mikveh* to honor significant times of transition or celebration, such as reaching a certain age, becoming a parent, or reading Torah for the first time.

In the sixteenth-century renewal of the Jewish mystical tradition called Kabbalah, Rabbi Chaim Vital taught in the name of his teacher, Rabbi Yitzchak Luria, that anger may be dispelled by immersing in a ritual bath.

While Rabbi Vital was speaking of literal immersion, figurative immersion in the form of meditation and visualization can also be effective.

This meditative *mikveh* practice is particularly helpful when we become aware that anger is building within us or anger is building against us. The meditation is not meant to deny the reality of anger but to free us from its domination so that we might be better able to deal with whatever issues stimulated the anger in the first place.

1. In a period of meditation, after allowing yourself to become as relaxed as possible, imagine that there is a pool of peaceful water in front of you. Let that image take shape in your mind.

2. When you feel comfortable, imagine stepping out of your clothes and gradually entering this pool of peaceful energies. You might wish to submerge yourself briefly, feeling the warm and soothing water cleanse you of your shell of anger and upset. You might allow yourself to gently float on the water, feeling totally supported.

3. The following statements, or their equivalents, can be helpful as you experience the healing waters: "This pool of peace naturally washes away any shell of anger that I have been carrying." "This water shields me from any anger that has been aimed at me." "I release myself to the deep peace of this water, and am profoundly refreshed." "My mind is clear. My breathing is easy; I am at peace."

4. Continue to imagine yourself in the water for as long as you wish. When you leave the pool, you will find that while your body is totally dry, you are able to feel the peaceful energies of the water in every cell.

Walking This Practice into the World

Water is a natural cleansing agent, and you can practice various forms of this meditation in your daily life. When feelings of anger arise within you, or when you become aware of the anger of another directed at you, find a washroom where you can allow water to flow over your hands. As you do so, imagine that this water carries the peaceful energies of the *mikveh*. If stepping into a washroom is not possible, see if you can take a few sips of water, affirming that you are inviting peaceful energies into every cell of your being.

Take a Breath and Center Yourself

Meditation and other spiritual practices help us become more sensitive to our feelings, so that we are less likely to respond reactively when anger arises. We learn how important it is to be gentle with ourselves, so that we do not try to fight anger with anger, or feel guilty should we become openly angry.

As the twentieth-century Lubavitcher rebbe, Rabbi Menachem Mendel Schneerson, taught, "As with anything else, the way to correct [the trait of anger] is step by step. The first step is to wait … [so] that the emotion will not gain momentum" (Igrot Kodesh, Letter 5239).

One way to instill this habit of waiting before expressing anger is through the breath. When you become aware of the anger of self-righteousness rising within you, or feel anger coming at you from another, take a few moments to settle into meditation. Quiet yourself. Repeating the phrase "This is not about me" is often helpful when someone else is angry. When the anger is within you, acknowledge it fully as you inhale. You might silently say, "I breathe in any anger awakening in my mind and in my body." Honor the feeling of anger as you might honor any feeling, without negative judgment and without resistance. Then, as you exhale, imagine releasing that anger, without harm. You might silently say, "I release any anger now without harm."

When you find that you have reached a point where you no longer feel angry or feel the sting of anger aimed at you, affirm the place of greater peace that you are experiencing. You can silently repeat, "I am at greater peace now. My mind is clear and my body free of tension. I am able to act more compassionately in the world now."

Walking This Practice into the World

You can do this practice even when others are around. Take a breath and draw in any anger you are experiencing. If anger is coming from another, mentally remind yourself, "This anger is not about me." Know that attacking another when he is angry will never be helpful. If you are feeling anger, acknowledge it and draw it into your breath. Release it as you exhale, and silently say, "I release any anger now without harm. I am able to be present more peacefully in this moment."

◌‿◌

How Christianity Views Anger

Two important themes concerning anger emerge in Christian scripture. Anger can be a force for good when it awakens us to things we have forgotten or missed. And anger can be a sin when it causes us to act in ways that are inconsistent with God's purposes.

Many times we do not identify anger as a force for good, yet it has the ability to open our eyes and hearts to the experiences of those around us. In James 1:19–20, we read, "You must understand this my beloved: let everyone be quick to listen, slow to speak, slow to anger; for your anger does not produce God's righteousness." This verse suggests that when anger arises because another says something that hurts your feelings, you should listen beyond the words to hear how it feels to be the other. Taking time to explore the reasons for the hurtful words or actions can help you understand the other's experience. In this way, anger can lead to empathy for the other; it can express a depth of concern and help increase your capacity for compassion.

Yet when anger is self-serving, Christianity sees it as a sin. We read in Ephesians 4:26, "Be angry, but do not sin; do not let the sun go down on your anger, and do not make room for the devil." Self-serving anger stems from injured feelings concerning the self without concern for others. It often results in pain or sorrow for other people.

Anger amplifies aspects of what it means to be human. It tends to highlight the age-old struggle between the needs of the self and concern for the other. Examples of Jesus's anger in Christian scripture take us even more deeply into this topic. We read in Mark 3:1–6:

> Again he entered the synagogue, and a man was there who had a withered hand. [The Pharisees] watched him to see

whether he would cure him on the Sabbath, so that they might accuse him. And he said to the man with the withered hand, "Come forward." Then he said to [the Pharisees], "Is it lawful to do good or to do harm on the Sabbath, to save life or to kill?" But they were silent. He looked at them with anger; he was grieved at their hardness of heart and said to the man, "Stretch out your hand." He stretched it out, and his hand was restored. The Pharisees went out and immediately conspired with the Herodians against him, how to destroy him.

Here we see Jesus's anger framed by grief and the recognition of "hardness of heart" or that all-too-human egocentrism. Anger framed by grief points toward concern for others and the recognition of the "hardness of heart" connects that with sorrow. In this way anger is an expression of compassion. It is not because of an injured ego that Jesus speaks. He speaks from a place of concern, not just for others but also for the healing of a community.

We see another example of Jesus's anger in Matthew 11:20–24:

Woe to you, Chorazin! Woe to you, Bethsaida! For if the deeds of power done in you had been done in Tyre and Sidon, they would have repented long ago in sackcloth and ashes. But I tell you, on the day of judgment it will be more tolerable for Tyre and Sidon than for you. And you, Capernaum, will you be exalted to heaven? No, you will be brought down to Hades.

This passage is often understood as an act of cursing the inhabitants of these towns where Jesus's message of peace and healing has been neither understood nor embraced. But in Jesus's anger we see a deep concern for others. Would we curse something we did not care about? Jesus's care is based in the belief that we are all interconnected and that such interconnectedness reflects the oneness of God. His view encompasses a bigger picture, a broader perspective, a higher spiritual awareness. Here he is expressing deep compassion for people whose lives will include suffering and unhappiness because of this essential lack of awareness.

In Matthew 21:12–13 (also Mark 11:15–19; Luke 19:45–48; and John 2:13–25), we see Jesus's anger in defense of morality:

> Then Jesus entered the temple and drove out all who were selling and buying in the temple, and he overturned the table of the money changers and the seats of those who sold doves. He said to them, "It is written, 'My house shall be called a house of prayer,' but you are making it a den of robbers."

Jesus is expressing deep anger and frustration. He hopes to get the attention of the Jewish community, along with those in charge of the day-to-day business of the temple, because the temple originally was built as a place of sacrifice. Sacrifice had been understood to be a way of coming closer to God. But by the time of Jesus, the temple had become big business, foreclosing on the property of Jewish peasants who were unable to pay their temple tax. Those in charge of the temple would stand to lose considerable wealth if Jesus's message had been heeded. He knows that this supreme challenge to the status quo will likely end in his death. Today Jesus's actions against those at the temple would be the equivalent of a challenge against the wealthiest 1 percent of the world's population. This was righteous anger, coming forcefully from a deep place of moral concern for the welfare of the Jewish community.

These examples from Christian scripture show us that anger, when understood through the lens of a higher spiritual awareness, can be useful and positive, and can successfully challenge obstacles to justice and healing. Contemporary theologian Patrick D. Miller has said, "We might better ask whether such thoughts as expressed [in anger] have any other permissible context than conversation with God, from whom no secrets are hid, from whom no rage or anger can be concealed."[1] When expressed in service to justice and healing, to the purposes of God, anger can even become a form of prayer, part of a conversation with God.

A Christian Spiritual Practice for Moving beyond Anger

Challenging God

In the heat of the moment, it is always difficult to be objective when it comes to anger. It takes practice to see it for what it is, how it is working, and what you can do about it.

When you become angry, take deep breaths and find a centered place. When you have found some calm, ask yourself whether the anger concerns you or whether it concerns someone else or something else. Speak to God. Ask questions. Express anger to God. The psalms, in particular, teach us that all human emotions are properly expressed to God in prayer. Once, I cursed God and instead of feeling the punishment that, as a child, I thought I might, I felt my curse "hit" something. It felt as if it had been received. It was, in effect, an affirmation of faith.

There is sharing in these moments that can be both useful and healing.

Walking This Practice into the World

As you resume your life's activities, use the phrase "hard-heartedness requires compassion" as a way to see the causes of anger and the possibilities for anger in a larger and more constructive context.

How Islam Views Anger

The Qur'an says that God has created for us the faculties of sight, hearing, feelings, and understanding (23:78 and 32:9), and grants us laughter and tears (53:43). Spiritual teachers take this to mean that all feelings are a gift from God, regardless of whether they are pleasant or difficult. It is easy to be grateful for joyous feelings, but the human ego tends to avoid, deny, and minimize feelings that

make it feel threatened or unhappy. We don't realize that inconvenient feelings, such as anger, fear, sorrow, and guilt, are simply
energies that are begging to be acknowledged, healed, and integrated. We perceive them as something separate from ourselves.
Yet when we embrace these feelings with courage and compassion, we grow in authentic empowerment. There is no need to run
toward difficult feelings so that you can grasp their lessons and
insights; just don't run away from them.

Someone asked the Prophet for a teaching that was essential
and practical. The Prophet replied, "Do not become angry and furious." The man repeated his question several times and each time
the answer was the same: "Do not become angry and furious." This
anecdote illustrates the great need to pay attention to our anger
before it overwhelms us. Thus, Sufi masters ask us to be excep-
tionally mindful of our feelings of anger. These feelings are highly
susceptible to the wiles of our slinking whisperer, or the voice of
our lower self, whose mission it is to cause us to "rebel and go
astray" (Qur'an 38:82). If we are unmindful, that slinking whisperer stirs up the underlying cause of anger, be it fear, frustration,
guilt, or some other unpleasant feeling. It then exploits our weak-
nesses of pride, jealousy, and low self-esteem. That mix is volatile.
Anger might turn into rage and fury. Our body stiffens, our emotions become numb, and our thoughts get muddled. We say and do
terrible things.

The Qur'an cautions us against allowing our hearts to become
clenched and blinded. When this happens, we lose control, balance, and any sense of proportion. In times of rage and fury, if we
cannot control our vengeful impulses, the Qur'an commands us
to at least remember in those times that "mandated is the law of
equality" (2:194). What the law means is clarified in another verse:
"The recompense for an injury is an injury thereto [in degree]:
but if a person forgives and makes reconciliation, his reward is
due from Allah: for Allah loveth not those who do wrong" (42:40).
In moments of uncontrollable anger, strive to remember the
divine commandment not to overstep bounds and overreact in

retaliation. More importantly, know that Divinity would like us to rise above our vindictive compulsions. We are promised heavenly rewards if we engage in the difficult process of forgiveness and reconciliation.

The practice of forgiveness is divine. However, Sufi teachers are quick and eager to reiterate that forgiveness is not possible without also doing the work of healing the anger or wound caused by the wrongdoing. It is unwise to overlay anger or pain by mere intentions and words. That is like whitewashing a burning house. There is a profound teaching in a story about the Prophet and an opponent named Wahshi, who had murdered the Prophet's uncle. When Wahshi asked for forgiveness, the Prophet readily forgave him and welcomed him into his community, but asked that Wahshi should keep his distance from the Prophet for some time. True forgiveness needs to be accompanied by healing and integrating the pain, anger, and suffering caused by the injury, and this process takes time.

Being patient and forgiving does not mean that we allow ourselves to be abused by unjustified anger from another. Our noble aspirations to follow the high road must be tempered with a sense of due measure and proportion, as delightfully illustrated by a teaching story about a snake that had been terrorizing a village. The frightened villagers enlisted the help of a sage who was known for his ability to communicate with animals, and the sage spoke at length with the snake. Deeply repentant, the snake asked for forgiveness and made a commitment to practice nonviolence. After a year or so, the holy man revisited the village and found the snake in a ragged and pitiable condition. "O Seer, what did you teach me?" complained the snake. "Children practice throwing stones at me, and grown-ups delight in kicking me." "O snake," replied the seer, "I simply asked you to stop biting. When did I ever ask you to stop hissing?"

Rumi cautions us that the energy of anger is fiery and powerful; it is a "king over kings." It needs to be bridled. Even if our anger is justified and we believe that our righteous anger awakens us and energizes us to engage in righteous action, we need to be ever vigilant about the workings of our lower self. We may indeed experience righteous anger when someone commits a terrible wrong, and justify our indignation by calling it defense of truth or honoring a religious principle. But it is all too possible to become arrogant in our righteousness, and if we do not notice our arrogance it will have serious consequences: In fighting extremism, we ourselves might become extreme; in combating injustice, we become unjust; in destroying institutions that we consider elitist or self-serving, we replace them with institutions that reflect our anger and fear.

Islamic Spiritual Practices for Moving beyond Anger

Refuge in God, Water, and Nature

Traditionally, upon feeling anger, a Muslim is advised to invoke God's help immediately by repeating into the heart, "I seek refuge in God from the wiles of Satan." Or, you can repeat one of the divine names of God, such as Peace or Patience. Some choose the mantra *Astakhfurillah*, which means "I beg repentance." God promises in the Qur'an: "So remember Me; I will remember you" (2:152).

The Prophet suggests an additional remedy: perform ablution with water, for "anger is from Satan, Satan is from fire, and water extinguishes fire."[2] Some choose to swirl and swish water in their mouth until the anger subsides.

Another technique is to lie down—preferably directly on the ground—and feel the nurturing and healing properties of Mother Earth enveloping your being.

Walking These Practices into the World

In times of anger, rest attention on the heart and repeat words like, "Peace, dear heart." Whenever possible, make contact with water and nature. Feel the healing touch of water on any part of your body. Gaze upon a flower; touch a tree; lie on the grass. These actions will soften the sharp edges of anger, keep it within bounds, and transform it into vitality and vigor.

Sacred Expression

Repeatedly, the Holy Book asks us to be mindful, pay attention, and listen. In this practice, we honor our feelings of anger and give them permission to express themselves in invisible realms. By removing inner blockages, caused by denial or repression of anger, we expand our inner spaciousness.

1. Close your eyes and enter into a meditative state. Focus on your nostrils and follow your breath as you inhale and exhale for a few minutes. Then, focus on your heart and silently count from ten to one, telling yourself that at the count of one, you are ushered into your sacred sanctuary. Sacred sanctuary is an imaginative place you create in your inner landscape. It could be indoors or outdoors. Make it a place of absolute safety and astonishing beauty, filled with energies of healing and love. Endow it with enchanted and magical properties. It is a place of infinite possibilities; you can fly here if you want to.

2. Summon the person you have issues with. In this place of safety and possibilities, the person arrives accompanied by her soul. That person's soul gives you permission to express your anger. Souls love the truth. Express your feelings and grievances little by little. Whatever you say is perfect. Remind yourself as often as possible that souls love the truth. In this realm, the only consequences of expressing the truth of your feelings are healing and empowerment. Take your time, but do not overdo it.

3. In the next step, reflect on your heartfelt aspiration. What is it you want or need in relation to this person? Put it in the form of a prayer. Then, express your sacred prayer in the presence of the Universe and her soul. End the prayer with the sentence, "This, or whatever is in my highest interest, is manifesting for me now."

4. In the last step, thank the person's soul for giving you permission to express your feelings fully. Then, listen to her soul also thanking you for your expression of truth and asking to be released. Give your permission. See or sense that person fading from your vision and returning into the embrace of Spirit.

Remain in silence and, after a while, focus on your heart and breathe in and out of it. Feel your breath nourishing and nurturing your heart. Come into awareness when you are ready.

Walking This Practice into the World

Practice sacred expression with a person, with a situation, or with Spirit. Repeat this practice several times, as needed. You might be astonished at how this work in the imaginal realm affects the situation in the earthly realm. You experience a sense of release. Amazingly, anger becomes defused.

Sacred Holding

Sacred holding acknowledges the feelings of anger and embraces them with tenderness and compassion. Not only does anger soften, but also once integrated it becomes a valuable source of self-knowledge, empowerment, and blessing.

Sacred holding is a six-step process that is best done close to the time when you have experienced a difficult feeling like anger. But to ensure that you have the technique readily available when you need it, study the steps and practice them at the earliest opportunity.

1. In a state of meditation, give yourself permission to feel your feelings of anger, no matter how difficult or awkward. Do this little by little, always with compassion for yourself. Remind yourself that all feelings are sacred.

2. Ask yourself, "Where do I hold this feeling of anger in my body?" Feelings have a resting place, and we experience them as sensations in the physical body: the head, the throat, the heart, the solar plexus, and the belly—all are likely sites for emotional

distress to settle. Patiently direct your consciousness so that you locate the site of what is called "physical holding."

3. Once you have located the feelings as sensations in your body, acknowledge them with your consciousness, again with mercy for yourself. You can use sacred naming to talk to yourself. You might say affectionately, "Dear Heart, I am sorry for the difficult feelings and sensations you are experiencing. Allow me to support you as you grapple with this difficulty." Hold the sensations with the tender embrace of the soul. Continuously shine the light of merciful awareness on them and abide with them. If the sensations move to another location, move your attention to that place. At this time there is no need to fix or analyze the sensations; simply be present with the holding as long as you want. Spiritual guides explain that, by doing this, you allow for a "streaming beauty" to flow through you. The Qur'an has a lovely metaphor for this light of gentle awareness that softens and transmutes: it is akin to "the dawn as it breathes away the darkness" (81:18).

4. Lovingly direct some questions to the center of sensations in your body: "Do you have a message for me?" Simply listen. Be attentive and respectful, even if you hear nothing.

5. Ask tenderly, "How may I befriend you? How may I love you and integrate you?" Again, just listen sincerely.

6. Set an intention to allow your breath to flow through that physical locus of your feelings as you inhale and exhale. Allow the Divine Breath to caress that focal point. Little by little, you will experience healing, integration, and transformation of the difficult feelings.

Walking This Practice into the World

By respecting the energy of anger and by being willing to embrace it with love, you will transform it into vitality and inner strength. You will palpably feel as though a parched ground has turned green in a spring shower.

When Stagnant Anger Leads to Burnout

"Burnout," a term first coined in 1974 by the psychologist Herbert Freudenberger, refers to a kind of depression characterized by exhaustion, cynicism, and inefficacy. Many people from all walks of life, especially those who work in human services where the stress and emotional demands are uncommonly high, complain of feeling withdrawn, antisocial, spiritually empty, and hopeless. Besides stress, a core cause of burnout seems to be an inability to live one's own values in the corporate world. Young resident doctors, for example, often despair because economic values are placed ahead of human values, compromising their commitment to provide the best possible care, regardless of cost or the patient's ability to pay.[3] The insidious danger of burnout is that it happens little by little and we may not recognize that it is happening until we are already caught in its downward spiral. As with anger, the best defense is to be hypervigilant to signs of it in our own psyches and behaviors, and to employ spiritual practices that calm our souls, refresh our minds, and connect our hearts to the Source of hope, love, and a sense of purpose in life.

Judaism on Burnout

Elijah is the prophet whose story unfolds in the biblical book of 1 Kings. Even though he has demonstrated the power of his God, he is rejected by his society and feels that his work has been a failure. In the face of feeling totally overwhelmed and defeated, he flees into the wilderness, sits down under a tree, and prays for his own death. "It is enough!" he cries. "Please, Eternal One, take my life, for I am no better than my fathers" (1 Kings 19:4).

Many who strive to remedy the deep injustices of persistent racism, the apparent destruction of the middle class, and the immense challenges of a deteriorating environment become overwhelmed by what appear to be insurmountable tasks and the expectation of failure. The attendant anxiety and anger overwhelm both mind and body. In the condition of overwhelm, possible positive outcomes seem to disappear and hope is lost. The mental and physical impact of such overwhelm is destructive to the individual as well as to the group.

Rabbi Nachman of Breslov, the late-eighteenth-century Hasidic master, knew such feelings himself. Many believe that he was plagued by overwhelming depression, despair, and hopelessness. From such experiences, a critical teaching emerged: "When a person needs to ascend from one level to another, he must undergo a descent before the ascent, for the descent is for the purpose of the ascent" (Likutey Moharan I:22).

Nachman continues:

> And each time one rises from one level to another according to his situation, the impure husks rise anew to block him, these being the cravings and imaginations and thoughts and confusions and obstacles, and they spread out before him abundantly at every point.... But in truth, this is not a fall at all, rather it is because they need to ascend to a new level. (Likutey Moharan I:24)

Elijah's experience of overwhelm is expressed as his yearning to die. He sees no hope. The answer he receives is deeply meaningful. He has gone alone into a cave in the side of a mountain, and experiences himself called by God:

> Go out and stand upon the mountain ... for the Eternal is about to pass by. Now there was a great wind, so strong that it was splitting mountains and breaking rocks in pieces ... but the Eternal was not in the wind; and after the wind an earthquake, but the Eternal was not in the earthquake; and after the earthquake a fire, but the Eternal was not in the fire; and after the fire, a sound of absolute silence [often translated as a still small voice]. (1 Kings 19:11, 12)

What changes things for Elijah is not the dramatic power orchestrated by a heavenly Being. Rather, Elijah finds solace and rejuvenation in that which had been within him always. The experience of being overwhelmed is a response when our attention focuses on externals that we have been unable to affect through our actions. The restorative awakening returns the prophet, and ourselves, to the essential nature of our own being.

ℐ𝒻𝒻𝒻 Jewish Spiritual Practices for Avoiding Burnout

The Silence of the Still Small Voice

When the world appears to weigh heavy upon us, and we experience ourselves unable to achieve our goals, we are invited to an action called *teshuvah*, the return to the essence within us. Faced with your own experience of overwhelm and impending burnout, meditation can be an essential spiritual practice. This meditation is not aimed at solving any external issues. Rather, it prompts you to remember the deeper nature of your own identity and renew your connection to the Ultimate Source from which springs the motivation for significant action in the world.

1. In meditation, after finding yourself drifting into a state of deep calmness, focus your attention on the sensations you experience in your body. Allow yourself to move into a place of witness, from which you can observe your body without being caught up in any tensions or stress you discover. Simply practice witnessing.

2. Become aware of the activity of your mind. Witness the thoughts that continually arise. When you witness, you are not grabbed by any particular thought, judgment, memory, or yearning. You simply witness from an increasingly calm place.

3. From this place of witness, you are not particularly involved with the sensations of the body and thoughts of the mind that are before you. In this place, you may begin to feel an awareness of profound silence. This silence is restorative. From this silence flows an energy of compassion that is beyond words, an energy seeking to support you and help you embrace the personal self gently and lovingly. Rest in this silence, and allow

that greater compassion and love to flow outward, through the witness consciousness into every cell of your body and every level of your being.

4. Taking a few deep breaths can bring you back into your body. Allow yourself time to experience what continues to unfold from the whispers of that silence, from the still small voice within yourself.

Walking This Practice into the World

It is difficult to open to the deeper silence in the midst of our daily activities, particularly as we grapple with our struggles, upsets, and disappointments. But this can help: Take a breath and silently say, "I am more than this." Hold the breath for just a few seconds, and then release it as you silently repeat, "A deeper wisdom awakens within me now."

When threatened with energy-draining burnout, release the need to fix things. Release the idea that you are required to do it all. As we are reminded in an ancient text, "It is not incumbent upon you to complete the task, but you are not free when you desist from it altogether" (Ethics of the Fathers 2:21).

Reframing Apparent Defeat

Rabbi Nachman counseled that a descent into the experience of being overwhelmed by failure may actually precede an ascent into greater awareness. Here is a simple practice that draws from his teaching. When faced with issues in your life that seem overwhelming, and when you find obstacles that seem to block your attempts to get ahead, remind yourself that these very obstacles may be a signal not of defeat but of an important growth spurt in your life.

1. In meditation, think about the obstacles that seem so overwhelming. Observe them from a place of calmness. Imagine that they are not your enemies, but are actually signs that you are ready to ascend to a greater level of understanding. Don't try to circumvent the obstacles or the conditions that seem to block you. Instead, imagine them surrounded by light. If the obstacles are other people, see them surrounded by light. Even if you have experienced them as your enemies, hold them in light. And if the

obstacles are specific conditions in your world, surround those conditions with light.

2. Maintain this meditation until you are able to remain relaxed and calm while imagining (or pretending, if the image itself does not appear) that all perceived obstacles are held in light. Affirm silently, "My way is filled with light. I am held in light," as you complete and conclude this meditative practice.

Walking This Practice into the World

There are times when it feels like the roof is caving in. Perhaps we already have a full workload, yet additional emergencies come up that need to be handled yesterday. Perhaps we've been looking forward to some time off when another project lands in our lap. And then traffic on the freeway grinds to a halt on the way home. Those are the times when repeating "My way is filled with light. I am held in light" can relieve the stress of the moment. Particularly when we feel the darkness close over us, these words can usher in a cascade of relief.

When you feel your body begin to relax—overwhelm is always accompanied by body tension—it may be time for a gentle inquiry, such as, "I wonder how this condition [or this person] will actually be helpful in the greater healing I seek."

Christianity on Burnout

Burnout is commonplace and painful. It represents a total loss of focus, a feeling of helplessness, hopelessness, and desperation. Jesus reveals his thinking about this important topic in Mark 9:33–37:

> Then they came to Capernaum and when he was in the house he asked them, "What were you arguing about on the way?" But they were silent, for on the way they had argued with one another [about] who was the greatest. He sat down, called the twelve, and said to them, "Whoever wants to be first must be last of all and servant of all." Then he took a little child and put it among them; and taking it in his arms, he said to them, "Whoever welcomes one such child

in my name welcomes me, and whoever welcomes me welcomes not me but the one who sent me."

Why is this important? By expressing concern for other people, Jesus shows us a way to pull back from the kinds of all-encompassing thoughts and actions that lead to burnout. He provides us with a model for doing this: Children have less clutter in their lives and more imagination that can help create the perspective that is lacking when we feel burned out.

The ability to summon a new perspective helps us in many ways:

> Beloved, I do not consider that I have made it my own; but this one thing I do: forgetting what lies behind and straining forward to what lies ahead, I press on toward the goal for the prize of the heavenly call of God in Christ Jesus. Let those of us then who are mature be of the same mind; and if you think differently about anything, this too God will reveal to you. (Philippians 3:13–15)

With a new perspective we are more likely to let go of the past and look forward to the challenges on the road ahead. It will help us avoid the distractions that not only divert our attention but also drag us down with negative energy.

Jesus is aware of the complexities of the human spirit. He accepts the reality of being human and provides us with the spiritual tools to help us crawl out of the holes of burnout and back to a place of perspective and energy. These tools also help us recover that essential balance among our own needs, the needs of others, and the needs of the planet.

A Christian Spiritual Practice for Avoiding Burnout

Centering through Journaling

In one way, maintaining a sense of centeredness is the best defense against burnout. Spiritual practices help us maintain—or regain—our center.

One such spiritual practice for helping with burnout is journaling. Try writing about the reality of burnout in the particulars of your situation. Writing about the stressors that lead to burnout puts them in a place where you can "see" them. In that way they become less powerful. As you read over what you have written, enter a meditative mode and use this phrase: "I can see." Then, just as Jesus said, by welcoming him we welcome the one who sent him. So use the phrase "I welcome you" to make peace with the challenges that are throwing you off center.

Walking This Practice into the World

Repeat the phrases "I can see" and "I welcome you," especially in moments when you no longer feel centered.

Islam on Overwhelm and Burnout

Feeling overwhelmed or burned out is a sign of imbalance in our lives. We become so involved in our activities that we forget that a fulfilling life requires us to nurture both body and soul and that we must work equally in both the visible and the invisible worlds. If we work mostly in the material world to achieve our physical and financial goals, without regard for the mysteries and nourishment of the invisible realms, we are, in the words of Sufi teachers, nothing more than "wretched employees." We may earn a good livelihood but we become slaves to material needs and outcomes. Over time we will experience exhaustion and emptiness and feel drained. The material world, the mystics remind us, is a place of expenditure. To balance our personal accounts, we also need to spend time and energy in the invisible world, a place of spiritual income.

On the other hand, if we denounce and devalue this material world and spend too much of our time in prayer and meditation, Sufis ask with incredulity, "Why are you here on earth?" To a companion who fasted all day and prayed all night, the Prophet warned against this imbalance: "Your body has a right over you, your soul has a right over you, and your family and wife have a right over you. So give everyone the right it has over you."[4]

Keep in mind also that soul and body have different needs. We require nourishment from both invisible and visible worlds to experience fulfillment and joy. Pray, fast, and be conscious of God but also "do not deprive yourselves of the good things of life which God has made lawful for you" (Qur'an 5:87).

The relationship between body and soul is mystically represented in Islamic spirituality by Jesus and his donkey. Jesus, greatly revered in Islam as a prophet, is a symbol of our higher self. His donkey is a symbol of our material self. Not all ecstasies are the same: Jesus was drunk on love for God; his donkey was drunk on barley. This metaphor of Jesus as soul and the donkey as body is extended to discern the different loads both carry. Alas, says Rumi, we sometimes put the saddle on Jesus and set the donkey loose in the pasture. When a Bedouin once asked the Prophet whether he should tie his camel to a post when going for prayers or just trust in God, the Prophet replied, "First tether the camel and then trust in God."

Islamic Spiritual Practices for Avoiding Burnout

Aliveness

In our retreats and workshops on overcoming depression and burnout, we ask a central question: At this time in your life, what would bring you joy, peace, and a sense of being alive? Some choose silence. In their hectic pursuit of material results, they can never seem to make time for practices like meditation. They realize they have been like fish quivering and thrashing on the banks of the material world. How life-giving it feels to enter the waters of silence! Others want to move their bodies, do yoga, or go running. They realize the joy of nurturing their bodies, temple of their souls. A few want to listen to music or read poetry. They yearn for that connection with beauty that resonates inside. Some realign their life purpose. One retreat participant was forever changed by contemplating an insight from Rumi: "Give up this ten days of famousness and revolve with me around the Sun that never sets."

Walking This Practice into the World

Whatever makes you come alive, and feel joyous and authentic, make a commitment to incorporate that into your life. "I wish I could show you when you are lonely or in the darkness," exudes the fourteenth-century poet Hafiz, "the astonishing light of your being."

Listening

In our retreats, we break into groups and ask each person to talk about his or her disappointments, anger, fears, and anxiety. While that person talks, the others are asked to simply listen. Truly listen. We ask the listeners to metaphorically put their heads on the speaker's chest and sink into what is being said. It is astonishing what honest expression of feelings and true listening from the heart can do for healing and hope. We advise our participants to create time in their schedules to regularly gather in circles of love and participate in this process.

Walking This Practice into the World

Identify one or more people in your life whom you feel close to, whom you trust, and who love the truth. Gather regularly with this circle of love, every two weeks or monthly, to participate in this practice of taking turns to express feelings and listen.

If you have difficulty connecting with such a circle, create an "inner circle of love" (described on page 131) in the imaginal realm. In your meditative state, express your feelings as fully as possible to members of your inner circle. Know that they receive your expressions of anger and disappointment with tender affection and understanding. When it comes time to practice listening, touch your heart and listen to the rhythm of your heart. The sages say that there is a voice that doesn't use words. Just listen.

By doing this exercise, you will feel unburdened, with a greater capacity to experience joy.

Closest to the Light

A popular request from workshop participants is for a practice or an insight to prioritize and manage the preponderance of daily tasks. How can one balance the needs of self, family, work, and community? Sufis use a technique called "Closest to the Light." This practice is based on the following hadith: "Make all your concerns one single concern and God will look after all your other concerns." Simply ask yourself which of the things on your to-do list are closest to the Light and attend to them. Use whatever time and energy are left for the other tasks on the list, and you will find that the Light takes care of them.

As an example, let's say that you need to raise money for your organization, prepare for a lawsuit, attend a religious ceremony, and care for your ailing mother. Ask yourself which activity holds the greatest sacredness and meaning for you. Maybe you decide that taking care of your mother is closest to the Light. Willingly and lovingly focus your activities on tending to her and, as for the others—the fund-raising, the lawsuit, and the religious ceremony—give to them whatever is left of your energy and time without avoidance or aversion. The Light will bless you for honoring it and will take care of your other concerns. Islamic sages say that there is a great secret in this for anyone who can grasp it.

Walking This Practice into the World

Do this practice daily and you will feel a radiance of light in your heart. Rumi promises that if light grows in your heart, "You will find your way home."

Inner Circle of Love

One of the best ways to heal from burnout is to spend time with members of your circle of love: These are selected friends, family members, and others whom you love, trust, and honor for their integrity, morals, and ideals. Very few of us are actually blessed with this kind of authentic community. Not to worry, say Sufi teachers. You can always use your imagination to create an extraordinary inner circle of love in your inner landscape, and bask in the love and affection they hold for you. Here are the steps:

1. Close your eyes and enter into a state of silence. After some time, allow yourself to drift into your sacred sanctuary. The place could be indoors or outdoors. Remember, it is a place of infinite possibilities.
2. From that place, summon your inner circle of love, comprising loved ones living or deceased, prophets and saints, historical figures, animals, trees—anyone or anything your heart yearns to invite. The only limitation is your belief system.
3. Remember that it is in the nature of these members to love you. They shower you with love and light. Some or all of them come up to you and hold you tenderly. Allow yourself to be cherished, nurtured, and nourished. Surrender into the love and compassion they hold for you. Spend some time here.
4. When it is time to come into awareness, say good-bye to each member of your circle. Receive their thanks and blessings, and come into awareness.

Walking This Practice into the World

Make it a daily practice to go into your sacred sanctuary and bask in the love of your inner circle. You will experience an abiding sense of inner peace, joy, and hope that will refresh and strengthen you as you return to the demands of the visible world.

6

Meeting Fear without Violence

Transcending Defensiveness

In his classic 1965 science fiction novel *Dune*, Frank Herbert introduces a litany to be repeated in the face of fear. It begins, "I must not fear. Fear is the mind-killer."

Fear is not only the mind-killer, but also an effective civilized-behavior killer. Controlled by the fear of harm coming from another, human beings over the centuries have acted more violently than even they could have imagined. Yet, at the same time, fear is a natural feeling that is crucial to our survival. Without healthy and realistic fear, we could not ensure our safety as we negotiate the myriad situations of daily living. But healthy and realistic fear is quite different from the fear that debilitates and moves us to violence.

Fear, the *Merriam-Webster* dictionary says, is "an unpleasant and often strong emotion caused by anticipation or awareness of danger." Such fear can help us recognize dangerous situations and respond in ways that support our survival. But fear can also be exaggerated, arising from a recollection of past situations, past conditioning, or beliefs. Fear in this form can lead us to act in irrational ways that can escalate conflict.

James F. Mattil, managing editor of *Flashpoints: The Guide to World Conflict*, writes, "The common thread that weaves violent political movements together is fear.... Whenever we ask why people hate, or why they are willing to kill or die for a cause, the answer is invariably fear."[1]

Anxiety is a form of fear based on what might happen, not necessarily a real and objective threat. Anxiety is an indiscriminate and debilitating form of fear that inhibits our ability to live our lives freely. According to the National Institute of Mental Health, anxiety has become the prominent psychological ailment in our culture.[2]

Fear and anxiety hold us hostage and impact our health on all levels. Physiologically, they raise our blood pressure and increase the production of adrenaline, with negative consequences for our cardiovascular system. Psychologically, fear and anxiety rob us of our ability to discriminate between immediate and imagined threats, and lead us to act without the benefit of rational thought. Mentally, fear clouds our thinking, inhibiting our ability to be present in the moment.

Fear's effects on our daily lives are pervasive. We find ourselves afraid of abandonment, of being alone, of giving up control, of being totally honest, of missing out. And when we focus our fears and anxiety on our body, we may live in constant fear of impending accident, disease, and death.

One of the only guarantees in this life is that we all will experience fear. It has been a constant companion throughout human evolution. But if we are to resolve conflicts without violence, we will have to learn to deal with our fear. If we are to live our lives with a degree of confidence and joy, we will need to decrease the plague of anxiety.

Meeting Fear in the Jewish Tradition

Among the ways fear manifests in the Jewish tradition are fear of God, fear of being vulnerable, and fear of being powerful.

The Fear of God

Fearing God is commanded in the Jewish tradition. According to the *Jewish Encyclopedia*, the fear of God is synonymous with love and service. Unlike other kinds of fear, God is to be feared because of the radical All-ness of God. We stand as representatives of the Ultimate Reality, yet we are not to fear God because we are concerned about being punished for our wrongdoings. We are to fear God through the way we live our lives. This fear is a motivation for action.

> And now, Israel, what does the Eternal require of you, but to fear the Eternal your God, to walk in God's ways, to love God, and to serve the Eternal with all your heart and with all your soul. (Deuteronomy 10:12)

The fear of God inspires righteousness and peace, distancing us from evil and wrongdoing. "You shall not curse the deaf, or put a stumbling block before the blind, but you shall fear your God" (Leviticus 19:14).

"Fear of the Eternal is the beginning of wisdom," declares the psalmist (111:10). We might translate this kind of fear as "reverence" or "awe," appreciating the majesty and the eternality of the One. Fear of God in Jewish tradition is not to be associated with the possibility of punishment for wrongdoing, but, rather, with an awareness of the One Presence awake within us always.

There is only one Ultimate Source of life. To know this is to experience a profound sense of awe and fear. We are like single cells in a cosmic body whose dimensions are beyond comprehension.

The Fear of Being Vulnerable

Despite the command to fear God, the command most often stated in the Jewish Scriptures is "Do not fear." It appears so often because time after time in scripture we collapse into fear, and that fear robs us of the mental, emotional, and physical strength to deal with the obstacles before us. When he first sets out beyond the world he knows, Abraham, the forefather of Judaism, is told, *al tira*, "do not fear" (Genesis 15:1). Later, when Hagar, the mother of Ishmael, is about to despair, she hears an angel of God calling out, *al tir'i*, "do not fear" (Genesis 21:17). That command is repeated to Isaac, to Jacob, to Joseph, and to generations of other biblical characters.

The command *al tira* is heard and transmitted by the great prophets. Isaiah hears, "Do not fear, for I am with you, do not be afraid, for I am your God" (Isaiah 41:10). And, as *al tira* echoes through the centuries, it is accompanied by the reassurance that God can be trusted, that "I am" is always present.

But in our fear such an awareness is exactly what is absent. Instead, we feel our aloneness, our vulnerability. We are afraid that others might discover just how imperfect we really are, how vulnerable we are. We are afraid because of our awareness of our own mortality.

The Fear of Being Powerful

There is another kind of fear that Marianne Williamson, the Jewish-American writer and spiritual activist, speaks of in her book, *A Return to Love*: "Our deepest fear is not that we are inadequate. Our deepest fear is that we are powerful beyond measure. It is our light, not our darkness, that most frightens us."[3]

Her words seem to echo the psalmist's poetic vision:

> Yet You have made [human beings] a little lower than God, and crowned them with glory and honor. You have given them dominion over the works of Your hands; You have put all things under their feet. (Psalm 8:5–6)

The fear that we focus on in this chapter is the fear of our vulnerability. At the same time, however, we might consider our response to our own abilities. We have capacities to heal and we have capacities to destroy. Perhaps a fear of our destructive inclinations is profoundly appropriate.

Dealing with Our Fears

In *The Secret of the Rebbe*, Yechiel Harari shares a teaching that inspired the last Lubavitcher rebbe, Rabbi Menachem Mendel Schneersohn (1902–1994), "to meet the absolute truth of each moment, and to experience the fullness of creation. Practicing the present moment allowed those who sought his counsel to feel deep connection with him, and showed them how to avoid collapsing into fear, for that, too, was simply the product of a particular passing moment."4

The secret of dealing with fear, like dealing with any uncomfortable and upsetting emotion, is to honor the feeling. Denial is among the least functional of defense mechanisms. Instead, we must be present with the feeling and invite it to reveal its deeper wisdom.

Jewish Spiritual Practices for Honoring Our Fear

Since many of our fears keep us safe, doing away with fear altogether would not be helpful. We would not want to remove the fear of burning our hands by reaching for items in the oven without protection. Fear of driving intoxicated is a good and proper fear, and it would not be helpful to eliminate it. There are legitimate fears stimulated when encountering illness or death. And there are also fears prompted by anticipation of pain.

But many fears hinder our ability to live freely and inhibit our ability to be true to ourselves. Some of us fear heights, elevators, being alone, public speaking, being shamed, or getting ill, among many others. It's as if there is an endless list of fears and anxieties that we encounter.

The pervasiveness of *al tira* commandments in Jewish scripture reflects the universality of the feeling of fear.

Honoring the Moment

Learning from the way of the rebbe, rather than trying to avoid the moment of fear, we need to allow it, examine it, and explore it. When experiencing fear that is not brought on by an immediate situation demanding action, begin to simply honor it as it is, in the present moment.

Begin with physical sensations. Feelings of fear will be reflected somewhere in the core of the body. Perhaps you will feel it in your belly or it might be in your chest or throat. The feeling might manifest in your neck or head. Gently inquire into the sensations in your body that accompany the feeling of fear.

Honoring the sensations of the body is one way of honoring the truth of the moment. The sensations simply are as they are. Our feelings simply are as they are.

Just as there are physical sensations of emotional feelings, there will also be thoughts. After attending to the physical sensations, explore the voice of fear. What does it think will happen? What is it afraid of?

Being fully present in the moment, focusing awareness on the sensations, feelings, and thoughts, changes everything. There is no more resistance. You can try this out the next time you experience anxiety or fear.

Walking This Practice into the World

Wherever you are, when fear or anxiety arises that is unconnected to an immediate threat, honor the feeling. See what happens when you explore the facets of that experience.

The Words We Tell Ourselves

Proverbs 12:25 tells us, "Anxiety weighs down the human heart, but a good word cheers it up." When we feel anxious or fearful, we exacerbate that condition with negative inner self-talk. Such thoughts magnify the negative experience we are having. In such cases, we can consciously choose to replace those thoughts with "good words."

When feeling fear or anxiety about something that may or may not happen in the future, simply notice the messages that are reinforcing your experience in that moment. Be gently curious. Don't try to change anything. Just listen to the anxious ramblings of your mind.

Then, begin to replace those sentences with "good words," affirmations that lead you out of unnecessary fear. Here are some possibilities for you to learn and repeat in such situations. Silently repeat each statement until you feel it's time to go on to the next.

In this moment, I am safe.

I find five things I can see, five things I can hear, and five things I can touch.

I respond to this moment with greater calmness and clarity.

Walking This Practice into the World

This practice is meant to be used in the world, wherever you experience a moment of fear or anxiety.

The 3-3-3 Breath

When we're particularly anxious, changing our self-talk may aggravate the situation. Sometimes what we feel is panic, and the last thing we want is to more fully experience a moment of panic. At such times this threefold breathing technique can be extremely helpful.

Inhale to the count of 3, hold the breath for the count of 3, and exhale to the count of 3. Do that a few times, and then begin to extend the length of the inhale and the exhale. You can still hold for a count of 3, but you can inhale and exhale to a count of 5, 6, or 7.

Notice what happens to your entire system as you practice this 3-3-3 breath.

Walking This Practice into the World

Just before a public speaking presentation, boarding a plane, or other nonthreatening situations that make you fearful, you may find the 3-3-3 breath practice especially helpful. Whether sitting or standing, you can inhale to the count of 3, hold the breath for the count of 3, and then exhale to the count of 3. Do that several times, and notice how your fear subsides.

Meeting Fear in the Christian Tradition

Fear accounts for much of the negative energy experienced by human beings. We worry about many things. And we worry because we are afraid. This is why the admonition not to be afraid appears over a hundred times in the Christian Scriptures. Such references point to fear and its negative consequences. We do not need to be afraid.

Here is my favorite teaching by Jesus on the topic of fear and worry:

> Therefore I tell you, do not worry about your life, what you will eat or what you will drink, or about your body, what you will wear. Is not life more than food, and the body more than clothing? Look at the birds of the air; they neither sow nor reap nor gather into barns, and yet the Holy One feeds them. Are you not of more value than they? And can any of you by worrying add a single hour to your span of life? And why do you worry about clothing? Consider the lilies of the field, how they grow; they neither toil nor spin, yet I tell you even Solomon in all his glory was not clothed as one of these. But if God so clothes the grass of the field, which is alive today and tomorrow is thrown into the oven, will he not much more clothe you—you of little faith? Therefore do not worry, saying "What will we eat?" or "What will we drink?" or "What will we wear?" For it is the Gentiles who strive for all these things; and indeed it is the Holy One who knows you need all these things. But strive first for the kingdom of God and his justice and all these things will be given to you as well. So do not worry about tomorrow, for tomorrow will bring worries of its own. Today's trouble is enough for today. (Matthew 6:25–34, adapted)

The standard rendering of this passage typically translates the "Holy One" as "Heavenly Father." But it is almost impossible to understand the admonition not to worry in the context of the masculine otherness of God. It does not necessarily point to an inclusiveness that can help us see that we are actually held in and embraced by the presence of God, which is the key to letting go of our worries. Otherwise, it might feel simply like going out on a limb and not knowing (and fearing) when it might break. That doesn't work here.

Here are some other references to fear in the Christian Scriptures:

> Do not be anxious about anything, but in everything, by prayer and petition, with thanksgiving, present your requests to God. And the peace of God, which transcends all understanding, will guard your hearts and your minds in Christ Jesus. (Philippians 4:6–7)

> Do not let your hearts be troubled. Believe in God, believe also in me. (John 14:1)

Each of these passages recognizes the natural human inclination to fear. Life does prompt fear. The antidote to fear is the hope of sharing in the peace of God through belief, that is, through an understanding that the peace of God is stronger than anything one might fear.

Perhaps the most significant of all are two passages that appear near the beginning of Luke's gospel:

> In the sixth month the angel Gabriel was sent by God to a town in Galilee called Nazareth, to a virgin engaged to a man whose name was Joseph, of the house of David. The virgin's name was Mary. And he came to her and said, "Greetings, favored one! The Lord is with you." But she was much perplexed by his words and pondered what sort of greeting this might be. The angel said to her, "Do not be afraid, Mary, for you have found favor with God. And now you will conceive in your womb and bear a son and you will name him Jesus." (Luke 1:26–31)

> In that region there were shepherds living in the fields, keeping watch over their flock by night. Then an angel of the Lord stood before them, and the glory of the Lord shone around them, and they were terrified. But the angel said to them, "Do not be afraid; for see—I am bringing you good news of great joy for all the people: to you is born this day in the city of David a Savior." (Luke 2:8–11)

The symbolism of the angel Gabriel and the unnamed angel in the second passage suggests a message of high importance. It is critical that each of these messages from the angels begins with the words "Do not be afraid." Some of that refers to the sudden and stunning intrusion into ordinary life. It comes to a young woman of no particular accomplishment or station, and it comes to a group of shepherds, who in those days were regarded as outcasts of society. But the intrusion also penetrates all of life in its ordinariness and in its extraordinariness. It helps frame the nature and function of the revelation and becomes part of the foundation of Jesus's ministry. It addresses the deeply human experience of fear.

As part of this Christian contribution, it should be noted that, at times, fear has been used as a tool of the Christian church to control the laity and to take advantage of resources. Some of this control stems from the word "fear" in the phrase "fear of God." It has been used to equate the fear of God with the fear of punishment. Fear is a natural human experience and can be countered by God, but only if God is understood to be loving and not harshly judging and punishing. As Rabbi Ted has said, in Judaism, the fear of God is synonymous with love and service.

A Christian Spiritual Practice for Honoring Our Fear

The Prodigal Son Revisited

Fear is a distant country from which each of us longs to be liberated. For this practice, we will use *visio divina*, or sacred seeing, a traditional practice in the Eastern Orthodox churches, to free us from that distant country.

In chapter 1, we used the story of the Prodigal Son for the practice called *lectio divina*. We return now to that story.

You will need to find Rembrandt's painting, *The Return of the Prodigal Son*, on the Internet. You may also wish to purchase a poster of this painting, regarded by many as the best oil painting in Western culture. It is now in the Hermitage Museum in St. Petersburg, Russia.

It will be helpful for you to reread the story of the Prodigal Son in Luke 11:15–32 before doing the practice.

1. Come into a centered place using the meditative practices of sitting up straight, closing your eyes, and paying attention to the air moving in and out of your nose.

2. Now, gently open your eyes and focus on Rembrandt's painting. Notice the unconditional love of the parent, the skepticism of the older brother and the others. Most of all, notice how the younger son, the one who has come home from a distant country, is being held in love, forgiveness, and compassion.

3. Continue to focus on the painting and, as you do, consider once again your own distant countries, your desire to come home, and what that might mean. This could very well include a conversation with God, the Holy One, using questions, supplications, and declarations. Feel the calm in this image, the centeredness it exudes, and its ability to re-create that miraculous feeling of returning, of being set free from that distant country.

Walking This Practice into the World

Use this phrase every time you feel fear: "I am held in love." Picture yourself as the Prodigal Son in Rembrandt's painting and sink into that assurance.

Meeting Fear in the Islamic Tradition

Some degree of fear is inevitable in all our lives, no matter how much we may try to live in a state of surrender to divine will. "Certainly," God says in the Qur'an, "we shall test you with something of fear, hunger, loss of wealth, lives, and fruits" (2:155). It is not that God wants to prey on our uncertainties and make us suffer acute anxiety over things we cannot control. Rather, God wants to cultivate within us an inner strength that we can access only by exercising our spiritual muscles of faith, patience, and trust in the face of challenge and unease. Have you not noticed, Sufi teachers ask, that fruits don't grow on the trunks of trees? They hang from branches. To receive the blush of the Beloved, they need to quiver and tremble in the breeze. Once again, remember the spiritual adage: Don't run toward fears; just don't run away from them. Embrace them as opportunities to grow in wisdom, grace, and trust in a Power that enfolds and supports you as you make your way through life.

Perhaps the most common anxiety to which we all are prey is fear of the unknown and dread of uncertainty in our lives. Rumi uses the metaphor of a white cow that lives on an island green with grass. All day long the cow eats the grass but at night it is filled with fear and anxiety. "Oh my! What shall I eat tomorrow? I'm doomed." Tomorrow comes and the grass has grown. The cow chomps and munches the grass during the day. Night comes, and again the cow shakes with fear and anxiety, thinking, "What will happen tomorrow?" This is the story of our lives. We have a minuscule understanding of the mysteries of the invisible world or how the grass continues to grow. We have little faith in the Mystery that sustains us moment to moment.

To overcome fear, we have to develop faith in God. However, faith cannot simply abide in words. We have to move through three stages, instructs the Qur'an (102:5, 102:7, 69:51). Move from mere belief, or what is called "borrowed certainty," to becoming a witness to Spirit in your life. Engage in life, explore, discern, and learn from your mistakes. In the final stage, allow for an inner knowing to emerge from within. From your life experiences, create space for trust and faith in God to grow in you. Allow faith to grow into a subtle and unique bond with the invisible world. A Bedouin was once asked if he had faith in God. He replied, "You mean the God who has sent me afflictions, poverty, and made me wander from country to country?" But as he spoke, he entered into a state of ecstasy.

Another major fear we humans share is what psychologists call dread of our mortality: Simply put, we are afraid of dying. But we can ease our fear and use it to gain major insights about life. "The only preacher you ever need is awareness that you will die," said the Prophet Muhammad, and he meditated regularly on his own death. Sufi teachers advise that when you need to make important decisions, think about your death. Priorities rearrange themselves and you make good decisions. Another practice of the Prophet was to visit graveyards and pray for the departed. This, he explained, expands understanding of the mystery of life and the impermanence of the created world; it deepens in us the divine qualities of humility and compassion.

Reminders about our mortality or visiting graveyards might not be a favorite practice for many of us. However, we can grow spiritually if we allow ourselves to experience with compassion and grace our feelings about the inevitable "deaths," little and big, that occur in our lives: death of aspirations, job loss, failure of relationships, death of friends and loved ones. Slowly, it dawns on us that our fear is not about loss or death but about the tragic waste of not having lived, of not having loved enough, of not having been true to ourselves. The fourteenth-century poet Hafiz says that on our deathbed, our greatest regret might be, "Dear World, I did not kiss you enough."

In the context of this book, one of the ways we do not "live" enough is by allowing fear to keep us from speaking and living our truth. We betray ourselves when we fail to challenge outdated beliefs and unfair traditions that do not serve the common good. In the case of Islam, many Muslims are aware that our religion has gone astray when it blatantly preaches exclusivity, condones violence, supports patriarchal bias, and engages in homophobia. In many societies, the poor are treated with disdain and constantly suffer injustice and indignities. Too often, we fail to speak up lest we incur the displeasure and wrath of entrenched interests and corrupt authorities. The pressure to conform to the status quo is great. Spiritual teachers tell us that we are at a stage of history when we must operate from a state of higher consciousness and sacred courage. We have to live the injunction of the Qur'an: "Stand out firmly for justice, as witnesses to Allah, even as against yourselves, or your parents, or your kin, and whether it be against rich or poor ..." (4:135). In another verse, the Holy Book says, "Fear not humankind; fear Me" (5:44).

What can assuage the fear and insecurity that minorities and vulnerable groups experience in societies that are authoritarian and do not respect the rule of law? Sincerely reaching out to make personal connections and interacting with others, both within one's minority group and in the dominant society, is an important first step. In every society, people of decency, goodwill, and courage are drawn to help the disadvantaged. They will provide a protective bulwark against violence and harm. Engaging in cross-cultural collaborative projects to promote social justice and rescue our injured earth is another excellent way to soften the lines between "our" group and "theirs."

Before we can do the important outer work, however, we need to attend to our own spiritual health. The mystics plead with us to be in regular attendance at the divine court. God is aware of injustices and mindful of our fear and pain. When Moses and Aaron were afraid of Pharaoh's tyranny and ruthlessness, Allah said, "Do not fear. Indeed I am with you. I hear and I see" (Qur'an 20:45–46). In another passage, God says: "If God helps you, no one can overcome you" (Qur'an 3:160).

If we doubt the power of the invisible world to overthrow seemingly invincible regimes, all we have to do is look closely at history. Did we ever think that, in our lifetime, the brutal apartheid regime of South Africa would crumble or that the Berlin wall and the ideology of communism would collapse?

Sufi teachers repeatedly caution us not to use exaggerated fear, individually or collectively, to manipulate others into serving our selfish needs for vengeance or political victory. Fear is like fire: When used recklessly, it easily gets out of control and consumes everything in its path. The mulla learned that lesson when a mother asked him to use fear to convince her young son not to be so incorrigibly rude and rebellious. "Please put some fear in his heart," she pleaded. So the mulla stared fiercely into the boy's eyes, contorted his face, and with ghoulish growls commanded him to listen to his mother. His performance was so ferocious that the mother fainted and the mulla rushed out of the room. When the mother regained consciousness, she berated the mulla, "I asked you to frighten my *son*, not *me*." "Madam," replied the mulla, "when you invoke fear, it consumes everyone. Fear has no favorites. Did you not notice that I myself got so scared that I had to leave the room?"

Islamic Spiritual Practices for Honoring Our Fear

Be Present

Give yourself permission to look at your fears and experience the attendant feelings. Do this little by little and with mercy for yourself. Do not avoid or deny your feelings. Fears grow in the dark and assume monstrous shapes that can quickly overwhelm us. Use sacred naming (page 54) to reassure yourself that you have loving support. If possible, do some sacred holding (page 120). With compassion for yourself, acknowledge your fear and allow yourself to experience and embrace the feeling. Locate the sensations in your body. Make a conscious intention to breathe in and out through that physical location. With mercy and tenderness be present with your fear sensations. Perhaps have a little conversation with your fear, and then release it to Spirit.

Walking This Practice into the World

When you give yourself permission to face your fears with gentleness, the light of awareness slowly softens the distortions caused by fear. At a deep level we realize that, in essence, everything that frightens us is something that needs our attention and love.

Sacred Writing

Spend some time writing a list of your fears and allow yourself to express in writing your feelings about them as fully as possible. Then be silent for a while, with your hand on your heart, and make an intention to get in touch with your higher self. When you are ready, write a response to yourself, beginning with the words, "Dear one, this is your Beloved speaking. I have read your notes, felt your trembling, and heard your sighs, and I want to tell you ..." Finish the letter on a note of mercy and compassion, allowing your higher self to speak freely to your heart. You will be amazed at the insights and creativity that pour out of you. An inner peace will envelop you.

Walking This Practice into the World

Do this writing practice regularly, dealing with any difficult feeling or situation in your life. Over time, you will connect to your inner teacher, whose wisdom, counsel, and love have the potential to transform your life.

When Fear Inspires Violence and the Breakdown of Social Justice

Perhaps you are participating in a peaceful demonstration—protesting war, promoting racial justice, supporting financial justice—and things begin to turn violent. Acting out of anger, someone throws a rock that shatters a store window. Someone in a counterdemonstration moves toward you in a threatening way. The police, themselves acting out of fear, begin confrontational maneuvers.

Perhaps a friend of yours was beaten up because of his religion or his sexual orientation. He asks you for answers. What do you do?

Maybe a very close friend or relative has had a severe accident and is in intensive care. You want to visit, but you feel afraid. The last thing you want to do is show up at the hospital and have a panic attack. What do you do?

How can spiritual practice support us when encountering fear-based violence or the consequences of it?

Jewish Responses to Violence Done to Us or by Us

As we have seen above, many fears and harmful anxieties can be managed through constructive self-talk and meditative practices.

But when confronted by actual violence, we are no longer dealing with imagined realities—our fears have become real.

Obviously, if we find ourselves in the midst of violence, it is wise to distance ourselves from danger. But there are times when running away is not right. When we witness violence against someone because of her religion, race, or sexual orientation, we need to do everything we can to bring an end to the bullying. Sometimes, the responsibility rests with those who witness such behavior. They need to be urged to step in to stop violent behavior.

To stop an Egyptian taskmaster from beating a Hebrew slave, Moses intervenes, and kills the Egyptian (Exodus 2:11, 12). He then actively stops shepherds from driving the daughters of Reuel (Jethro) away from the well. Jewish tradition does not prohibit physical violence in the service of stopping violence, but peaceful interventions are always preferable.

For example, the violence that God seems to command in Torah against those who had previously occupied the Promised Land (Deuteronomy 7:1–4, 20:16) comes from the fear that the children of Israel will fall into idolatry if they interact. It is easy to see how violence is a consequence of our fears.

We are learning to deal with our fears without resorting to violence. When our anger causes pain to another, witnessing that pain might well serve to awaken us from the trance of anger. As soon as possible, we need to figure out how we might contribute to the healing rather than standing idly by.

Jewish Spiritual Practices for Dealing with Violence

Preparing for Conflict

In his work *Hayim v'Hesed* (Life and Lovingkindness), the Hasidic Lithuanian rabbi Hayka of Amdur writes, "O man! O woman! Know that every day there will come to you some new test, either insults and abuse, or monetary loss, and you should see to it that you are prepared for everything before it happens, and then you will receive it with joy" (*Erech Apayim*, 3:8).

When anticipating a difficult meeting, it can help to visualize yourself encountering any abuse without collapsing into anger yourself. Before such a possible conflict, take time in meditation to visualize the challenges you anticipate, and imagine staying centered. Consider that such conflicts are tests that encourage you to develop calmer ways of acting in the world. In your meditation, experience yourself responding with greater clarity. Another's anger need not ignite your own.

Walking This Practice into the World

When you find yourself in a conflict situation, experiencing criticism and anger, remind yourself that this is an opportunity to practice acceptance. Stay aware of how easy it would be to respond with anger, but notice that you are able to witness anger without sinking into it. Cultivate a greater equanimity that allows you to respond more effectively, even when you are criticized.

Visiting the Injured, the Sick, and the Dying

Many of us feel fear and anxiety in anticipation of seeing those we love in painful situations. Here is where the fear of God reminds us that all is One. We appear separate, and we appear vulnerable, but our essential nature is part of a greater shared Presence. Imagine that the Presence in you will be meeting the Presence in the other(s). It is important to honor your feelings, and deal compassionately with those who are suffering. And it is critical from a spiritual perspective to remember the greater Presence we share. Visiting the sick, called *Bikur Cholim*, is one of the prime directives in Jewish tradition. The Talmud even says that "one who visits a sick person takes away one-sixtieth of their illness" (Bava Metzia 30b). A caring visitation can bring a little piece of healing.

After you move into the calm space of your meditation, honor any feelings of fear that arise when thinking about visiting someone who is injured, ill, or dying. Accept those fears without negative judgment, and release them as they appear. Move just a little bit behind your mind and its chatter to the place of witness. Just as you are able to calmly observe the workings of your mind, imagine that you meet those who are suffering with this same sense of witnessing. You do not need things to be any different than they are. In your meditation, imagine that the witness within you meets the witness within the other. Behind all the words you share, there is a connection that brings healing.

Walking This Practice into the World

We never know when we will encounter someone who is the victim of anger, violence, or illness. Our task is to remain present, and avoid the temptation to simply indulge anger and upset. When faced with challenging situations, remaining aware of one's surroundings can be very helpful. The crisis situation is part of something greater. Although the situation may be dire, there is always more that is going on. Keep alert and aware. Remind yourself to survey the greater environment, to help center yourself, and to avoid falling prey to fear and anger.

Christian Responses to Violence Done to Us or by Us

In the time of Jesus there was an awakening to the possibilities of nonviolent resistance to violence. It is amazing to think that such an awareness was developing then, because the only religious leaders with high visibility to promote nonviolent resistance since then have been Mohandas Gandhi and Martin Luther King Jr. nineteen centuries later.

Nonviolent resistance makes sense because when the response to violence is violence it always leads, in one way or another, to more violence. The tendency to use violence to respond to violence is what theologian Walter Wink calls "the myth of redemptive violence." He writes,

> The belief that violence "saves" is so successful because it doesn't seem to be mythic in the least. Violence simply

appears to be the nature of things. It's what works. It seems inevitable, the last and, often, the first resort in conflicts. If a god is what you turn to when all else fails, violence certainly functions as a god. What people overlook, then, is the religious character of violence. It demands from its devotees an absolute obedience-unto-death.[5]

He goes on to say that violence—not Judaism or Christianity or Islam—is the dominant religion in our society today.

These two statements express the drama and force of violence, which is a major obstacle to peace. Wink reports that this myth dates back as far as 1250 BCE, when leaders of the empires of the ancient Near East perpetrated violence as a way, ostensibly, to bring about peace. Force is correct, he adds, either as an initiator of conflict or as a response to conflict. And in war, the powerful and the rich benefit from violence while the poor suffer from it.

But there are other kinds of violence, and all kinds of violence must be resisted. Jesus did not advocate pacifism in the sense of doing nothing. Instead, he advocated resistance. In the Sermon on the Mount, Jesus says that if someone were to strike you on the cheek, turn the other cheek (Matthew 5:39). This has most often been misinterpreted as a call to pacifism—doing nothing. But in the time of Jesus, if someone were to strike someone's cheek it would be done with the right hand. Further, it would be done with the back of the hand, as an expression of power. But if the one who has been struck turns, the one who is striking would have to use the palm of the hand and this would shame the one who is striking. It is a way to resist the violence. This strategy would not be useful today, but it points to the important idea of resistance. Given the conviction that we must love without conditions, nonviolent resistance becomes the only viable Christian response to violence.

I believe it would be possible to mobilize nonviolent responses to violence today using military discipline. On a large scale it would result initially in much death and suffering among those offering resistance. But it would also hold the possibility of breaking the cycle of violence. That would bring new meaning to the word "hero." Modern examples of nonviolent resistance include the lunch counter sit-ins in the South during the civil rights movement of the 1960s and the Women in Black in Israel/Palestine today.

When Rabbi Ted, Imam Jamal, and I were interviewed by John Blackstone for the *CBS Evening News* (aired December 26, 2009), he asked us if we wanted to eliminate conflict. We replied that as long as there are egos there will be conflict. Instead, our work is to help us move to a place where the consequences of conflict will be positive, creative, imaginative, and healing. That is how violence can cease to be a religion of such power, permitting the potential of all spiritual paths to contribute to the healing of the world—the people and the planet.

A Christian Spiritual Practice for Dealing with Violence

Journaling Responses to Violence

Take some time to write in your journal about three important topics: How is your nation dealing with violence in terms of war, domestic violence, gun violence, and violent crime? How do you respond, personally, to violence? Do you seek revenge? If so, you are human! Now reflect on Jesus's teachings about nonviolent resistance and unconditional love and ask yourself where changes might be made in your life, in your community, and in your nation.

Walking This Practice into the World

Think about one of the topics you journaled about and come up with a strategy to address it using nonviolent resistance. Then join with others to put that plan into action.

Islamic Responses to Violence Done to Us or by Us

In seventh-century Arabia, the fledging and nascent Islamic community in Medina was in constant danger of being decimated by attacks from the armies of the Qurayish tribe and its allies, which were vastly superior in numbers and armaments. Under these circumstances, the Qur'an gave Muslims permission to resist and fight "until war lays down its burden" (47:4). Oppression is worse than killing, says the Qur'an (2:191), and "if God had not enabled people to defend themselves against one another, monasteries and churches and synagogues and mosques—in which God's name is abundantly extolled—would surely have been destroyed" (Qur'an 22:40). The insights about resisting violence from the other side are summarized in the following Qur'anic passage: "Fight in God's cause against those who wage war against you, but do not commit aggression—for, verily, God does not love aggressors" (2:190).

The Prophet was aware that any fighting, no matter how moral and justifiable, has the capacity to bring out the worst in us. According to one tradition, the Prophet, after returning from the Battle of Tabuk, told his followers, "We have returned from the 'lesser jihad'; let us now engage in the 'greater jihad.'" The Arabic word *jihad* literally means "effort" or "struggle." "Lesser jihad" refers to battle; "greater jihad" refers to the essential inner work of taming and transforming the ego. The real enemy, the Prophet explained, is inside of us. Aware that the conditions of warfare can blind the heart, the Prophet was eager to turn the attention of his followers to the sacred work of curbing the ego's appetite for the spoils of war and for domination and revenge, which easily lead to unchecked violence and cruelty.

In a telling passage, the Qur'an counsels humanity that when victory comes your way, "Extol thy Sustainer's limitless glory, and praise Him, and seek His forgiveness" (110:3). Why seek forgiveness? Because this is a highly effective spiritual practice to prevent the ego from gloating and corrupting us with a false sense of pride and arrogance.

One aspect of the greater jihad is to become aware of our angry and vengeful thoughts, which can lead to imaginary scenarios of violence that too easily become manifest on the outer level of reality. The subconscious does not distinguish between real and imaginary. It absorbs and reacts to the negativity as if it were real, manifesting in outer violence. I recently attended a workshop where the presenter pointed to a shocking statistic: Every twenty-eight hours an African-American is killed by state-sponsored violence. But the heart of the problem, he continued, is that African-Americans are killed a billion times a day by the devastating power of society's demeaning thoughts and stereotyping against them. These poisonous vibrations, which are caused by fear and ignorance, have a dreadful impact on our collective consciousness, including that of both the sender and the receiver. It is absolutely paramount that we become aware of our conditioned biases and the negative, often violent, scenarios that our imaginations create in response to our fear.

An Islamic Spiritual Practice for Dealing with Violence

Awareness of Violent Imaginary Scenarios

The moment you become aware of negative thoughts and feelings, focus your attention to initiate a spiritual intervention. It is paramount to become aware of any unchecked negative imaginary scenarios swirling in our minds, based on thoughts of fear, ignorance, and hate. Intervene immediately. Sufis say, *"Tauba! Tauba!"* the moment they recognize that this is happening. The word *tauba* implies forgiveness and the intention to turn to God for help. We may acknowledge the scenario and turn away from it by saying, "Not true! Not true!" or "Not real! Not real!" or "Letting go! Letting go!" This spiritual intervention will break the pattern and, by the grace of God, allow space for beautiful patterns of thoughts and feelings to take root.

Walking This Practice into the World

By the constant practice of compassionate awareness and self-talk, we can diminish our negative thoughts and forestall the creation of imaginary scenarios that are filled with harmful energies. With our minds thus unburdened and cleansed, we greatly decrease the likelihood of dramatic conflict in our lives and we open our hearts to greater hope and joy.

7

Love as a Force for Change

Focusing on the Positive

We have been focusing on some of the ways spiritual practices can relieve the psychological and physical challenges of those working toward greater social justice and more effective earth care. We have also been encouraging spiritual seekers to appreciate that true spirituality is always reflected in the way we live our lives. Spirituality and social activism are mutually supportive. In this chapter, we turn our focus to love, an energy we believe enhances both spiritual practice and meaningful activism in the world.

Mahatma Gandhi taught that true peace between countries must rest on the solid foundation of love between individuals. He felt that love was the strongest force in the world.

Martin Luther King Jr., clearly a student of Gandhi, affirmed, "Darkness cannot drive out darkness: only light can do that. Hate cannot drive out hate: only love can do that."[1] He also said, "Power at its best is love implementing the demands of justice, and justice at its best is power correcting everything that stands against love."

So now we consider, from our own traditions, how the power of love can help us heal personal pain, address social injustice, and respond to environmental degradation.

Love in Judaism

Judaism has often been characterized, particularly in traditional Christian writings, as a religion of law, rather than a religion of love. But the texts of Judaism do not support this view. Certainly, there are rules and regulations in Jewish tradition but, ultimately, those laws are in the service of love. In the early years of the second century, Rabbi Akiba, one of Judaism's greatest sages, taught, "'Love your neighbor as yourself' (Leviticus 19:18) is the greatest principle in the whole of Torah" (Jerusalem Talmud, Nedarim 30b; also Sifra 2:12). Jewish tradition speaks of two main focuses of love: the love of persons, illustrated by Rabbi Akiba's statement above, and the love of God.

Loving God

We noted in chapter 2 that Judaism focuses on Oneness in the central text called the *Sh'ma* (Deuteronomy 6:4). But that text leads to the *V'ahavta*, "And you shall love":

> And you shall love the Eternal your God with all your heart,
> with all your soul, and with all your might. (Deuteronomy 6:5)

In a Torah commentary, the Polish Hasidic teacher Sefat Emet, Rabbi Yehudah Leib Alter of Ger (1847–1905), refers to a teaching of Maimonides (1135–1204) in which that great scholar contests the idea that love can be commanded at all. How can an emotion be commanded? Perhaps that's a question we all might ask.

The Sefat Emet's answer to that question is that it is the very nature of an individual's heart and soul to love God, for "this natural inclination is buried deep within the heart, the willful longing to seek out this love."[2]

But if it is our nature to love God, why isn't this love expressed more readily within us and around us? Furthermore, what would this love look like?

The Torah directs us to love God with "all your heart, with all your soul, and with all your might." The rabbinic commentators note that the Hebrew word for "your heart," *levav'cha*, indicates that you are to love "with both your inclinations, with the good inclination and with the evil inclination" (Berachot 9:5). As Rabbi Abraham Isaac Kook (1865–1935), one of the most influential rabbis of the early twentieth century, writes, "Love is complete and flows well from the source of pure unity only when both the inclinations are integrated and the evil inclination bonds with the good inclination."[3]

We saw earlier that the good inclination, the *yetzer tov*, motivates us toward acts benefiting others as well as ourselves. The evil inclination, the *yetzer ha-ra*, motivates us to act only in our own self-interests. Both are part of us, since they are manifestations of the ego, our personal identity. But how are we to integrate them? We cannot do so with our more limited identity, since that identity knows itself and the world in terms of contrasts. To know good, we need to know evil; to know behavior that makes things better for everyone, we need to know self-serving behavior.

The words that follow the biblical injunction to love God with "all your heart" are "with all your soul." The word used here for soul is *nefesh*, which refers to the separate self, our personal identity in the world. This soul contains both the good and the evil inclinations, as well as the physical, emotional, and mental aspects of our being. Although we usually experience this personal identity as separate from others, in truth, it is not. Remember that the essential teaching of Judaism is that God is One. Rabbi Kook speaks of this Oneness:

> This is the teaching: the meaning of "YHVH is one" [Deuteronomy 6:4] is not that God is the only God, negating other gods (though this too is true!), but the meaning is deeper than that: there is no being other than God.... The content is as follows: everything that exists in the world, spiritual and physical, is God.[4]

Nothing is separate because everything is part of One Being. We use the word "God" to indicate the interconnectedness of all being. But the *nefesh* itself, because it is a conditional self, responding to changing inner and outer conditions, is unable to sustain a love for itself, much less for others or for God. However, the *nefesh* is realized as whole and complete by the more inclusive identity within each person called the *ruach*. Even though we have encountered these words before, it is essential to appreciate how these aspects of self operate in the context of loving God. The Greater Self we often relate to as the heart-space is naturally able to hold the contrasting inclinations as one, and realize the *nefesh* as whole.

Love of God flows from the whole heart and the whole soul. When we know ourselves as whole, love is the natural state of our being. Yet there is one further part of this verse. We are to love God (All Being) with "all our heart, with all our soul, and with all our might." The Hebrew word *m'odecha*, usually translated as, "with all your might," explains Rabbi Adin Steinsaltz, one of the greatest Jewish scholars of our time, "really means 'with all your more.' It means giving your life and everything that you possess, and then you give more. What is the more? The things that you cannot do."[5]

We open to loving God when our heart is at peace, our soul is held in love, and our consciousness is expanding. In the moment of such love, there is always "more." The love of God is always evolving, being more.

What Loving God Looks Like

Loving God means opening to the wonder of all existence. Loving God means stepping into the field of love, the consciousness of love. This is not a personal experience. In fact, it's not an experience at all. It's a way of being. Loving God is not something we do; it's something we are. We might describe it with feelings of awe, wonder, profound peace, and intimate connection, which lead us right to the commandment "And you shall love your neighbor as yourself" (Leviticus 19:18).

Once again, let's consider teachings from Rabbi Kook, the first chief rabbi of Palestine:

> I love all people. I am not able *not* to love all people and all nations. I desire from my deepest depths that all be raised to glory, that all be fully brought to perfection.[6]

> My love for all God's creations, for all reality is great. Far be it from me to allow even the slightest dislike or hatred for God's creatures into my heart.... I do not want the honor of any human diminished. I want all to be elevated, all to be honored.[7]

We are taught to love our neighbor and then, more specifically, to love the stranger. In the first case, the text says, "You shall love your neighbor as yourself: I am the Eternal" (Leviticus 19:18). Then, we read, "You shall love the stranger as yourself, for you were strangers in the land of Egypt: I am the Eternal your God" (19:34). Loving neighbor and loving stranger are both consequences of loving God; they are also paths to loving God. Truly loving others means realizing the depth of our connection, that each and every one of us is a unique expression of a shared Being. Martin Buber taught, "This love of others is higher than any other service that one can give to God. Without it there is simply no love of God."[8] The Hasidic masters taught:

> To love God truly, one must first love persons. And if anyone tells you that they love God and do not love people, you will know that such a person is lying.[9]

But what if your neighbor has caused you pain? What if you see another person's behavior creating havoc in the world, making that person difficult to love? The Hasidic sage, Rabbi Shmelke of Nikolsburg, answered that question:

> Love your neighbor like something which you yourself are. For all souls are one. Each is a spark from the original soul, and this soul is wholly inherent in all souls, just as your soul is in all the members of your body. It may come to pass that your hand makes a mistake and strikes you. But would you then take a stick and chastise your hand, because it lacked understanding, and so increase your pain? ... [I]f you punish your neighbor, you only hurt yourself.[10]

The Activist Consequence of Loving God

Simply put, loving God removes the barriers our separate selves erect. We no longer seek punishment for those who have hurt us, because we know their actions spring from their own lack of love. Social activism springing from the love of God transcends the polarization that inhibits truly effective change. Resisting the ego's tendencies to demonize the other, responding to anger with love—this is the ground for the kind of nonviolent resistance that has been an ideal in our world since the work of Gandhi.

Jewish Spiritual Practices for Opening Our Hearts to Self and Others

The divisions among self-love, love of other, and love of God are less clear than one might think. Love of God is inclusive and unconditional, and so it is a path to unconditional love of self and of other. To open our hearts to the cosmic Eternal Presence, to the Life expressing through all forms, allows us more easily to include ourselves and others in that love. Spiritual practices, then, are not only meant to open us to the greater field of Love but also to support the service to ourselves and to others that flows from that field.

The Heart-Space Meditation

Remember that opening to the love of God is not something we *do*, it's something we *are*. What allows us to move beyond the constant judgments of the mind is the willingness to simply accept whatever we are experiencing at the moment.

Find a comfortable position and allow yourself to drift into an easy place of relaxation. Begin to notice your breathing. Without trying to change anything, notice how your body breathes. Then do a body scan, gently moving through your body to discover how it's doing at the moment. Once again, there is no need to change anything. This is a meditation of allowing.

Bring your focus to the space of your heart. Imagine that you are moving your center of awareness into the area of your heart. Be aware of how that feels.

Imagine that there is an energy of acceptance that opens at the level of your heart. Whatever you perceive, simply accept it as it is. Notice the flow of your thoughts and feelings with a very gentle curiosity. From the place of your heart, you can become aware of your thoughts, and of the conversation your mind is continually producing. There is no need to change anything; simply notice and accept.

Rest in the quiet of the heart for as long as you wish. This is the space of *ruach*, the greater and more inclusive self that is able to hold your mind, your feelings, and your body in an embrace of simple acceptance.

Bring to mind some of the people in your life. Once again, do so without any need to change them. Allow them to be held in the field of unconditional acceptance. When you are ready, bring to mind some of the people with whom you have disagreements. Hold them in this same field. Remember that, at heart, all of us need the same things. We need to love and be loved. We need to support and be supported. And, most of all, we need to accept ourselves exactly as we are in the moment, and we need to accept others exactly as they are. This unconditional acceptance brings us into the field of love, and the field of love supports the healing that we seek.

Walking This Practice into the World

As you go about your day, practice simply noticing your perceptions, judgments, feelings, and thoughts. Notice the stories you tell yourself about the things and the people you see. Take time to be aware of your breathing, and remember that there is a heart-space in which you accept so profoundly that you and others naturally become unlocked from more limiting points of view.

Shechinah Meditation (Affirming the Presence in Self and Others)

Shechinah means "indweller," and is the indwelling Presence of Life within each and every one of us. Behind our uniqueness as separate beings, we contain within us that greater Being in whom we are always connected.

In your meditation, take time to discover where you experience this Presence awakening within you now. Perhaps it is in your head, behind your mind. Perhaps it awakens within your heart. You might feel that Presence in different areas of your body at different times.

Seek it gently. You will know it by the deeper sense of calmness encountered there. You will know it by the gentle sense of vitality. Within you is that Presence that has not aged in the same way that your physical body has aged. That Presence may or may not appear to have a form. Each time you practice this *Shechinah* meditation, allow the Presence to meet you in its own way.

Rest in the indweller for as long as you wish. You may sense a blessing expressed from that Presence and flowing through every cell of your body and every level of your being. Trust the love that flows naturally from that Presence, for love is its nature.

Walking This Practice into the World

See if you can sense the Presence within you as you go about your daily activities. As you interact with others, perhaps you can sense that Presence within them, behind each one's personality. This is something you share with every other being. Perhaps you can even imagine that the Presence within you greets the Presence within the other.

It's Not a Snowball, It's a Light Ball

In the Creation myth, light was born from the chaos. When we find ourselves caught in anger, resenting others, harboring grievances, our minds are in chaos. Sometimes we find ourselves reinforcing our inner chaos by replaying painful events over and over again in our minds.

Here is a powerful as well as a fun way to use light to help release such negative energies. In your meditation, as people come to mind with whom you feel uncomfortable, imagine forming a ball of light in the same way that you would make a snowball. You can enjoy the process, making the light ball as small or as large as you like. Then throw that light ball at those with whom you feel uncomfortable.

Imagine that your aim is perfect, and that you hit them exactly where you are aiming.

As the light ball hits them, it gradually melts over them, so that the light gently surrounds them. Keep throwing light balls. As you do so, notice how you are feeling about the person who is the target of your light balls.

Should you wish, make a very large light ball for yourself, and imagine stepping right into it. Allow that light to melt over your entire body, and feel it soothing you. You might notice that the light melts right into you, so that you are not only surrounded by light, but you are also filled with light.

As you conclude this meditation, once again notice whether you feel any different than you did when you began.

Walking This Practice into the World

You might find times during your day when someone around you is in need of a light ball. At certain moments you might wish to create one for yourself. Instead of indulging resentments or bad feelings as they arise, imagine using light balls as missiles of love. Fire at will!

Love in Christianity

In Hebrew, the word *hesed* is translated as both "loving-kindness" and "steadfast love." "Steadfast" could hardly refer to anything but loving without conditions. How else could such love be steadfast— unable to be moved or changed by anything? This became the central or core teaching of Jesus's ministry. Loving without conditions is what Christians often call "grace." This radical idea did not originate with Jesus. In fact, he was drawing on one of the deepest and most important teachings in his tradition, Judaism. Jesus was quoting from Deuteronomy and Leviticus in this passage we read in Matthew 22:36–40:

> "Teacher, which commandment in the law [Torah] is the greatest?" He answered him, "'You shall love the Lord your

> God with all your heart, and with all your soul, and with
> all your mind.' This is the greatest and first commandment.
> And a second is like it, 'You shall love your neighbor as
> yourself.' On these two commandments hang all the law
> [Torah] and the prophets."

Jesus teaches us to open the heart, first to God—to Being itself—
and second to others. In each case love permits and energizes the
capacity to open the heart, to move out from the ego into a deeper
sense of our interconnectedness.

Yet it is very difficult for each of us to imagine loving in this
way, wholeheartedly, without conditions. If we think of those we
love the most, we all can pinpoint things we would change about
those people. They are the conditions that prevent us from fully
loving. If we could let go of those conditions, there would literally
be nothing that would keep us from experiencing the grace that
Jesus embodied, as stated in John 15:12: "This is my commandment, that you love one another as I have loved you."

In the story of the Prodigal Son (Luke 15:11–32), the father forgives the son who has wasted the money given him and welcomes
him home—unconditionally. The role of the older son, who does
not understand what is happening, is to show just how difficult it is
to move from conditional to unconditional love.

Radical change is possible when we love without conditions. For
example, we would be able to love our enemies, as Jesus instructs
us, "I say to you, love your enemies and pray for those who persecute you" (Matthew 5:44). And it is possible that they, feeling our
love, would no longer be our enemies.

The apostle Paul stresses the importance of unconditional love,
though he never uses that phrase, when drawing on what he under-
stands as the wisdom of Jesus's teaching:

> If I speak in the tongues of mortals and of angels, but do
> not have love, I am a noisy gong or a clanging cymbal. And
> if I have prophetic powers, and understand all mysteries
> and all knowledge, and if I have all faith, so as to remove

mountains, but do not have love, I am nothing. If I give away all my possessions, and if I hand over my body so that I may boast, but do not have love, I gain nothing.

Love is patient; love is kind; love is not envious or boastful or arrogant or rude. It does not insist on its own way; it is not irritable or resentful; it does not rejoice in wrongdoing, but rejoices in the truth. It bears all things, believes all things, hopes all things, endures all things.

Love never ends. But as for prophecies, they will come to any end; as for tongues they will cease; as for knowledge, it will come to an end. For we know only in part and we prophesy only in part; but when the complete comes, the partial will come to an end. When I was a child, I spoke like a child, I thought like a child, I reasoned like a child; when I became an adult, I put an end to childish ways. For now we see in a mirror dimly, but then we will see face-to-face. Now I know only in part; then I will know fully, even as I have been fully known. And now faith, hope, and love abide, these three; and the greatest of these is love. (1 Corinthians 13:1–13)

His words are truly beautiful and reach deeply into our souls. But if we do not understand the importance of unconditional love, they can be left on the shelf. We can walk away being glad for having heard them, but not having heard both the challenge and the promise they hold.

The most impressive and hopeful depiction of love in the Christian Scriptures is one that is almost always missed: the resurrection of Jesus. The story is told to underscore and proclaim the good news (the gospel) that God can always make everything new, can always forgive us, can always help us start afresh—even under what we might otherwise regard as impossible circumstances. This is unconditional love.

Love is a force for change because it brings people together, it invites cooperation and collaboration. It strengthens our egos by making them more porous, while at the same time affirming our dignity. It inspires us to long for and make use of an open heart that is able to empathize and to have compassion for other people.

ℰℓℓ℘ Christian Spiritual Practices for Opening Our Hearts to Self and Others

Lectio Divina Revisited

I like the Christian spiritual practice of *lectio divina* because it involves the reading of scripture as well as meditation and contemplative prayer. For Christians, reading scripture is important not just because of the wisdom that can be found in it,[11] but also because it is one of the best ways for Christians to feel connected to that bigger picture, that thing we feebly call Eternity. It can help center us and give us a place in our own tradition.

For this practice, read each selection of scripture on pages 165 to 167, meditate using a verse or a phrase or even just a word from it, and then pray using your sense of the connection to the power of love to change the world.

> With Matthew 22:36–40, trying using the phrase "God and neighbor." You may also use "Holy One and neighbor."
> With Luke 15:11–32, try "We begin to celebrate."
> With John 15:12, try "Love one another."
> With Matthew 5:44, try "No longer enemies."
> With 1 Corinthians 13, try "And the greatest of these is love."
> And when reflecting on the resurrection, try "I am made new."

Be still and reflect on each of these experiences.

Walking This Practice into the World

As you go through your day, carry a phrase you've chosen. Let it come to mind frequently, and notice the surprising ways the words may connect with your activities, personal encounters, and thoughts.

Love in Islam

Love, according to the dictionary, is a profoundly tender, passionate affection for another being. Heartwarming though this definition may be, it doesn't begin to describe the power contained in that four-letter word. Love, according to Islamic mystics, is the ultimate divine mystery, the force that brought the universe and, indeed, each one of us, into being. "I was a secret Treasure," God revealed to the Prophet Muhammad, "and I longed to be known, so I created the worlds, visible and invisible." The secret Treasure, in Sufi writings, is *Al-Wadud*, the One Who Loves. This Divine Lover appointed us humans as God's representatives on earth and, says the Qur'an, has made Her Bounties flow to us "in abundant measure, seen and unseen" (31:20). All we are asked in return is to worship none other than Allah. And what is worship? Again the dictionary provides the basic answer: It is to adore, and to adore is to regard with utmost love and esteem.

How does one begin to explain love? If we use intellect to fathom love, we shall be left far behind in life's journey. Overthinking leads us to shrink from the smallest obstacles to love, and we often experience love as subtle degrees of domination and servitude. "But this is not love!" exclaims Rumi. From the depths of his being he pours out poetic insights about the true nature of love. Love arrives complete, like the moon in the sky, he says. It is an ocean whose depths cannot be fathomed. The garden of love is green without limit and yields many fruits other than joy and sorrow. To understand the beauty, mystery, and power of love, we must experience this divine attribute not in our minds but in our hearts. With hearts truly open to love, we no longer shrink from its obstacles and are ready to take on dragons!

We humans tend to "love" all kinds of things other than our fellow beings. We love our new cars, our technological gizmos, our favorite foods. Many of us also love peace, social justice, earth care, and other worthy causes. What we may not realize is that in all our pursuits of people, things, and causes, what we are really longing for is the ultimate satisfaction of being in a loving relationship with the Divine Source of Love. "There is a disease in my breast that no doctor can cure," said the early Sufi saint Rabia; only union with the Divine Friend could cure her malady. All our longings for emotional and material satisfaction are really a deeper yearning for Absolute Mystery, veiled and obscure. "Friend!" cried out the sixteenth-century sage Kabir, "Ask yourself, who is it we spend our entire lives loving?"

This leads to a deeper mystery: Loving God is about widening and deepening our inner capacity to encompass love for the Source. The absolute splendor of the Beloved and our capacity to hold love for the Beloved are revealed as one and the same. This is a wondrous insight. This is the crux of love.

How Do We Deepen Our Capacity to Love?

Love's call is at the center of our being, but we are not aware of its deepest purpose until we open our hearts through the faithful practice of compassion for ourselves and for all of God's creation, both animate and inanimate. Compassion is love made manifest, according to many spiritual traditions, including Islam, and the divine attribute of compassion is mentioned more than two hundred times in the Qur'an. By loving ourselves and others and by doing righteous deeds, says the Qur'an, we will be brought into the presence of Supreme Love itself. "The Compassionate will endow with Love" (19:96).

Self-compassion means to accept and embrace ourselves just as we are, whether happy or sad, confident or fearful, satisfied or frustrated. When we continuously allow ourselves to lovingly enfold both our laughter and our tears, both the light and the shadow aspects of our being, something awakens and shifts deep within us, and we open into an expanded capacity to love and be loved.

With an increased capacity to love comes the realization that true love of God involves love and care for God's creation. In a hadith qudsi (sayings of the Prophet in which he quotes Allah), God says, "Son of Adam, why did you not visit Me when I was ill?" The human stutters, "How could I visit You, when You are the Lord of the Worlds?" And God replies, "When one of My children is ill, you will find Me there."

Similarly, the hadith concludes, when we offer drink to the thirsty or food to the hungry, we are actually offering them to God. In the same vein, we are called to love and protect our fellow creatures in the animal kingdom. "Animals and birds are communities like your own and are a part of the living world," says the Qur'an, "and in the end, they will also gather before the Protector of all" (6:38). We can show our compassion for animals in numerous ways, for example, by treating our household pets with kindness, making conscious choices in our consumption of meat, demanding humane treatment of animals in slaughterhouses, and advocating for the well-being of laboratory animals.

Finally, in the spirit of love for all of God's creation, our hearts will bow before the inestimable gifts of Mother Earth and move us to defend her against the ceaseless assaults that threaten her forests, her mineral and energy resources, and, above all, her life-giving waters.

With so much at stake, it behooves us to keep moving more deeply into love, no matter how many times we feel disappointed, helpless, rejected, or hurt. In all your relationships, love with a sense of joy, sacredness, and commitment. Don't ever give up on love. Eventually, you will be graced and blessed by the Love that truly satisfies.

Islamic Spiritual Practices for Opening Our Hearts to Self and Others

In the language of the Qur'an, God is both *zahir* and *batin*, both manifest and hidden (57:3). Sufis take this to mean that God is both outside and inside each one of us. The Holy Book reveals, "We will show them Our signs on the farthest horizons and within their own selves" (41:53). By opening our heart to Divinity within and without, we fulfill the purpose for our existence.

Spiritual teachers rhapsodize over the insight that Divinity resides in the chambers of the human heart. In a hadith qudsi quoted in an earlier chapter, God says: "I cannot be contained in the space of the earth, I cannot be contained in the space of the heavens, but I can be contained in the space of the pure loving heart of my devotee." In another hadith qudsi, God speaks about the veils of separation between Divine Heart and human heart: "There are seventy thousand veils between you and Me, but there are no veils between Me and you." Sufis take the seventy thousand veils to mean the layers and layers of self-centeredness that must fall away before we can achieve full consciousness of God, who already knows us intimately and yearns for us to come closer to the Light.

The heart is a critical organ in Islamic spirituality, mentioned 132 times in the Qur'an. "O my Lord! Expand my breast!" is the plea of Moses recorded in the Qur'an (20:25). The Prophet Moses begs God to relieve his human limitations, "that we may celebrate Your praise continually, and remember You unceasingly" (20:33–34). "Granted is your prayer," God replies (20:36), as God will surely reply to us if we do the hard work of opening our hearts by practicing compassion, awareness, dedication, and discipline every day of our lives.

Sadly, we do not normally volunteer for such work until life circumstances force us to. According to Rumi, there are two primary veils that keep us from becoming seekers: the veils of health and wealth. When our health or that of our loved ones is fine and we are financially secure, we feel unshakable and maybe even a little irritated by all this talk about spirituality and opening up the heart. But should one of the veils shatter because of a medical crisis or a drastic change in our material circumstances, we stir from our self-satisfied slumber, asking deeper questions and yearning for deeper meaning. In Rumi's poetic language, our hearts realize that there is a kiss we have been wanting all our lives: a touch of Spirit on our body. Our hearts long to open up to deeper and mysterious truths. We long to come closer to the Light, just as our Creator longs for us to do. "Take one step toward God," the Prophet says, "and God takes seven steps toward you; walk to God, and God comes running to you."

Diminishing Negative Traits

How do we remove the metaphorical veils to come closer to Divine Heart? A major practice is to "render your innermost heart pure of all dross" (Qur'an 3:154) so that you can "bring to God a sound heart" (Qur'an 26:89). By reducing our negative ego energies, we can expand our loving and divine qualities. Islamic sages say that we are lugging around a metaphorical bag in our life journey. Discern whether what is inside is "sweet or bitter." Redeem yourself from "fruitless effort and disgrace." Put into your bag only that which is worth bringing to a righteous sovereign.

The Prophet Muhammad counsels us to let go of three negative energies that are at the root of all wrongdoing: pride, greed, and envy. To overcome pride, whenever you achieve victory or receive a blessing of good fortune, immediately remind your heart to express gratitude to the Source, and also tell the heart, "Please forgive me." This combination of gratitude and seeking forgiveness for self-congratulation will counter the rise of arrogance. Fight your greed by reminding yourself that, on the day of your death, all your hoarding of acquisitions will be left behind in your palace. What takes you forward beyond the grave is "righteous deeds" (Qur'an 16:30). To counter envy, the Qur'an asks us to pray, "I seek refuge with God ... from the evil of the slinking whisperer" (114:1–4).

Walking This Practice into the World

Every step we take to cleanse the heart rewards us with the joy of sacredness, beauty, and hope. Spiritual teachers implore us to persist. "If you get irritated by every rub," asks Rumi, "how will the mirror of your heart ever be polished?"

Deepening Divine Qualities

What are some divine attributes that will purify the heart and dissolve some of the veils separating us from God? Perhaps the four most frequently mentioned by spiritual teachers are patience, humility, sincerity, and truthfulness. Meditating on metaphors from nature can help deepen these qualities. The patience shown by the rose to the thorn is what keeps it fragrant. When the seed humbly falls to the ground, it germinates, grows, and becomes a tree. Plant a mango seed in the soil and it remains sincere and true to its nature, growing into a mango tree that delights rich and poor alike.

Walking This Practice into the World

By purifying the heart, over time we grow a mysterious light in the heart. This radiance attracts to itself the light of Divinity, creating what the Qur'an calls an effulgence of "Light upon light" (24:35). No matter how difficult our life circumstances, our being becomes graced by peace, centeredness, and guidance.

Honoring Difficult Feelings

Another major way to open our hearts to the Light is to honor our feelings, especially the difficult ones. Feelings register as sensations in the body, and, if we pay attention, our bodies will tell us what needs our attention and love. When difficult feelings arise, such as arrogance, impatience, or jealousy, they present an opportunity for growth. Thus, when we get into an argument with someone, the circumstances of the disagreement may be important, but even more significant may be personal baggage that is surfacing in order to be acknowledged, loved, healed, and integrated. The feelings that arise are exactly what we need for healing and empowerment. If, in the midst of difficult feelings, we sincerely try to make choices based on love, compassion, and awareness, many veils of separation will dissolve and we will move closer to the Light.

Walking This Practice into the World

Acknowledge and be present with your difficult feelings and, whenever possible, see them as opportunities for empowerment and development. Meditate on the insight of Rumi that when you encounter difficult feelings of anger, shame, and malice, "greet them at the door laughing, because they have been sent as a guide from beyond."

Divine Remembrance

Continuously remind yourself of the astonishing mystery that Divine Heart resides in human heart. Rest your attention on your heart-space during quiet moments and even as you are engaged in speech and action. Touch your heart frequently with love and gratitude. Plant words of endearment into your heart. "To God belong the most beautiful Names," says the Qur'an several times. Your loving attention and planting of words of beauty can pierce many veils separating heart and Heart. You will become bathed with love and peace.

Walking This Practice into the World

Do this practice long enough and your heart will celebrate a traditional prayer exclamation of Sufi practitioners: "I have remembered You so much that I have become You head to toe; little by little, You arrived and little by little, I departed."

Opening Our Heart to Others

If we truly understand the Prophet's saying that God resides in every human heart, then, in the words of spiritual leader Hazrat Inayat Khan, "to treat every human being as a shrine of God is to fulfill all religion." As soon as we begin to consider the feelings of another, we begin to worship God.

How do we treat the poor, the disadvantaged, and the people in our lives who offer us no material advantage? The Qur'an asks us to be especially mindful about this important subject. Even advanced beings need reminding, as the Qur'an describes in a chapter titled "*Abasa*," which means "He frowned." Deep in conversation with a tribal chieftain whom he was trying to win over as an ally for his embattled group of Muslims, the Prophet was irritated by a poor old blind man who interrupted with a question about the Qur'an. "He frowned," the Qur'an says of the Prophet, and soon afterward he received an admonition from on high: "And the one who regards himself as self-sufficient, to him you pay attention ... but as for the one who came eagerly to you and with an inner awe, him you disregarded" (Qur'an 80:5–10). The Prophet was deeply repentant, and ever afterward treated the old man with honor. The blind man became a Muslim and twice the Prophet appointed him governor of Medina.

"Who can be better in religion than one who submits his whole self to God, does good, and follows the way of Abraham," asks the Qur'an, "for God did take Abraham for a friend" (4:125). Indeed, Islamic tradition holds that Abraham (or Ibrahim in Arabic) was the first Muslim in the sense of being a self-surrendering "Friend of the Merciful." But in a legend similar to a Jewish midrash, even this revered prophet and father of monotheism had to learn about respecting and honoring the feelings of those whose beliefs and ways of worship were different from his own. The Prophet Abraham had a daily practice of delaying his breakfast until a hungry stranger could join him. One day the guest happened to be a Zoroastrian, a so-called "fire-worshipper," and his unfamiliar prayers so infuriated Abraham that he told him to leave immediately. But God reproached Abraham, saying, "I have given this man life and food for over seventy years. Could you not feed him even one day?" At once Abraham ran after the man, brought him back to his tent, and treated him with exquisite hospitality and respect. If our prophets and founding fathers had to move beyond their prejudices and human self-interest, how much more is it necessary for us lesser beings to break through our biases and grow in graciousness?

Walking This Practice into the World

It is almost a cliché to say it, but one of the best ways to open our hearts to others is to pay more attention to their feelings and ask ourselves how we would feel in a similar situation. Even in difficult circumstances, such as a confrontation with an unfriendly or threatening person, we should do our best not to create unnecessary hurt while taking righteous action to resolve or neutralize the situation. That other person is a face of God, and the loving heart will respond with deep regard for the Divine in that other person's heart. Rumi exclaims, "O God, You have created this I, you, we, they to play the game of adoration with Yourself." We need to engage in this cosmic game with mercy, graciousness, and generosity!

8

Making Spiritual Practice a Way of Life

The Daily Inner Work of Peace

Our goal is a consistent celebration of spiritual practices that reinforce effective action in the world. Spirituality can provide the direction and the energy needed to move into the world with enough compassion to avoid polarization as we work toward greater justice and healing. The fuller inclusivity of the spiritual dimension allows us to grasp possibilities that then must be walked into our world.

So now we look at making spiritual practice and compassionate action part of our daily lives. In this chapter, we three share spiritual practices from each of our traditions that can inform all of our days, our years, and our lifetimes. Some are specifically related to religious holidays. These practices can usually be practiced alone or with a group, where spiritual practices can not only increase cohesiveness of purpose but also encourage group action.

This is about how we live our lives, day by day.

Jewish Spiritual Practices for Daily Use

Morning Practice upon Arising: Modeh Ani— I Am Grateful

The very first words to be recited upon arising in the morning express gratitude: *Modeh* (women say *Modah*) *ani* ... "I give thanks ..." The entire passage says:

Modeh/Modah ani l'fanecha, Melech chai v'kayam,
sheh-heh-cheh-zarta bi nishmati b'chemlah;
rabbah emunatecha.

I give thanks in Your Presence, Living and Enduring Being,
for You have mercifully returned my soul to me;
great is Your faithfulness.

When repeating these words, understand that the Presence awakening within us is absolutely inclusive, beyond limitation of space or time. That Presence is the Life of our life, the Soul of our soul, the Heart of our heart. That Presence is the ultimate source of all life. We are grateful for the level of the soul (*neshamah*) that connects us to that enduring Presence. We are not alone.

Walking This Practice into the World

Gratitude changes everything. Keeping a gratitude journal can help you focus. Imagine being grateful for all the opportunities you are offered each day to express kindness and caring.

Blessings before Eating

Spiritual practices invite us into the present moment. Blessings before eating inspire greater awareness of all who have contributed to the food we are about to eat, and encourage us to consume that food more consciously. The most common blessing before eating is called the *motzi*, the blessing over bread.

Baruch Atah Adonai, Eloheinu Melech ha-olam,
Ha-motzi lechem min ha-aretz.

Blessed are You, Eternal One our God, Universal Creative Presence, the One who brings forth bread from the earth.

You might wish to add a second blessing that is traditionally said when doing something for the very first time, for, if we are truly present, each moment is totally unique. The *Shehechiyanu* calls us into greater appreciation for each new now:

*Baruch Atah Adonai, Eloheinu Melech ha-olam,
sheh-heh-chi-yanu, v'key'manu, v'higiyanu laz'man
   ha-zeh.*

Blessed are You, Eternal One our God, Universal Creative Presence, who holds us in life always, who supports the unfolding of our uniqueness, and who brings us to this very moment for
   blessing.

Walking This Practice into the World

If you wish, you can develop your own words to express blessings before eating. You can also find your own ways to honor the uniqueness of each moment. The specific words are less important than the intention behind them. A simple affirmation can serve quite well. For instance, "I am grateful for this food I am about to eat" is simple and direct. "I am grateful for this unique and special moment" conveys the essence of the more traditional words. Find your own words and your own ways to express blessing and gratitude as you are about to eat each meal.

A Daily Prayer Practice

The central prayers in the traditional Jewish daily worship service are collectively called the *Amidah*, a word that means, "standing," since their recitation is done standing. This part of the service is also called simply the *Tefillah*, the "prayer."

The *Amidah* has three basic sections. First, we express praise, then we focus on what we are praying for, and then we speak words of gratitude. We begin with praise for a universe that can fulfill our needs, then turn to the fulfillment of those needs, and then express thankfulness for having our needs fulfilled.

With praise, express awe at the beauty of this living universe of which you are a part. Praise the Presence of Life and Love residing within you and within each and every aspect of creation. Praise the power of consciousness to support creation through words and images.

When moving into petition, rather than expressing, "I want ..." or "I need...," affirm having that for which you pray. Imagine the fulfillment of what you need. Inwardly, experience the feelings you will have when your prayers are answered. Let this part of your prayer support you as you imagine the life you seek.

Then express gratitude. Express thankfulness for the ability to experience the fulfillment of your prayers. Share gratitude for the Presence within you that awakens you to greater Life and more profound Love. Voice your appreciation for a universe that allows you to live and grow, and to be who you most truly are.

This threefold cycle of prayer can be done at any time you choose. When you focus on a specific issue in your life or in your world, the cycle gets very clear. Affirm that there is a greater Presence in this world who supports the good you wish to bring into the world. Become as calm as possible, and feel what it would be like when that prayer is made real in the world. Imagine the world you wish to live in. When you feel the uplift of having, doing, or being what you seek, turn to thanksgiving. Be grateful for the energy that is now supporting the realization of your prayer.

Walking This Practice into the World

This prayer cycle can be done very quickly or it can be done at greater length. You can write your blessings of praise, your affirmations accepting the life, the change, and the world you seek, and your statements of gratitude. Use the words you have written until it's time to revise them. This threefold prayer can profoundly support the changes we seek to bring to ourselves, to each other, and to our world.

Ending the Day with Forgiveness: *Ribono shel Olam*

A spiritual ritual for ending the day can be very helpful. In Jewish tradition, prayers recited before sleep contain the *Sh'ma*, which you have encountered before, and this remarkable prayer of forgiveness:

> *Ribono shel olam*, Source of All Being, I now seek to forgive all who have hurt me, all who have done me wrong, whether deliberately or by accident, whether by words, by deed, or by thought, whether against my pride, my person, or my property,

in this incarnation or in any other. May no one be punished on my account.

And may it be Your Will, Eternal One, my God and the God of my fathers and mothers, that I be no more bound by the wrongs I have committed, that I be free from patterns that cause pain to me and to others, that I no longer do that which is evil in Your sight.

May my past failings be wiped away in Your great Mercy, Eternal One, and may they not manifest through pain and suffering.

Let my words, my thoughts, my meditations, and my acts flow from the fullness of Your Being, Eternal One, Source of my being and my Redeemer.

Forgiveness itself is a spiritual path. Our resentments and anger, our sense of guilt and shame, hold us back. To forgive is not to deny painful moments, but to accept that the past was simply as it was. Forgiveness does not excuse another's words or behavior; rather, it sets us free. Without forgiveness, we hold on to old wounds and carry them with us always. Forgiveness allows us to release a painful past and live more freely.

Walking This Practice into the World

Forgiveness releases us from the blame and shame game. As you go about your day, become aware of the automatic judgments you make about yourself and others, and forgive yourself immediately for any negativity you generate. When others say or do things that irritate you, imagine what it would feel like if you forgave them and let go of the grievance that weighs you down.

Jewish Spiritual Practices for the Rhythms of the Year

The cycle of holidays through the year provides opportunities for celebrating the core energies each festival or holy day expresses. On a spiritual level, these energies can be welcomed at any time of the year when they can support you in your life. Here are the major holidays through the Jewish year and a basic spiritual practice that expresses their uniqueness.

Shabbat

The most important Jewish holiday concludes each and every week of the year. The seventh day begins Friday evening and extends until Saturday evening, and invites a celebration of Creation. In the biblical myth, God celebrates the first Shabbat after affirming that all creation is "very good!" (Genesis 1:31). That absolute appreciation for all that exists is the essence of Shabbat. Each week, we are invited to embrace it all, allowing our unconditional acceptance to support the unfolding evolution of life.

Walking This Practice into the World

A Shabbat moment is one in which we rest in the absolute wonder of creation. There is no need to change anything, simply a willingness to experience gratitude. Unconditional acceptance of ourselves and others pierces separation and quiets the judging mind. You can find blessing in the ordinary and beauty within you and all around you, as you open your heart and know, "This is very good!"

Rosh Hashanah

Rosh Hashanah celebrates the Jewish New Year, which begins each fall. It is also called the "Day of Judgment," because one of the traditional themes of this holiday is being called to judgment by God. It is most likely that God's judgment is far more loving than our own. Our ego-driven minds tend to focus on our failings and our failures, but a more inclusive Presence expresses profound acceptance and love. When we are judged by the greater Presence, we open ourselves to be loved.

A meditation of self-acceptance and self-love frees us to act more kindly to ourselves and to others. Imagine standing in the presence of the One. You may imagine that Presence as a being of light, perhaps as a feeling of warmth, or even as a musical chord or chant. Imagine that you are totally known by that greater Awareness, and feel the love that radiates toward you. You are loved exactly as you are.

Walking This Practice into the World

Our minds automatically judge all kinds of things as we move through our days, and we notice most clearly things that are not as we might wish them to be. As you become more aware of your judgments, imagine that everyone is perfect exactly as he or she is. Each of us is at the perfect place from which we can grow, and our awareness of this reality supports this growing. Imagine that all those you meet are at just the right place on their path. Notice how this practice impacts your day.

Yom Kippur

Yom Kippur is the Day of Atonement, which can also be read as At-One-ment. It's a day of prayer and fasting through which we strive to release all that keeps us from opening more fully to the Presence behind our personalities, and to the love in our hearts. So it's a day of forgiveness for self and for others, a day for releasing grievances.

A Yom Kippur spiritual practice is a meditation in which we continually release whatever comes into consciousness. In a space of greater calmness, accept all the sensations that arise within your body, and then release them by moving your consciousness behind them. A particular sensation may or may not change, but you are no longer identifying with it. Become aware of any feelings you experience, accept them as they are, and then move behind them. Do the same with your thoughts. Notice them, accept them, and then move your awareness behind them. You have sensations, feelings, and thoughts, but they do not define you. You are more than any and all of them. Keep noticing, accepting, and releasing, as you move your point of awareness deeper into the more inclusive streams of consciousness. Touch the inner silence that is always One.

Walking This Practice into the World

When negative feelings and thoughts arise, realize that they are simply your feelings and your thoughts. Remind yourself that you are more than those feelings and thoughts, and so is everyone else. Even though it's tempting to identify ourselves with a particular feeling or thought, we do not have to do so.

Sukkot

Sukkot celebrates the fall harvest of the land, as well as the spiritual harvest that follows Rosh Hashanah and Yom Kippur. *Sukkot* means "booths," and traditional Jews build temporary three-walled huts, with leafy ceilings open to the sky, and enjoy eating and even sleeping in them. These booths are reminiscent of the temporary dwellings we made when we were helping each other with the harvest, moving from field to field just as we had when we planted the seeds months before.

A Sukkot meditation invites us to know a peace so deep that we feel safe without locked doors and windows. Imagine that even those who are sleeping on the streets are safe. Imagine that we are once again helping each other as we did in the fields so long ago. This meditation encourages us to experience greater safety and security in our world, and to support that for others.

Walking This Practice into the World

Imagine that working together toward social justice and environmental healing is the natural state of things, but we get trapped into polarizing positions when we forget the greater Life we share. How can you help those you meet with their "harvest"? What can you do now to create safer communities that all can enjoy?

Hanukkah

Hanukkah is the eight-day Celebration of Light that comes in the late fall or early winter each year. While it began as a celebration of a second-century BCE military victory over forces of oppression and occupation, it was refocused on the Light of Spirit by the early rabbis.

A Hanukkah meditation is a Light-bringing meditation. In your meditation, imagine that a golden sphere of Light totally surrounds you. Take some time to allow this image to form. Realize that this Light supports healing and wholeness within it, and automatically draws out any negativity without harm. Affirm that this Light surrounding you automatically welcomes supportive energies from others, and reflects any negative energies back to their source without harm. Rest in this Light. When you are ready, imagine others supported in their own spheres of golden Light.

Walking This Practice into the World

Remind yourself often that every person you meet is held in Light. You might silently tell yourself, "[Use his or her name] is held in Light." Silently remind yourself, "I am held in Light." Notice the difference such an affirmation can make.

Purim

Purim celebrates the victory of good over evil, chronicled in the biblical book of Esther. But the more mystical Jewish teachers realized that it is crucial to understand that both good and evil live within each of us. It is not our task to kill the evil within us but to become more aware of it, so we are less likely to act it out in the world. On a spiritual level, Purim calls on us to embrace all polarities as contrasting expressions of the One.

A Purim spiritual practice encourages us to acknowledge good as well as evil intentions within ourselves, and to simply accept them. Our acceptance frees us to act more compassionately in the world, appreciating that we all contain both self-serving as well as service-oriented aspects of self. Even though you would rather show just the good parts to the world, in your meditation, accept both. Learn to appreciate when each aspect is activated in yourself and in others.

Walking This Practice into the World

Notice more carefully how people around you are acting. Witness the form as well as the specific content of their actions and their words. See if you can identify those parts within yourself that mirror what they are expressing. Become more aware of both sides of your personal identity.

Passover

Passover, the spring Festival of Freedom, celebrates our redemption from enslavement in ancient Egypt. We are encouraged to discover ways in which we are still enslaved, perhaps stuck in the tight places in our own lives, so that we might act to free ourselves. Passover calls us to become more aware of those who are still enslaved in our world, and to dedicate ourselves to acting in support of their greater freedom.

A Passover spiritual practice focuses on discovering the ways in which we keep ourselves stuck. In meditation, gently consider the things you would most like to do in your life, and notice what beliefs and actions keep you from doing those things. Consider what you would like to be, and look at how you have learned to hold yourself back. In meditation, give thought to what you would do if you were not afraid, what you would do if you could not fail. Move beyond your current stuck places into being the person you wish to be.

Walking This Practice into the World

Notice how you inhibit yourself, how you automatically make assumptions that limit your possibilities. Consider how you would like to act, and how you would like to be, particularly at those moments when you feel uncomfortable. Become more sensitive to the ways others are limited, not only by their own beliefs but also by inequalities in our society. What can you do to support greater freedom for all?

Shavuot

Shavuot, the Festival of Weeks, comes seven weeks after Passover. While originally celebrating the early summer wheat harvest, it has come to be known as the time of revelation at Mount Sinai following the Exodus from Egypt.

A Shavuot practice focuses on becoming available for more profound inner teachings. Following the initial relaxation as you enter meditation, set an intention to listen to a deeper wisdom that rises within you, behind the activity of the mind. If you have a specific issue or question, bring it with you into the quiet within. And listen. When you find yourself caught up in thoughts of the mind, step back behind those thoughts. And listen. It can be helpful to have a journal with you to record your experience following this kind of spiritual practice.

Walking This Practice into the World

Because our minds are so swift to present us with answers, we often don't take time for a deeper consultation. Learn to say, "I need to think about that," instead of offering the first response that comes to mind. See if you can usher a deeper wisdom into your daily life.

Jewish Spiritual Practices for the Cycles of Life

Here are the major Jewish life-cycle events that provide opportunities for spiritual practice. A meditative practice is associated with each one.

Birth

Birth is a time for naming and blessing new intentions in our lives. In silence, consider what is ready to be born now within you. What greater purpose is yearning to be fulfilled as you walk in your world?

Bar/Bat Mitzvah

Bar/Bat Mitzvah, a rite of passage originally marking the age of sexual maturity for Jewish boys and girls, calls on us to accept greater responsibility for our own actions. In meditation, allow yourself to own all the feelings and thoughts you experience. No outside person or agency is making you think or feel anything; you are generating your own thoughts and feelings. Release blame and understand that you are no longer the victim. You can take responsibility for greater contributions to your world.

Confirmation

Confirmation urges us to accept greater responsibility for our own spiritual life. In your meditation, appreciate that you have everything you need to awaken more fully to the wonder of the Life you are.

The calmness of meditation can support the deeper remembering of the more inclusive awareness you carry. Confirm your own spiritual authority.

Marriage

Marriage challenges us to step into deeper relationship as a spiritual practice. Meditating with a partner can be extremely meaningful. Sit together and let the silence embrace you both. Affirm the deeper purpose for which you have come together. Explore ways in which you can express that purpose in your life together and in your world.

Death and Dying

Death and dying are times for reaping the benefits of spiritual practice. In many ways, meditation is a kind of practice for dying, since conscious dying is a letting go of our connection to our body and to our personal, separate self. Regular spiritual practices can contribute to a calmness with which we can support others during their moments of transition. When our own turn comes to release our hold on this level of being, meditation can help us remember that we are always in the Presence of Being. Let your meditation be a practice for letting go.

Christian Spiritual Practices for Daily Use

The development of spiritual practices in the Christian tradition begins with descriptions of Jesus's own practices and continues through descriptions of practices in the early church described in the Christian Scriptures (e.g., "pray without ceasing" [1 Thessalonians 5:17]). But among the most important organized efforts to emulate Jesus's spiritual life is the experience of the Desert Fathers (*abbas*) and Mothers (*ammas*), beginning about the third century CE in Egypt. The practices of prayer, meditation, and fasting were the inspiration for practices in both Eastern and Western monastic traditions and were carried forward by them and in later attempts to revive Jesus's spiritual teachings.

In addition, the liturgies for corporate worship in Christianity attempt to connect the practices done privately, alone or among family members in the home, with the experience of the broader Christian community.

Upon Awakening

The great Christian mystic Meister Eckhart is reported to have said that if one simply said "thank you" every day, that would amount to a very deep spiritual practice. There is a Hebrew prayer, spoken upon awakening, that I have learned from Rabbi Ted and I use his translation: "I thank you, living and Eternal Being, for You have mercifully restored my soul within me. Your faithfulness is great." I like this practice because it shows a connection between Judaism and the development of spiritual practices in Christianity.

Walking This Practice into the World

The phrase "thank you" is like a crowbar opening the heart. Say it often and your life will be transformed.

Praying the Hours

The Book of Hours, which was developed during the medieval monastic period, specifies different prayers for different times of the day. This can be seen as an attempt to pray without ceasing. The Christian monastic movement was a highly organized experience of keeping a focus on God and away from more mundane concerns.

Taking between five and twenty minutes to meditate at specified times creates a strong framework for the work and play of the day and reflects the concerns of the *Book of Hours* as well as the practices of the early Christian community.

Walking This Practice into the World

Set reminders or alarms for a few times of day to pause, take a few deep breaths, and remember your connection to God. Call to mind the vast network of faithful people throughout history and around the world and join your prayers to theirs.

Reading Scripture

Reading a brief passage of scripture and thinking about it when moving through the day also contributes to a spiritual sensibility. The practice of *lectio divina* (see chapter 1) is an additional attempt to provide focus and substance to the need to focus on God. It began with the early Christian theologian Origen in the third century CE.

Walking This Practice into the World

In the morning, choose a line or two of a sacred text and write the words down in a place where you'll see them frequently throughout the day. Try to memorize them, and repeat them to yourself as you have a few moments between activities and tasks.

Blessing before Meals

A blessing before eating is an excellent way to be reminded of the privilege of having enough to eat. It is also a way to recognize those who do not have enough. For example, here is a traditional blessing with the addition of including others. "Bless us, O Lord, and these thy gifts which we have received from thy bounty. And keep us ever mindful of those in need." This reflects Jesus's own practices. For example, in Matthew 15:36 we read, "He took seven loaves and the fish and after giving thanks, he broke them and gave them to the disciples and the disciples gave them to the crowds."

Walking This Practice into the World

When you sit down to eat, pause to really notice the food in front of you. Offer a prayer of gratitude either silently or aloud. If you are eating with others, invite them to share in this blessing, or simply comment on the meal appreciatively.

Blessing after Meals

Getting into the habit of just saying "thank you" at the conclusion of a meal contributes to a spiritually gracious sensibility. This is suggested by a prayer from the Roman Catholic tradition: "We give thee thanks for all thy benefits, O Almighty God, who livest and reignest, world without end. Amen."

Walking This Practice into the World

Get into the habit of remembering after each meal, in the context of gratitude, the great blessing of having food at all, alongside an awareness of the multitudes with little or no food.

Singing Alone and Together

There are many references to singing in the Christian Scriptures. For example, in Matthew 26:30 we read, "And when they had sung a hymn they went out to the Mount of Olives." Singing together reflects the oneness of all; it is also a wonderful way to appreciate the preciousness of relationships and the great privilege of being together. Sometimes singing along with a recording or with the radio also brings us closer to God. It can enhance our spiritual development and strengthen our spiritual awareness.

Walking This Practice into the World

Throughout the course of the day, remember the phrase, "Singing takes me higher and closer to God, to other people, and to all of creation."

Prayers before Sleeping

Reflecting on the experiences of a day provides an additional opportunity for thanksgiving, and for remembering the needs of others and of the world. It mirrors the evening prayers that originated with the Desert Fathers and Mothers and continued through monasticism to this day. In addition, confession—specifying where mistakes have been made—is a way of emptying before sleep so that the new day can be a new beginning.

Walking This Practice into the World

As you look forward to the rest and peace of sleep, say to yourself, "Sleep welcomes me."

Each of these suggestions comes in addition to the spiritual practices offered at the conclusion of each chapter. These practices are habits that sometimes come after long periods of trial and error. But, as habits, they can seem easier as they become part of your daily routine. They provide the essential foundation for strengthening spiritual awareness, for developing a spiritual way of understanding experience, for cultivating a spiritual sensibility, and for enhancing our experience of corporate or communal worship.

Christian Spiritual Practices for the Rhythms of the Year

Advent

The calendar of the Christian year begins with Advent, the season of the four Sundays prior to Christmas Day. Advent means "coming" and during this season we wait for the coming of God in the person of Jesus of Nazareth. During this time the days are growing shorter and the light diminishes until the winter solstice, when it seems as if the whole world has gone to sleep with a light from a single star watching over us by night. Christmas represents light coming into the world; light in the person of Jesus helping us to see God's purposes, and light in the form of the wisdom of his teachings. Place an Advent wreath flat on a table with five candles. Four candles represent hope, joy, love, and peace. They are lit in the home on each of the four Sundays of Advent. Readings may accompany the candle lightings, along with prayers. On Christmas Eve, the fifth candle is lit. It is called the Christ candle and symbolizes the light of God coming into the world through the wisdom and healing of Jesus. Use the word associated with each candle as a focus for centering during the days of Advent.

Walking This Practice into the World

Use the phrase "light is coming into darkness" as a way to remember your need to increase your spiritual awareness.

Epiphany

This season, which comes right after Christmas, is the time when we remember the three magi whose journey to Bethlehem tells of the spreading of the message of Jesus into the world beyond Judea. An epiphany is an experience of revelation, a time of making something known. It is the time when we give thanks, once again, for the light of God being made known in the wisdom of Jesus's ministry. The practice is to remember the story of the magi as a way of understanding the wisdom required to recognize revelation in general and the teachings of Jesus in particular.

Walking This Practice into the World

Because the wisdom of Jesus is connected to the wisdom of the rest of the world, use the word "wisdom" as a cue to reflect on your life and wisdom.

Lent

The season of Lent is a deeply reflective time, preceding Palm Sunday, Holy Week, and Easter. It is a time to take stock, to be even more mindful than usual, a time to be emptied of all the superficial things clogging our souls. It is a time to prepare for Easter. People speak of "giving up things for Lent." What we need to give up are all the things that numb our souls, all the things that distract us, all the things that pull us away from our spiritual centers. When we say something like "I gave up chocolate for Lent," it trivializes and demeans the season. It also takes away the potential for healing because it contributes to our numbing instead of to our healing and the strengthening of our aware-ness. The season of Lent is similar to a prayer of confession writ large. It is not a time to express guilt. It is a time to clear away the rubble of our minds and spirits and specify where we want things to be different. Repentance is the act of turning, of turning around, or, at least, turning in a different direction. It can become a preparation for the transforma-tion and healing offered by Easter.

Walking This Practice into the World

Use the phrase "I am turning" to cue your thoughts and prayers about ways to strengthen your spiritual awareness.

Palm Sunday

This is the day when we remember the triumphal entry of Jesus into Jerusalem. It was not, however, the triumph that the Jewish community was expecting or hoping for. Jesus came into town on a donkey, a humble beast symbolizing the contrast with the military might of the Roman army of occupation. The community had hoped that Jesus would lead a revolt against the occupation, but Palm Sunday is a reminder, which often goes unnoticed even today by Christians, that Jesus came to make God's purposes better known. He came to call on us to do the inconvenient work of spiritual practices, to encourage concern for those less fortunate, and to demonstrate the importance of challenging the status quo. While the observance of Palm Sunday is primarily a practice for Sunday worship, it is an opportunity to remember that we do not always recognize God's purposes. In general, spiritual practices help increase our spiritual awareness and recognize the difference between our concerns as individuals and the purposes of God.

Holy Week

This week is the spiritual correlate of Passover and the Israelites' liberation from Egypt. While Palm Sunday invites us to think about Jesus's ministry in a way that points toward spirituality and away from human concerns and ego consciousness, Holy Week changes our direction. In this progression, we hear of Jesus's supreme challenge to the status quo when he overturns the tables of the money changers to call attention to the corrupt practices of those in charge of the temple. The temple bureaucracy sustained the ritual of temple sacrifice long after it had lost its spiritual significance and was using that as a cover for making money, principally by foreclosing on the property of Jewish peasants who were not able to pay their temple tax.

Maundy Thursday is the day of the Last Supper, a day when some think that Jesus and the disciples may have been observing the Passover meal. Following the meal, Jesus goes to the Garden of Gethsemane, where he is betrayed by Judas, arrested by the Romans, and imprisoned at the house of Caiaphas, the Jewish high priest. He is tried before the Roman governor, Pilate, and sentenced to death by crucifixion. He dies that Friday afternoon and is placed in a tomb donated by a man named Joseph of Arimathea. On Saturday, the tomb is sealed and guarded to prevent disciples from removing Jesus's body. On Sunday morning, the first day of the week, Mary Magdalene and another woman named Mary go to see the tomb. Mary spots a man she takes to be a caretaker of the tomb; the man asks her why she is crying. Mary finally recognizes the man as Jesus. He appears to some people that afternoon and to the rest of the disciples sometime later by the Sea of Tiberias.

While it is often argued whether or not Jesus really did come back to life, that argument misses the point of the story. I believe the point of the story is that God can always make everything new. This is the highest illustration of unconditional love. As a spiritual practice, Holy Week, observed both in our homes as well as in worship, helps us feel the transition from the concerns of our ego consciousness to the concerns of God. It is similar to the Jewish observance of Passover in the way it frees us from the imprisonment of our own egos to the liberation of experiencing the healing love to God.

Easter

The season of Easter carries forward the themes of Holy Week and Easter Sunday while also giving more focus to the creation of the Christian church. The spiritual practices of the season of Easter focus on the telling of the stories of the early church and how they sought to re-create the bridge between ego and openness to God's purposes, as illustrated by the movement from Palm Sunday to Easter Sunday.

Walking These Practices into the World

Use the phrase "I can be free" to recall the dynamics of this time, and the question "Why am I free?" to carry forward the meaning of Easter and the unconditional love of God.

Pentecost Sunday

This is a Sunday fifty days after Easter Sunday when the birth of the Christian church is celebrated. It celebrates how a diversity of people from all over the world came together and felt a communion and presence of the Spirit that became the foundation for the church. The practice of Pentecost Sunday focuses on an appreciation of the diversity of the early adherents of the church, who forged a cooperative approach to their common beliefs.

Pentecost

The season of Pentecost takes up half the church year, running from Pentecost Sunday to the first Sunday of Advent. It is sometimes known as the season of the church, a time to focus on the meaning of Jesus's teachings for the ministry of the church.

Walking These Practices into the World

Use the question "What is my purpose?" to reflect on the hopes of those who came together in Jerusalem and had that powerful collective experience of the spirit of the Holy One.

These rhythms of the church year, while experienced communally in worship, can also be and should be practiced in family or individual settings.

Christian Spiritual Practices for the Cycles of Life

Baptism

While interpretations of this sacrament vary, it is mentioned first in scripture with the baptism of Jesus by John the Baptist. It is practiced in various ways by different Christian denominations and always involves water, either by sprinkling on a baby's head or by complete immersion in water at a later age. It symbolizes inclusion in the Christian community of faith, it requests the support of the congregation of the child's parents as the child grows, and, perhaps more than anything, it reminds us that in a life filled with uncertainty, baptism points to a certainty of faith: We are created and sustained by God, the Holy One. We are recipients of the great miracle of life itself.

Remind yourself of this moment by using the phrase "I am baptized." (This was Martin Luther's favorite phrase, especially in times of difficulty or depression.)

Confirmation

In my tradition of the United Church of Christ, confirmation refers to the confirmation of the vows taken on our behalf at our baptisms. It is preceded by a class where spiritual practices, church history, and theology are now taught alongside introductions to other faith traditions.

Give thanks for the community that took vows when you were baptized by saying, "My baptism is confirmed."

Marriage

A wedding of two people makes public and asks for the support of "God and these witnesses" of something that has already happened privately: Two people have committed themselves to each other in marriage. When people make promises to each other publically, they connect themselves to the tradition of covenants, making promises in the presence of God and asking for the help of God as they move forward into a future that is mostly unknown.

Say, "I love [partner's name] unconditionally."

Divorce

Just as those entering into a marriage need the support of God and witnesses, those deciding to end a marriage need the same thing. Today many churches offer rituals to ease the pain of divorce and to help people move toward a new life with the support of the church.

Say, "I forgive and I am forgiven."

Funerals and Memorial Services

A worship service marking the death of a loved one or friend exists in almost all faith traditions. It is a time to give thanks, to remember one who has died, and, in the worship of God, to connect to that larger span that precedes life on earth and that moves beyond the death of the body.

Repeat the ancient Christian conviction, "Life does not end with death."

Islamic Spiritual Practices for Daily Use

Perhaps the most important practice in Islamic spirituality is cultivating a constant sense of the Presence of God. The Qur'an is full of admonitions to remember our Creator, and Sufi sages believe we are most fully human when we are conscious of God, while at the same time being engaged in the world around us.

Gratitude

A most effective way to be conscious of God is to express gratitude continuously for all the things, large and small, that enrich our lives. Start by greeting each day with words of praise for the gift of life itself. Just as in Jewish tradition, Islamic tradition holds that while we are asleep our souls are transported into the tender embrace of Divinity. The Qur'an says that God "makes the night as a robe for you and sleep as a repose and makes every day a resurrection" (25:47). So daily, upon awakening, I express deep gratitude for the return of my soul "for a term appointed" (Qur'an 39:42). Then I do my morning body prayers, bowing in adoration and praise of God and joining my voice to the cosmic chorus described in the Qur'an: "Everything that dwells upon the heavens and the earth extols the limitless glory of God" (62:1). Subsequently, I enter a period of silent meditation, which helps me feel centered and connected to the mysterious Source that nourishes and guides my soul.

During the course of the day I speak to the Divine Presence in my heart as often as I can remember, saying, "Thank you, Allah." When expressing thanks to others, I make it a habit to touch my heart, a practice that connects me to a deep core within. Sometimes I feel unusual joy come over me, and I say my favorite prayer of thanks: "O God, favor upon favor have You bestowed upon this handful of dust. Thank you." Even in times of affliction I strive to be grateful, for I believe that unknown blessings are already on their way. At these times I also repeat the Sufi prayer: "Dear God, save me from its harm but do not deprive me of its good."

Before retiring at night, I review my day and express gratitude to God for the day's many blessings and opportunities. I also reflect briefly on my shortcomings, especially in my dealings with others. If I have wronged someone I won't meet again, and cannot make amends to him in person, I create a ritual of forgiveness. In my heart I talk silently to the person and ask for his forgiveness. Then I invoke God's mercy and forgive myself.

Compassion

As I have said in chapter 7 and in nearly all my other writings, the most frequently mentioned names of God in the Qur'an are *Rahman* and *Rahim*, the twin sides of compassion. I make it a daily practice to cultivate compassion for myself and others. To deepen compassion for self, I tell my heart "I love you" as often as possible. To practice compassion for others, I remind myself frequently that they are manifestations of God. With people who are difficult, I strive to make a distinction between their behavior and their being. As I take the right action to deal with their behavior, I remind myself that their essence is sacred. Keeping this awareness in my heart infuses my actions, I believe, with sacredness, hope, and creativity.

Approval

Seeking approval from God or one's higher self, rather than from other people, is a profound spiritual practice. The truth is that no matter whose approval you seek, you become that person's captive. It is extremely useful to ask yourself frequently and honestly, "Whose approval am I seeking?" If I seek approval from others, I lose the freedom to follow my own inner guide. If you take this insight to heart, you are ready for the next Sufi wisdom: Choose your jailers with care and deliberation. Whenever I find myself struggling with a difficult decision or feel torn in my loyalties, my first essential practice is to ask myself, "Whose approval am I seeking, and to what end?" Pondering this question helps me distinguish between loyalty to my ego and commitment to God or a higher good.

Self-Awareness

Another form of divine consciousness is self-knowledge. As the Prophet said, "Know yourself and you shall know your Sustainer." To this day, I carry a piece of paper in my back pocket to record ego attributes and divine qualities I notice about myself in the course of my day. Every evening I gratefully shine the light of mindfulness over them in an effort to diminish my shadows and grow my better qualities.

In dealing with others, especially those I disagree with, I work hard to become aware of my conditioned biases and prejudices. In a hadith that expands our twenty-first-century understanding of human psychology, the Prophet said, "The faithful are mirrors to each other." Very often, an attribute we dislike in others is something that we need to acknowledge, heal, integrate, and empower in ourselves. We can accomplish this only when we connect to and become aware of our unconscious and conditioned self.

Living in the Moment

Another aspect of divine awareness is to live in the present moment and not be distracted by regrets over the past or anxiety about the future. When I find I have become unmindful, I immediately touch my heart and connect to my heartbeat. This transports me into the present moment. Sometimes I talk to myself and gently nudge myself to return to the present moment. Repeatedly, I remind myself that divine blessings are able to flow only through the present moment.

A commitment to be present does not mean that we avoid the past and ignore the future. We learn from past experiences and need to plan for the future. When I catch myself unconsciously regretting something in the past or worrying about something in the future, I realize that I am straying from the present moment. I resolve this through compassionate self-talk: "Brother Jamal, you are not present. Let's deal with this. I give you permission to regret or worry fully, for the next twenty minutes." This simple practice of conscious "allowing" makes me present with my regrets and worries. When the allotted time is over, I return myself gently but firmly to the present moment. Rather than feeling depleted, I become energized and hopeful.

Walking Softly on the Earth

Repeatedly, the Qur'an says that there are signs of God in nature. A daily walk in nature becomes a form of pilgrimage to holy places: It is the place where soul and world meet. I feel graced by nature's energies of healing, rejuvenation, and guidance. By sending out light, love, and gratitude to nature, I feel palpably loved in return. "Walk softly on the earth," urges the Qur'an (25:63), and many Sufis make a sacred practice of walking gently and mindfully in nature while silently invoking the mantra *Astakhfurillah*, which means, "I beg repentance." Among other things, this means that we should beg forgiveness from the tiny insects and worms, to which we unthinkingly cause widespread panic and pain simply by treading through their earth-based territory. By doing this exercise with sincerity and mindfulness, we earn unexpected blessings.

Service

The Qur'an says that our worship is incomplete if we do not extend it in service to God's creation. Sufi teachers ask us to be a "lamp, a lifeboat, or a ladder" to others in need, and to keep in mind three guidelines from the Holy Book: Give freely of what you love, give quietly without fanfare, and strive to bring about structural and systemic changes in society for the common good (3:92, 2:271, and 90:11–16). Each of us has a unique mission on earth, and this sacred purpose unfolds naturally and seamlessly when we develop a heartfelt aspiration and habit of service in our everyday life. The following hadith has always resonated in me: "Do good deeds according to your capacity. God never tires of giving rewards unless you tire of doing good. The good deeds most loved by God are those that are done regularly, even if they are small."

Community

We humans are social creatures and even the most introverted of us need authentic community to help sustain our inner work and to deepen our sense of contentment and fulfillment. A wall standing alone is useless, says Rumi, but add to it other walls and it can support a roof; only when ink joins with a pen can the blank paper say something. Ask yourself, are you blessed by genuine community, an intimate circle of companions who love you, whom you trust, and who cherish the truth? Those three gateways of love, trust, and truth are critical to determining which members comprise what Sufis call one's personal "circle of love." If you do not have such a circle in your life, you can still receive blessings and empowerment by creating a circle of love in your inner landscape. This practice, called "Inner Circle of Love," is described in chapter 5.

Genuine community is based not on outer similarities but on inner similarities. True friendship transcends the boundaries of race, culture, and religion; it is based on kinship of spirit. As a Muslim in twenty-first-century America, I have made it a spiritual practice to expand my circle from *umma* to *An Nas*, from the global Muslim community to humanity. This embrace of other religions and cultures by Muslims is already occurring in the United States. For example, several Pew Research studies of Muslims in America found that well over 40 percent of them said their best friends were non-Muslim.

Our sense of community also needs to extend to animals and nature. The Qur'an says that "animals are communities like your own" (6:38). A good spiritual practice might be to examine in what ways we honor this divine revelation and where we fall short. To honor the "signs of God in nature," it is a beautiful practice to hug a tree, lovingly stroke plants, and praise and thank nature for its beauty and selfless service.

Moral Courage

As our consciousness grows, so does the need to act with moral courage, even though it may not feel comfortable or convenient. Following this path is a spiritual practice of a very high order. It means telling ourselves and others the genuine truth and not the "truth of convenience"; doing what is right and not what is expedient; and acting upon our values, not merely paying lip service to them. It means that if I deplore corruption in religious institutions, I must challenge the status quo in my own religion by speaking out against spurious interpretations of the Qur'an, discriminatory religious traditions, and fabricated hadith that are rooted in social conditioning, blatant prejudice, and patriarchal bias, even though my speech may alarm my friends and agitate the self-appointed guardians of the faith. If I truly believe in kindness toward animals, it is an essential spiritual practice to witness the conditions of animals in zoos, labs, and slaughterhouses, and to make ethical choices about the animal products I consume. If I want to overcome racism, I must examine how I, as a South Asian, practice bias against dark-skinned people in my own community. As a spiritual practice I must speak out against this bias even when the offenders are elders or powerful members of society. And if I truly honor Mother Earth, my spiritual practices must include living a life of simplicity, even though our culture urges me to buy and consume far more than I need, and supporting those who risk livelihood and safety by challenging vested interests on our behalf.

Walking These Practices into the World

Clearly, the above-mentioned list of spiritual exercises is extensive and exhaustive. But by doing the practices and living the insights as often as we can remember, little by little we begin to experience what Sufis call a "Glow of Presence" in our life. Call this God, Invisible Force, or Higher Intelligence, but this Presence infuses our life with meaning, guidance, and motivation to serve the earth community. The words of a traditional Sufi saying, attributed to the Prophet Muhammad, resonate in our heart: "When you were born, everyone was smiling, but you were crying. Live such a life that when you depart, everyone is weeping but you are smiling."

Islamic Spiritual Practices for the Rhythms of the Year

Images of nature adorn the Qur'an, and Sufi teachers glean spiritual insights and practices from the cycle of the seasons. The season of autumn reminds us to be like a tree and let the dead leaves drop. Hafiz laments that too often we build a shrine to the past and do a "strange wail and worship"; he says that we simply have to stop being religious like that. Winter instructs us about the need to carve out regular time for reflection in our lives. The Prophet regularly spent time in silence, sometimes engaging in retreats that lasted forty days. Don't think the garden loses its ecstasy in winter, remarks Rumi: "It's quiet but the roots down there are riotous!" Spring teaches us that in our life there is a time of accelerated growth and renewal. Become humbled and crumbled like earth, advises Rumi, to "grow flowers of many colors." Summer demonstrates to us the beauty of inviting joy and radiance into our lives. Develop positive attitudes and celebrate life. The love and laughter bubbling up from within, says Hafiz, is the "sound of a soul waking up!"

Ramadan

For Muslims, perhaps the most spiritual period of awakening is the ninth month of the Islamic lunar calendar, called Ramadan. This word also describes the monthlong practice of cleansing the heart by abstaining from food, water, and sex from dawn to dusk. External fasting is accompanied by an internal fast to build "self-restraint" (Qur'an 2:183) against petty impulses and negative patterns of the ego, and to be conscious of God. Muslims engage in extra prayers of prostration in homes and mosques, especially in the "small watches of the morning" (Qur'an 17:79), to seek help from God and to ask for forgiveness. This is a month of intensive reflection, individually and collectively.

The underlying reason for the observance of Ramadan is gratitude for the Qur'an, the first transmissions of which began during the month of Ramadan. What can we humans offer to God in gratitude for the gift of the Qur'an? Anything we could think of, say the mystics, would be like taking gold to a gold mine or spices to the Orient. All we can truly offer is a polished heart that reflects God's face in it.

An integral part of Ramadan spiritual practices is community action to deal with injustice. At our Interfaith Community Sanctuary (ICS), the Muslim community has identified three areas where we need to make structural changes: bias against women, disrespect for the poor, and indifference to environmental degradation. To overcome patriarchal bias and attachment to outdated traditions, our Islamic Friday prayers for the last two years have been led by women, who also deliver sermons to a mixed congregation of men and women. To change their attitude about the poor and illiterate, the Muslims in our community, most of whom are immigrants, examine their inherited prejudice and misbehavior toward the "servant" and "worker" classes in their country of origin. In their hearts they beg forgiveness from those they mistreated. To overcome apathy and ignorance about the environment, Muslim members undertake specific earth care projects. In addition, the entire ICS community learns from Native American, Druid, and Wiccan teachers throughout the year about how to take care of the environment and the earth community. For example, the theme of weekly sermons for one entire year was "Spiritual Permaculture: Coming into Deeper Relationship with Earth."

Hajj

An immersion into God consciousness that happens every year is the six-day pilgrimage known as the hajj. In the twelfth month of the Islamic lunar calendar, millions of Muslims from all over the world gather in Mecca to perform a variety of practices, showing love and surrender to God in anonymous solidarity with their fellow Muslims. Men and women perform the practices together and wear the same white clothing, signifying purity and the truth that in the field of spirit there is no distinction. All Muslims, as allowed by physical health and financial means, are expected to perform this spiritual practice at least once in a lifetime. Those who cannot physically or financially afford to make the pilgrimage try to do it vicariously by saying extra prayers during the hajj and doing good deeds in solidarity with their global sisters and brothers who are actually doing the hajj.

New Year / *Hijra*

For many Muslims, the start of the new Islamic year is a time to reflect on the spiritual significance of *hijra*, the Prophet's dramatic move from Mecca to Medina in 622 CE. It seems to be a truism that no one is a prophet in his own country, and the Prophet encountered immense opposition to his message in Mecca, the city of his birth. After a prolonged period of persecution, the Prophet moved his community to Medina, where he achieved the nearly impossible task of uniting the warring Arab tribes and laid the foundation for the religion of Islam. By making this change, the Prophet was blessed by a phenomenal reversal of fortunes. So significant is the date of the "shift," called *hijra* in Arabic, that the Islamic calendar starts from the day of the *hijra* from Mecca to Medina.

Like the Prophet's *hijra*, shifts in our own lives can change our circumstances considerably. The shift could be internal, such as a change in attitude or higher awareness; it could be external, such as moving to a new job or to another residential location. Identify the *hijra* moment or moments in your life. Your awareness of them is sacred. Pray to God that your future internal and external changes may be blessed by the energies of the Prophet's *hijra*.

Walking These Practices into the World

Honor each cycle of season by reflecting on and living the unique message it has for your life.

If, for whatever reason, a Muslim is unable to fast during Ramadan, the Qur'an says, "It is incumbent on those who can afford it to make a sacrifice by feeding a needy person" (2:184). Because not all of us are able to travel to Mecca to perform hajj, we gain merit in heaven by pooling donations from family and friends and supporting a poor person eager to make the pilgrimage. This pilgrim prays on our behalf in the holy places in and around Mecca.

In the event that a *hijra* moment in your life led to negative consequences, identify and reflect on what positive attitudinal and physical change in your life might counter the decline. Pray for help, seek support from well-wishers, and act on your inner guidance. A little shift might result in a dramatic improvement.

Islamic Spiritual Practices for the Cycles of Life

Most of us pass through one version or another of three major stages of adult life: formation of life partnerships, the birth and rearing of children, and encounters with old age and death—first our parents' old age, and then our own. Each of these stages offers its own unique opportunities for us to increase our consciousness of the Divine in others and in ourselves.

Marriage

In relationships of commitment and love, often sealed by the sacred union of marriage, it is natural for our shadow side to come up repeatedly, so that through compassion and awareness we might embrace it and grow in vulnerability and surrender. A vital spiritual practice is to remember that our souls are seeking union to experience the mystery of Oneness. So spiritual is that longing that the Prophet called marriage "half of religion." Even in physical romance, our souls are seeking union through the body. Sexuality becomes the physical grammar of the soul.

Birth

The birth of a child is cause for both celebration and reflection on the mysteries of the invisible world. In a tender verse, the Qur'an says that when man embraces woman, a prayer from their soul rings out, "Bless us with a sound child" (7:189). Rumi exclaims that father and mother whisper gentle secrets to each other in the enchantment of the night and the child of the universe takes its first breath. Reflect on these signs of Mystery, and also on another sign of God: With the birth of a child, a mother and father also are born! Both parents have the opportunity to model what they want their children to become. The same opportunities apply to parents who adopt children and raise them as their own.

Caring for Our Parents

Caring for our parents is a profound act of love for God. Significantly, the Qur'an allows us not to obey our parents if they lead us to wrong-doing but instructs us that one of the ways to worship God is to "bear them company in this life with kindness" (31:15). "Say not a word of contempt" to them in their old age, but "address them in terms of honor" (17:23). "Tenderly lower to them the wings of humility," says the Qur'an, and hold them in your prayers: "O my Sustainer, bestow Your grace upon them, even as they cherished and nurtured me when I was but a child" (17:24).

Aging

Inevitably, if we live long enough, we too will become elderly and dependent on the kindness of our children and others. Aging is a time to consolidate the spiritual growth of a lifetime and to prepare for that long-desired reunion with our Source. It is also a time to enjoy the honor and respect mandated by the Holy Book and seconded by a hadith of the Prophet: "If a young person honors an elderly person on account of his age, Allah appoints someone to honor him in his old age." May we all live in such a way as to deserve a peaceful and blessed old age.

Passages

Conscious awareness of our death is an overarching spiritual practice. Because only God knows the moment of our death, it is important to complete what needs to be said or done at every stage of life. Whether it is telling someone you love him or her, making amends, or paying debts, do not delay. Even if it causes embarrassment or discomfort, take care of unfinished business. As the Prophet famously said, "It is better to blush in this world than in the next."

Our death is a wedding with Eternity. Our souls ache to return home. The unspeakable delight felt in the ultimate surrender is reflected in a beautiful utterance of Rumi: "A lovesick nightingale among owls, you caught the scent of roses and flew to the Rose garden."

Conclusion
Problems, Promises, and Possibilities

This book contains a wealth of spiritual practices, each of which encourages an awakening to the deeper aspects of our own being. Each spiritual practice is itself an authentic spiritual path: Each can help us get to the same place; each can be an authentic avenue to a shared Reality. So the practicing might be even more important than the specific practice. The unadorned awareness behind it all, often called enlightenment, is actually the remembering of who and what we already are. Words cannot adequately reflect that territory, but such remembering changes our lives.

The Problem with Spiritual Practices

The basic problem with spiritual practices is that we have to practice them. Meditative practice can, at times, be pretty boring and, at other times, deeply insightful. What are experienced as "breakthroughs," remarkable moments of a far more inclusive and shared identity, are not as frequent as we might wish. But the subtle as well as the more dramatic moments of spiritual practice contribute to significant inner changes that support more effective action in the world.

We know that, for some people, choosing a practice can be a problem in itself, and we hope we have made that process easier for you. Perhaps some of the exercises we have included inspire you to remember others, or to create your own. There is no limit to the possible focuses for meditative experience. One might even imagine that there is a unique focus meant for each and every one of us—that each of us has a particular spiritual practice best designed to support our own journey.

Our ego-driven minds want to judge a session of spiritual practice, but we can only do so by measuring that session against goals and expectations. True spiritual practice is not for the sake of another goal because the practice and the goal are one. Each spiritual practice session is complete in itself. It simply is as it is. Knowing this takes us away from the "better" or "worse" of the judging mind, relieves us of the weight of expectations, and allows us to be as we are.

The challenge is to engage with a spiritual practice regularly and allow each session to be perfect exactly as it was. "My meditation was successful" means "I did my practice." Whatever happened was exactly what was supposed to happen.

The Promise of Spiritual Practices

Spiritual practices provide a path to self-remembering. They help us detach from the compelling nature of our personal story and remember ourselves as creator rather than victim of that story. Along the way, there are physiological and psychological benefits of such practices. Increasingly, psychotherapists and others in the medical profession are recognizing the value of meditative practice in the process of self-healing. Spiritual practices are good for what ails us.

If this were all they accomplished, they would be valuable. But spiritual practice also allows us to deal with the deep frustrations, painful hopelessness, and frequent anger met while working to make the world a better place. It provides a reliable foundation to support us at moments of difficulty, and a springboard to effective and compassionate action in the world. These practices help us work toward significant change without adding to the polarization that makes things worse, rather than better. We are supported in moving beyond our past conditioning, however unconscious it might be, to work more freely toward equal rights and opportunities for all.

Spiritual practices, along with interfaith dialogue, provide all of us with one of the most hopeful paths toward the healing and the survival of person and of planet.

Possibilities Rising

Our work together as the Interfaith Amigos has given us greater hope for the survival of humankind. Through our sharing, we have each discovered more profound dimensions of spiritual wisdom within our own traditions. It's not a matter of which tradition is right, or better, or best. It's a matter of which tradition is right for each one of us—which tradition supports our journey toward a deep remembering.

We are each precious expressions of a single Being. We are given the opportunity to walk the love and the compassion of this shared Being into the world. On the way, we clothe our separateness with a personality to help us navigate material reality. But when we identify solely with this personality, we experience a life of constant comparison and judgment. We find a world of competing persons, groups, and countries. From that place of separateness, even when we strive to act more compassionately in the world, we are continually drawn into the drama of right and wrong, good and bad, righteous and evil. This ego drama confirms our personal identity, yet eclipses our more inclusive identity.

Hope comes when we remember our fundamental selves beyond the particular dramas of our personal selves and know that, ultimately, we all want and need the same thing. Sure, some of us are so caught up in our separateness that we demand that others be like us, but when we remember the Life we share, we know that demand to be a product of our competitive, fearful, separate self.

Hope rises when we allow our spiritual practice to infuse the way we live in the world. It then becomes our practice to love ourselves and others. Our practice is to treat ourselves and others with compassion. We want the very best for all of us, and we want to know how we can support ourselves and each other in this quest. Spiritual practices hold a key that allows everyone to thrive.

We are in this together, and it's a matter of our survival.

Acknowledgments

Writing a book is never an easy process, and it is rendered even more challenging when there are three authors participating in that adventure, especially when they no longer live in the same city where they can gather often during the writing process. So we need to express our appreciation to the support we received from each other along the way. We feel so blessed to have found each other, and to have found this calling to the expanding path of our interfaith dialogue.

We want to acknowledge the support we have received from the folks at SkyLight Paths Publishing, most especially to Emily Wichland and Rachel Shields, who helped us clarify our message to make it more accurately reflect our intentions. We are blessed by their skill as well as their interest in the work that we are doing.

We are grateful for Ruth Neuwald Falcon, our communications director, who helps keep us on track with our schedule of presentations. We suspect that herding a rabbi, a pastor, and an imam may even eclipse herding cats.

And we are grateful for all those over the years who have supported our work by providing venues for our presentations and questions that spur our learning. We also welcome comments and questions from our readers—you are all a part of this journey toward the greater spiritual awakening from which peace shall finally be born.

Pastor Don's Acknowledgments

I wish to acknowledge the extraordinary wisdom I have received from my beloved colleagues Rabbi Ted Falcon and Imam Jamal Rahman. What I have written in this book combines what I have learned from forty-five years of ministry and fifteen years of my association with

Ted and Jamal. And without the support of my wife, Judy, I would have not found the courage to persevere. Thanks be to all of you!

Rabbi Ted's Acknowledgments

I am so grateful for the teachers and students who have put up with me over so many years to support the evolution of my thinking, teaching, and writing. My wife, Ruth Neuwald Falcon, continues to see more in me than I see in myself, helping me to clarify what so often arises within me in fragmented ways. Her wise counsel and gentle goading helps keep me on track.

Ralph Waldo Emerson famously said, "All my best thoughts were stolen by the ancients." What I have been blessed to discover is what has been met before by those far wiser than I, and all those discoveries have been a profound blessing. I am grateful for all that has brought me to this moment, and I am grateful for those who keep me company here.

That my partnership and deep friendship with Pastor Don and Imam Jamal have grown ever more supportive over the years is something for which I am eternally grateful. Our meeting and our calling continues to be an inspiration.

Imam Jamal's Acknowledgments

I wish to express unending gratitude to my late parents, Ataur and Suraiya Rahman. They were my most treasured teachers.

Profound gratitude to my other beloved and cherished family members, especially sister Aysu, brother Kamal, and daughter Kristina. From them I have experienced unconditional love.

I am unimaginably blessed by my circle of love at Interfaith Community Sanctuary, notably by my lifelong friends Katayoon, Karen, and Sally Jo.

My friendship with my Interfaith Amigos, Ted and Don, is a source of abiding joy and learning for me.

I must make special mention of a family friend, Kate Elias, who selflessly continues to give me extraordinary help and support by virtue of her scholarship and editing skills.

Notes

Introduction

1. *New Revised Standard Version Bible* (New York: Division of Christian Education of the National Council of the Churches of Christ in the United States of America, 1989).
2. Yusuf Ali, trans., *The Meaning of the Holy Qur'an* (Beltsville, MD: Amana Publications, 1989); Muhammad Asad, trans., *The Message of the Qur'an* (Bath, UK: The Book Foundation, 2003); Camille Helminski, trans., *The Light of Dawn: Daily Readings from the Holy Qur'an* (Boston: Shambhala, 2000).

Chapter 1: Discovering the Need for Spiritual Practice

1. *The Collected Works of Mahatma Gandhi*, vol. 13 (Delhi: Ministry of Information and Broadcasting—Publication Division, 1964), 241.
2. The Gospel of Thomas is one of the Gnostic Gospels found in Egypt in 1945 at Nag Hammadi. It is not one of the four Gospels in the Bible, but many experts feel that some of the texts are an authentic representation of Jesus's wisdom.
3. Brian McLaren, *Finding Our Way Again: The Return of the Ancient Practices* (Nashville: Thomas Nelson, 2008), 89.
4. Al Ghazali in *Ihyaa Ulum*, vol. 2.

Chapter 2: Polarization: Our Basic Challenge

1. Aleksandr Solzhenitsyn, *The Gulag Archipelago, 1918–1956*, translated by Thomas P. Whitney (New York: Harper & Row, 1974).
2. Martin Buber, *Ten Rungs: Hasidic Sayings* (New York: Routledge, 2002), 89–90.
3. *The Portable Cervantes*, edited and translated by Samuel Putnam (New York: The Viking Press, 1949), 32.

Chapter 3: Moving beyond Past Conditioning

1. Danica Kirka, "Richest 1% Will Own More Than Half the World's Wealth by Next Year," *Toronto Star*, January 19, 2015. Kirka makes a projection to 2016.
2. Ibid.

3. Chuck Collins and Josh Hoxie, *Billionaire Bonanza: The Forbes 400 and the Rest of Us*, (Washington, DC: Institute for Policy Studies, 2015), www.ips-dc.org/billionaire-bonanza/.

4. Robin J. Anderson, "Dynamics of Economic Well-Being: 2004–2006 Poverty," *Household Economic Studies* (Washington, DC: U.S. Census Bureau), www.census.gov/prod/2011pubs/p70-123.pdf.

5. Kaiser Family Foundation estimates, based on the census bureau's March 2014 current population survey, www.prb.org.

6. William J. Sabol, Heather C. West, and Matthew Cooper, "Prisoners in 2008," *Bureau of Justice Statistics: Bulletin* (Washington, D.C.: U.S. Department of Justice, December 8, 2009), www.bjs.gov/content/pub/pdf/p08.pdf.

7. Report from the Stanford Center on Poverty and Inequality, 2015.

8. Equaldex 2016, www.equaldex.com.

9. Evan Soltas and Seth Stephens-Davidowitz, "Are All Muslims Terrorists?" *New York Times* (December 13, 2015), www.nytimes.com/2015/12/13/opinion/sunday/the-rise-of-hate-search.html.

10. FBI Hate Crime Statistics 2014, FBI National Press Office, November 16, 2015, www.fbi.gov/about-us/cjis/ucr/hate-crime/2014.

11. Betwa Sharma, "Meet the Muslim Girl Who Won the Bhagavad Gita Competition," *Huffington Post*, April 10, 2015, www.huffingtonpost.in/2015/04/10/bhagavad-gita_n_7022500.html.

12. Al-Mamun Al Suhrawardhy, *The Sayings of Muhammad* (London: Archibald Constable, 1905), 56.

13. Narrated by An-Nasaai and attributed to A'ishah, wife of the Prophet Muhammad.

Chapter 4: Overcoming Despair

1. Jeffrey Goldberg, "Is It Time for the Jews to Leave Europe?," *The Atlantic*, April 2015, www.theatlantic.com/magazine/archive/2015/04/is-it-time-for-the-jews-to-leave-europe/386279.

2. Viktor Frankl, *Man's Search for Meaning* (New York: Pocket Books, 1963), 104.

3. Tzvi Freeman, "How the Baal Shem Tov Changed the Way We Think about Happiness," Chabad.org, www.chabad.org/library/article_cdo/aid/1395566/jewish/In-Context.htm.

Chapter 5: In the Face of Failure

1. Patrick D. Miller, "The Hermeneutics of Imprecation," in *Theology in the Service of the Church: Essays in Honor of Thomas W. Gillespie* (Grand Rapids, MI: Eerdmans, 2000), 161.

2. Abu Dawud, book 36, Hadith 4766.

3. Richard Gunderman, "For the Young Doctor about to Burn Out," *The Atlantic*, February 21, 2014, www.theatlantic.com/health/archive/2014/02/for-the-young-doctor-about-to-burn-out/284005/.

4. Sahih Al-Bukhari, vol. 7, hadith 127.

Chapter 6: Meeting Fear without Violence

1 James F. Mattil, quoted in Phil Barker, "Fear," *Beyond Intractability*, July 2004, www.beyondintractability.org/essay/fear.
2 "Any Anxiety Disorder Among Adults," National Institute of Mental Health, www.nimh.nih.gov/health/statistics/prevalence/any-anxiety-disorder-among-adults.shtml.
3 Marianne Williamson, *A Return to Love* (San Francisco: HarperOne, 1996), 190.
4 Yehiel Hararai, *The Secret of the Rebbe* (Israel: Yediot, 2013).
5 Walter Wink, "The Myth of Redemptive Violence," *The Bible in Transmission* (Spring 1999): 1.

Chapter 7: Love as a Force for Change

1 Martin Luther King Jr., *Strength to Love* (New York: Harper & Row, 1963), chapter 5.
2 Arthur Green, *The Language of Truth: The Torah Commentary of the Sefat Emet, Rabbi Yehudah Leib Alter of Ger* (Philadelphia: Jewish Publication Society, 1998), 291.
3 *Orot: The Annotated Translation of Rabbi Abraham Isaac Kook's Seminal Work*, translated by Bezalel Naor (Northvale, NJ: Jason Aronson, 1993), 124–125.
4 *Otsar Mikhtavim u-Ma'amarim* (Jerusalem: Makhon Gahaley Esh, 1968), 75.
5 From an address delivered by Rabbi Adin Steinsaltz on June 17, 2004, at a gathering marking the tenth *yahrzeit* (anniversary of the death) of the Lubavitcher rebbe, Rabbi Menachem Mendel Schneerson, in the JFK Library in Boston.
6 Arpalet Tohar, quoted in Yitzhak Buxbaum, "An Open Heart: The Mystic Path of Loving People," in *The Jewish Spirit Booklet Series*, vol. 2 (1997): 22.
7 S. Raz and Malachim Kivnei Adam, quoted in Buxbaum, "An Open Heart," 22.
8 Donald J. Moore, *Martin Buber: Prophet of Religious Secularism*, 2nd ed. (New York: Fordham University Press, 1996), 47.
9 Buber, *Ten Rungs*, 82.
10 Martin Buber, *Tales of the Hasidim: The Early Masters* (New York: Schocken Books, 1961), 190.
11 We read to hear and understand God's Word. Not words, but Word. "Word" is a translation of the Greek *logos*, which in this case can be read as "purpose" or "purposes." So that when we read in the first verse of the Gospel of John, "In the beginning was the Word," we are reading that in the beginning was the purpose of God. This is complex and can be easily misunderstood, especially if we are inclined to take scripture literally.

Suggestions for Further Reading

Pastor Don's Suggestions for Further Reading

Bonhoeffer, Dietrich. *The Cost of Discipleship.* New York: MacMillan, 1963.

Brueggemann, Walter. *Living toward a Vision: Biblical Reflections on Shalom.* New York: United Church Press, 1982.

Chittister, Joan. *Wisdom Distilled from the Daily: Living the Rule of St. Benedict.* San Francisco: HarperSanFrancisco, 1990.

Coffin, William Sloane. *Credo.* Louisville, KY: Westminster John Knox, 2004.

McLaren, Brian. *Finding Our Way Again: The Return of the Ancient Practices.* Nashville: Thomas Nelson, 2008.

Martin-Schramm, James B., and Robert L. Stivers. *Christian Environmental Ethics: A Case Method Approach.* Maryknoll, NY: Orbis Books, 2003.

Merton, Thomas. *The Seven Storey Mountain.* New York: Harcourt Brace, 1998.

Ruether, Rosemary Radford. *Visionary Women: Three Medieval Mystics.* Minneapolis: Fortress Press, 2001.

Soelle, Dorothee. *The Silent Cry: Mysticism and Resistance.* Translated by Barbara Rumscheidt. Minneapolis: Fortress Press, 2001.

Wink, Walter. *Engaging the Powers: Discernment and Resistance in a World of Domination.* Minneapolis: Fortress Press, 1992.

Rabbi Ted's Suggestions for Further Reading

Amador, Xavier. *I'm Right, You're Wrong, Now What? Break the Impasse and Get What You Need.* New York: Hyperion, 2008.

Bernstein, Ellen, ed. *Ecology and the Jewish Spirit: Where Nature and the Sacred Meet.* Woodstock, VT: Jewish Lights, 2000.

———. *The Splendor of Creation: A Biblical Ecology.* Cleveland: Pilgrim Press, 2005.

Elgin, Duane. *The Living Universe: Where Are We? Who Are We? Where Are We Going?* San Francisco: Berrett-Koehler, 2009.

Falcon, Ted. *A Journey of Awakening: Kabbalistic Meditations on the Tree of Life.* Seattle: Skynear Press, 2003.

———, and David Blatner. *Judaism For Dummies.* Hoboken, NJ: Wiley, 2013.

Harvey, Andrew, ed. *The Essential Mystics: The Soul's Journey into Truth.* San Francisco: HarperSanFrancisco, 1996.

————. *The Hope: A Guide to Sacred Activism*. Carlsbad, CA: Hay House, 2009.

Korten, David C. *Change the Story, Change the Future: A Living Economy for a Living Earth*. San Francisco: Berrett-Koehler, 2015.

Kushner, Lawrence. *The Way Into Jewish Mystical Tradition*. Woodstock, VT: Jewish Lights, 2001.

Lamm, Norman. *The Shema: Spirituality and Law in Judaism*. Philadelphia: Jewish Publication Society, 2000.

Sacks, Jonathan. *Not in God's Name: Confronting Religious Violence*. New York: Schocken Books, 2015.

Sheldon, Lewis. *Torah of Reconciliation*. Jerusalem: Gefen, 2012.

Imam Jamal's Suggestions for Further Reading

Ali-Karamali, Sumbul. *The Muslim Next Door: The Qur'an, the Media, and That Veil Thing*. Ashland, OR: White Cloud Press, 2008.

Easwaran, Eknath. *Nonviolent Soldier of Islam: Badshah Khan, a Man to Match His Mountains*. Tomales, CA: Nilgiri Press, 1999.

Mackenzie, Don, Ted Falcon, and Jamal Rahman. *Getting to the Heart of Interfaith: The Eye-Opening, Hope-Filled Friendship of a Pastor, a Rabbi and an Imam*. Woodstock, VT: SkyLight Paths, 2009.

————. *Religion Gone Astray: What We Found at the Heart of Interfaith*. Woodstock, VT: SkyLight Paths, 2011.

Rahman, Jamal, Kathleen Elias, and Ann Redding. *Out of Darkness into Light: Spiritual Guidance in the Qur'an with Reflections from Christian and Jewish Sources*. Harrisburg: Morehouse, 2009.

Rahman, Jamal. *The Fragrance of Faith: The Enlightened Heart of Islam*. Bath, England: The Book Foundation, 2004.

————. *Spiritual Gems of Islam: Insights and Practices from the Qur'an, Hadith, Rumi and Muslim Teaching Stories to Enlighten the Heart and Mind*. Woodstock, VT: SkyLight Paths, 2013.

————. *Sacred Laughter of the Sufis: Awakening the Soul with the Mulla's Comic Teaching Stories and Other Islamic Wisdom*. Woodstock, VT: SkyLight Paths, 2014.

Yousafzai, Malala. *I Am Malala: The Girl Who Stood Up for Education and Was Shot by the Taliban*. New York: Little, Brown: 2013.

Index of Practices

8. Making Spiritual Practice a Way of Life

Inspiration

A Year of Spiritual Companionship
52 Weeks of Wisdom for a Life of Gratitude, Balance and Happiness
By Anne Kertz Kernion; Foreword by Rev. Carol Howard Merritt
Filled with engaging stories, practices and wisdom, this weekly guide provides insightful reflections and suggestions for incorporating mindfulness and gratitude into your daily life. 5 x 7¼, 176 pp, Quality PB, 978-1-59473-617-9 **$14.99**

The Golden Rule and the Games People Play
The Ultimate Strategy for a Meaning-Filled Life *By Rami Shapiro*
A guidebook for living a meaning-filled life—using the strategies of game theory and the wisdom of the Golden Rule.
6 x 9, 176 pp, Quality PB, 978-1-59473-598-1 **$16.99**

The Rebirthing of God: Christianity's Struggle for New Beginnings
By John Philip Newell Drawing on modern prophets from East and West, and using the holy island of Iona as an icon of new beginnings, Newell dares us to imagine a new birth from deep within Christianity, a fresh stirring of the Spirit.
6 x 9, 160 pp, HC, 978-1-59473-542-4 **$19.99**

Deepening Engagement
Essential Wisdom for Listening and Leading with Purpose, Meaning and Joy
By Diane M. Millis, PhD; Foreword by Rob Lehman
A toolkit for community building as well as a resource for personal growth and small group enrichment. 5 x 7¼, 176 pp, Quality PB, 978-1-59473-584-4 **$14.99**

Finding God Beyond Religion: A Guide for Skeptics, Agnostics & Unorthodox
Believers Inside & Outside the Church
By Tom Stella; Foreword by The Rev. Canon Marianne Wells Borg
Reinterprets traditional religious teachings central to the Christian faith for people who have outgrown the beliefs and devotional practices that once made sense to them.
6 x 9, 160 pp, Quality PB, 978-1-59473-485-4 **$16.99**

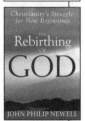

Fully Awake and Truly Alive: Spiritual Practices to Nurture Your Soul
By Rev. Jane E. Vennard; Foreword by Rami Shapiro
Illustrates the joys and frustrations of spiritual practice across religious traditions; provides exercises and meditations to help you become more fully alive.
6 x 9, 208 pp, Quality PB, 978-1-59473-473-1 **$16.99**

Journeys of Simplicity: Traveling Light with Thomas Merton, Bashō, Edward Abbey,
Annie Dillard & Others *By Philip Harnden*
5 x 7¼, 144 pp, Quality PB, 978-1-59473-181-5 **$12.99**

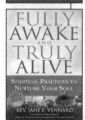

Perennial Wisdom for the Spiritually Independent
Sacred Teachings—Annotated & Explained
Annotation by Rami Shapiro; Foreword by Richard Rohr
Weaves sacred texts and teachings from the world's major religions into a coherent exploration of the five core questions at the heart of every religion's search.
5½ x 8½, 336 pp, Quality PB, 978-1-59473-515-8 **$16.99**

Whitman: The Mystic Poets *Preface by Gary David Comstock*
Walt Whitman was the most innovative and influential poet of the nineteenth century. This beautiful sampling of Whitman's most important poetry from *Leaves of Grass*, and selections from his prose writings, offers a glimpse into the spiritual side of his most radical themes—love for country, love for others and love of self.
5 x 7¼, 192 pp, HC, 978-1-59473-041-2 **$16.99**

Or phone, fax, mail or email to: SKYLIGHT PATHS Publishing
Sunset Farm Offices, Route 4 • P.O. Box 237 • Woodstock, Vermont 05091
Tel: (802) 457-4000 • Fax: (802) 457-4004 • www.skylightpaths.com
Credit card orders: (800) 962-4544 (8:30AM–5:30PM EST Monday–Friday)
Generous discounts on quantity orders. SATISFACTION GUARANTEED. Prices subject to change.

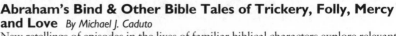

Bible Stories / Folktales

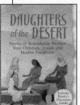

Abraham's Bind & Other Bible Tales of Trickery, Folly, Mercy and Love By Michael J. Caduto
New retellings of episodes in the lives of familiar biblical characters explore relevant life lessons. 6 x 9, 224 pp, HC, 978-1-59473-186-0 **$19.99**

Daughters of the Desert: Stories of Remarkable Women from Christian, Jewish and Muslim Traditions By Claire Rudolf Murphy,
Meghan Nuttall Sayres, Mary Cronk Farrell, Sarah Conover and Betsy Wharton
Breathes new life into the old tales of our female ancestors in faith. Uses traditional scriptural passages as starting points, then with vivid detail fills in historical context and place. Chapters reveal the voices of Sarah, Hagar, Huldah, Esther, Salome, Mary Magdalene, Lydia, Khadija, Fatima and many more. Historical fiction ideal for readers of all ages.
5½ x 8½, 192 pp, Quality PB, 978-1-59473-106-8 **$18.99** *Inc. reader's discussion guide*

The Triumph of Eve & Other Subversive Bible Tales
By Matt Biers-Ariel These engaging retellings of familiar Bible stories are witty, often hilarious and always profound. They invite you to grapple with questions and issues that are often hidden in the original texts.
5½ x 8½, 192 pp, Quality PB, 978-1-59473-176-1 **$14.99**

Also available: **The Triumph of Eve Teacher's Guide**
8½ x 11, 44 pp, PB, 978-1-59473-152-5 **$8.99**

Religious Etiquette / Reference

How to Be a Perfect Stranger, 6th Edition: The Essential Religious Etiquette Handbook Edited by Stuart M. Matlins and Arthur J. Magida
The indispensable guidebook to help the well-meaning guest when visiting other people's religious ceremonies. A straightforward guide to the rituals and celebrations of the major religions and denominations in the United States and Canada from the perspective of an interested guest of any other faith, based on information obtained from authorities of each religion. Belongs in every living room, library and office. Covers:

African American Methodist Churches • Assemblies of God • Bahá'í Faith • Baptist • Buddhist • Christian Church (Disciples of Christ) • Christian Science (Church of Christ, Scientist) • Churches of Christ • Episcopalian and Anglican • Hindu • Islam • Jehovah's Witnesses • Jewish • Lutheran • Mennonite/Amish • Methodist • Mormon (Church of Jesus Christ of Latter-day Saints) • Native American/First Nations • Orthodox Churches • Pentecostal Church of God • Presbyterian • Quaker (Religious Society of Friends) • Reformed Church in America/Canada • Roman Catholic • Seventh-day Adventist • Sikh • Unitarian Universalist • United Church of Canada • United Church of Christ

"The things Miss Manners forgot to tell us about religion."
—*Los Angeles Times*

"Finally, for those inclined to undertake their own spiritual journeys ...
tells visitors what to expect."
—*New York Times*

6 x 9, 416 pp, Quality PB, 978-1-59473-593-6 **$19.99**

Struggling in Good Faith
LGBTQI Inclusion from 13 American Religious Perspectives
Edited by Mychal Copeland and D'vorah Rose; Foreword by Bishop Gene Robinson
A multifaceted sourcebook telling the story of reconciliation, celebration and struggle for LGBTQI inclusion across the religious landscape in America.
6 x 9, 240 pp, Quality PB, 978-1-59473-602-5 **$19.99**

The Perfect Stranger's Guide to Funerals and Grieving Practices
A Guide to Etiquette in Other People's Religious Ceremonies
Edited by Stuart M. Matlins 6 x 9, 240 pp, Quality PB, 978-1-893361-20-1 **$16.95**

The Perfect Stranger's Guide to Wedding Ceremonies
A Guide to Etiquette in Other People's Religious Ceremonies
Edited by Stuart M. Matlins 6 x 9, 208 pp, Quality PB, 978-1-893361-19-5 **$16.95**

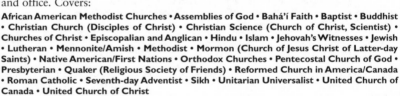

CONTENTS

ABOUT THIS BOOK

This book is not only a practical guide for the independent traveller, but is also invaluable for those who would like to know more about the country.

It is divided into four regions, each containing between four and ten tours. The tours start and finish in the towns and cities which we consider to be the best centres for exploration. Each tour has details of the most interesting places to visit en route. Highlighted panels dotted throughout each tour cater for special interests and requirements and cover a range of categories – for those whose interest is in history, wildlife or walking, and those who have children. There are also panels which highlight scenic stretches of road along the route and which give details of special events, crafts and customs.

The route directions are accompanied by an easy-to-use map at the beginning of each tour along with a simple chart showing how far it is from one town to the next in miles and kilometres. These can help you to decide where to take a break and stop overnight, for example. (All distances quoted are approximate.)

Before setting off it is advisable to check with the tourist information centre (addresses are given after the symbol $\boxed{i}$ at the end of town entries) at the start of the tour, for recommendations on where to break your journey and for additional information on what to see and do, and when best to visit.

Tour Information

See pages 165–73 for addresses, telephone numbers and opening times of the attractions mentioned in the tours, including telephone numbers of tourist offices.

Accommodation

See pages 159–64 for a list of recommended hotels for each tour.

Business Hours

Banks: there are many Bureaux de Change in Ireland, but banks are the best place to change money. Opening hours vary, but the majority of banks are open 9.30am–4pm, with some extended hours, including limited Saturday morning opening, in Northern Ireland. Foreign exchange counters in the main airports give decent rates: Belfast, open Monday 5.30am–10pm, Tuesday to Thursday 5.30am–11pm, Friday to Sunday 5.30am–midnight; Dublin, open daily 5.30am–9pm; Shannon, open daily 6.30am–5.30pm; Cork, open Monday to Friday 9am–5pm, Saturday and Sunday 11am–5pm. There is also a wide network of automatic cash points where credit and bank cards can be used.

Post offices: in the Republic, standard post office opening times are 8.30am–5.30pm, Monday to Saturday. The General Post Office in O'Connell Street, Dublin, is open Monday to Saturday, 8am–8pm and 10am–6.30pm on Sundays and bank holidays Post boxes are green; Republic of Ireland stamps must be used.

In Northern Ireland, standard opening times are 9am–5.30pm, Monday to Friday, and 9am–12.30pm on Saturdays. Throughout Ireland sub post offices close one other afternoon each week. Post boxes are red; British stamps must be used.

Credit Cards

Throughout Ireland American Express, Visa, MasterCard, Access and Diners cards are widely accepted, though not by some smaller restaurants and independent traders. Personal cheques can be cashed using a Eurocheque card. A few bed and breakfast establishments may expect to be paid in cash.

Currency

The monetary units are (in the Republic) the Irish pound (punt), abbreviated as IR£, and (in Northern Ireland) the pound sterling (£), each divided into 100 pence. These are not interchangeable.

Customs Regulations

Standard EU customs regulations apply when travelling between the Republic or Northern Ireland and another EU country, and if crossing the border between the two. Travellers may import or export goods for their personal use, up to certain limits depending on whether the goods were bought in ordinary shops (tax paid) or duty-free shops.

Electricity

220 volts AC (50 cycles) is standard. Sockets for small appliances are the three-pin flat or two-pin round wall types.

Embassies and Consulates

Embassies in the Republic:
Australia: Fitzwilton House, Wilton Terrace, Dublin 2 (tel: (01) 6761 517)
Canada: 65 St Stephen's Green, Dublin 2 (tel: (01) 4781 988)
UK: 29 Merrion Road, Dublin 4 (tel: (01) 205 3700)
US: 42 Elgin Road, Dublin 4 (tel: (01) 6688 777)
Consular offices for Northern Ireland:
Australia High Commission, Australia House, The Strand, London WC2B 4LA (tel: 0171 379 4334)
Canada: Honorary Consul, 378 Stranmillis Road, Belfast BT9 5EU (tel: (01232) 669 140)
New Zealand: Honorary Consul,

Ballance 118A, Lisburn Road, Glenavy, Crumlin, BT29 4NY (tel: (01846) 648 098) US: US Consul General, Queens House, 14 Queen Street, Belfast 1 (tel: (01232) 328 239).

Emergency Telephone Numbers

In both the Republic and Northern Ireland, dial 999 for police, fire or ambulance.

Entry Regulations

No passport is needed if you are a British citizen born in the UK and travelling from Britain. Other EU visitors must have a passport or suitable identity documents. All other nationalities need a passport and a very few need visas.

Health

There are no special health requirements or regulations for visitors to the Republic or Northern Ireland. It is best to take out medical insurance, though EU visitors are covered by a reciprocal agreement. Contact the post office for form E111 or equivalent.

Motoring

For information on all aspects of motoring in Ireland, including accidents, breakdowns and speed limits, see pages 158–59.

Public Holiday

(R) Republic only
(NI) Northern Ireland only
1 January – New Year's Day
17 March – St Patrick's Day
Good Friday & Easter Monday
1st Monday in May – May Day
Last Monday in May (NI)
1st Monday in June (R)
12 July – Orangemen's Day (NI)
1st Monday in August (R)
Last Monday in August (NI)
Last Monday in October (R)
25 December – Christmas Day
26 December – St Stephen's Day (Boxing Day)

Route Directions

Throughout the book the following abbreviations are used for roads:
M – motorways

Northern Ireland only:
A – main roads
B – local roads
Republic of Ireland only:
N – national primary/secondary roads
R – regional roads.

Telephones

To call a number in Ireland, first dial the access code: Australia 0011; Canada 011; New Zealand 00; UK (for the Republic only) 00. Then dial 353 for the Republic or 44 for Northern Ireland, and then the full number (omitting the first zero of the area code).

For international calls out of Ireland dial 00, then the country code: Australia 61; Canada 1; New Zealand 64; UK 44; US 1. Then dial the full number omitting the first zero.

New-style glass and metal call boxes have largely replaced the old ones which are blue and cream in the Republic, and red in Northern Ireland. Phones using cards (which can be bought at newsagents) are widely available.

Time

Both the Republic of Ireland and Northern Ireland follow GMT, or GMT plus 1 hour from late March to late October.

Traditional music sessions in pubs are part of the Irish culture

Tourist Offices

Republic of Ireland Tourist Board (Bord Failte): Suffolk Street, Dublin 2 (tel: 01602 4000).
Northern Ireland Tourist Board: St Anne's Court, 59 North Street, Belfast, BT1 1NB (tel: 0232 231221).
Both Tourist Boards maintain offices abroad.
Republic of Ireland Tourist Board (Bord Failte):
Australia: 5th Level, 36 Carrington Street, Sydney, NSW 2000 (tel: (02) 299 6177).
Canada: 160 Bloor Street East, Suite 1150, Toronto, Ontario M4w 1B9 (tel: (416) 929 2777).
UK: 150 New Bond Street, London, W1Y OAQ (tel: 0171 493 3210 – becomes 020 7493 3210 from 22nd April 2000).
US: 345 Park Avenue, New York, NY 10154 (tel: (212) 418 0800).
Northern Ireland Tourist Board:
UK: 11 Berkeley Street, London, W1X 5AD (tel: 0171 493 0601 – becomes 020 7493 0601 from 22nd April 2000).
US: Suite 701, 551 Fifth Avenue, New York, NY 10176 (tel: (212) 922 0101).

MUNSTER

The province of Munster is made up of the counties of Waterford, Cork, Kerry, Limerick, Clare and Tipperary. Its fertile ever-changing landscapes form a microcosm of Ireland.

Soaring, surf-fringed cliffs rise above tiny coves and sandy beaches. Mountains, awash with colours of rhododendrons and the delicate hues of heather, are slashed by deep gaps and scenic passes. The Knockmealdown and Comeragh ranges guard east Munster, while to the west the peaks of Macgillycuddy's Reeks include Ireland's highest, 3,400-foot (1,036m) Carrantouhill. The Slieve Mish range marches out to the tip of the Dingle Peninsula, and the Galtees, Slieve Felims, and Silvermines straggle across the interior.

A variety of fish fill Munster's rivers: the mighty Shannon that draws a watery line along the boundaries of counties Kerry, Clare, Limerick and Tipperary; the Lee that rises in the hills of Gougane Barra and flows eastward to split into two forks that make an island of Cork city's centre; the tidal Blackwater whose scenic beauty has earned it the title of the 'Rhine of Ireland'; and the Suir, Slaney and Nire whose waters trace their way across eastern Munster.

The beautiful Italian Gardens on Garinish Island benefit from the warming effects of the Gulf Stream (Tour 6)

Fertile fields are ringed by stone walls and verdant woodlands. Small fishing villages along the coast and prosperous inland market towns dot the landscape. Three of Ireland's largest industrial cities and most important ports – Waterford, Cork and Limerick – ring the coastline, while inland lies the great Golden Plain of Tipperary.

Ancient ringforts, dolmens, and cairns predate recorded history, while massive castles, monasteries and round towers speak of Christians, Vikings and Normans. The stone promontory fort of Dunbeg stands guard on the Dingle Peninsula, while adjacent fields contain the still-intact beehive huts of early Christians. The lofty Rock of Cashel is a reminder both of the days of Celtic kings of Munster and of the coming of Christianity.

The breathtaking scenery and the juxtaposition of history with progress leave the visitor with an almost overwhelming sense of the enduring nature of the region. There is a feeling that time has not stood still in this ancient land, but is marching on into eternity, its past a solid foundation for the future.

Tour 1
The strange barren landscape of the Burren is the most evocative sight of this region, though the towering grandeur of the Cliffs of Moher forms another unforgettable vista. For history lovers, Clare is a county of castles. Ennis, which readily claims the affection of the visitor, is the base for the tour.

Tour 2
From the Viking city of Limerick, this tour takes you west along the banks of the Shannon estuary, tracing the footsteps of the mighty Desmond clan who left massive castles in their wake. The route turns south, where history merges with culture in northern County Kerry and continues east and north for medieval ruins in Newcastle West and the picturesque beauty of Adare.

Tour 3
Turning east from Limerick city, it is not such a long way to Tipperary town, in the heart of that county's Golden Vale. Further east is the great Rock of Cashel, with its impressive ruins and folk village, then on to Thurles, Roscrea and Nenagh.

Dunguaire Castle looks out over Kinvarra Bay (Tour 1)

Tour 4
Tralee is the gateway to a tour of the antiquities of the Dingle Peninsula, through tiny seaside villages and over the breathtaking Connor Pass to Dingle town. Prehistoric forts, beehive huts and a drystone oratory that has stood watertight for over 1,000 years are only a few relics of this magical place.

Tour 5
The 112-mile (180km) Ring of Kerry takes top billing on this tour as you travel from one scenic wonder to the next. Mountains, lakes, sandy beaches and offshore islands form an unforgettable panorama, and Killarney town has its own fair share of splendid lakes, antiquities and legends.

Tour 6
From Kenmare, this tour takes you south to Glengarriff and the semitropical Italianate gardens on Garinish Island. It continues along wild seascapes and mountain passes of the Beara Peninsula.

Tour 7
This tour takes you to Blarney to kiss the famous stone and northwest through historic towns before turning east and south for Cahir's Norman castle, the spectacular drive across The Vee, Lismore's fairy–tale castle perched above the Blackwater river, and Youghal's harbour, haunted by Sir Walter Raleigh.

Tour 8
Turning south and west from Cork, the splendours of West Cork unfold along this tour. Delightful little coves and sandy beaches are backed by wooded hills. A turn inland takes you through a mountain to remote Gougane Barra.

Tour 9
After exploring historic Bantry, with its great house and attractive harbour, the route takes you to picturesque Skibbereen and Baltimore, a tiny village which has seen more than its share of violent events, and circles the unspoiled peninsula that stretches to Mizen Head, the southernmost mainland point of Ireland.

Tour 10
Waterford is the starting point for a journey along dramatic coastal cliffs and coves, picturesque castles, panoramic mountain views, and lush farmland. The Vee opens up unforgettable views of heather-covered mountains and bogs and Tipperary's fertile landscape.

Clare

The pleasant town of Ennis, the capital of County Clare, winds around low hills on both sides of the River Fergus. It was at the forefront of the struggle for emancipation, and has strong associations with Daniel O'Connell and Eamon de Valera. The life and influence of the latter is recorded in a small museum in the town.

2/3 DAYS • 159 MILES • 256KM

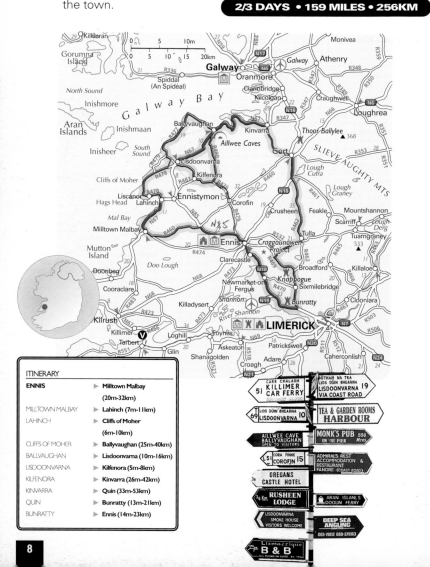